D0148478

Richard M. Weaver
1910–1963

Richard M. Weaver
1910–1963
A Life of the Mind

FRED DOUGLAS YOUNG

UNIVERSITY OF MISSOURI PRESS
Columbia and London

Library of Congress Cataloging-in-Publication Data

Young, Fred Douglas, 1942-
   Richard M. Weaver, 1910–1963 : a life of the mind / Fred
Douglas Young.
      p. cm.
   Includes bibliographical references (p.   ) and index.
   ISBN 0-8262-1030-9 (cloth : alk. paper)
   1. Weaver, Richard M., 1910–1963.   2. American
literature—Southern States—History and criticism—Theory, etc.
3. Libertarianism—United States—History—20th century.
4. Conservatism—United States—History—20th century.
5. United States—Intellectual life—20th century.
6. Criticism—United States—History—20th century.   7. English
teachers—Illinois—Chicago—Biography.   8. Critics—United
States—Biography.   9. Rhetoric—Philosophy.   I. Title.
PS29.W43Y68   1995
814'.54—dc20   95-35199
                                              CIP

Text Design: Elizabeth K. Fett
Jacket Design: Stephanie Foley
Typesetter: BOOKCOMP
Printer and Binder: Thomson-Shore, Inc.
Typeface: Schneidler

For credits, see page 217.

For:

Karin

Stephen

and David

Contents

Acknowledgments

Whatever is laudable about this work is the result of a great deal of help from many people, some of whom deserve special mention. Love of learning and especially of aptly spoken words are only a small part of a priceless legacy from my parents.

I thank Professor Clifford Amyx and Miss Catherine Dunne of Lexington, Kentucky, Professor Wilma Ebbitt of Newport, Rhode Island, and Mrs. Polly Weaver Beaton of Brevard, North Carolina, all of whom kindly let me interview them. Professor Cleanth Brooks, Professor Robert Heilman, and Dr. Russell Kirk provided important insights about Richard Weaver based on their having personally known him.

I am particularly indebted to Mr. George M. Core, editor of *The Sewanee Review,* for putting me in touch with people who had known Weaver over the years, for his careful, critical reading of this study, and for many other helpful suggestions.

Good friends and gifted students at The Westminster Schools in Atlanta have provided an intellectually stimulating environment where it has been my privilege to teach for two decades.

When I was an undergraduate at Northeast Louisiana University, Professor William A. Walker Jr. combined a quiet enthusiasm with a strong emphasis on using primary sources and developing critical skills to show me how much fun studying history can be.

Above all others, I thank my wife, Karin, for encouraging me in so many ways on innumerable occasions. Her love, support, and understanding have been the most important helps of all.

Richard M. Weaver
1910–1963

Introduction

THAT WAS YOUR SOUTH, A MANY-LAYERED TRACT

OF MIND AND SOIL, ITS TRAGIC PAST MADE WHOLE

BY PROVIDENTIAL GUILT AND TRUE DEFEAT.[1]

In the chapters that follow I trace the curve of Richard M. Weaver's intellectual life. Weaver was so solitary and remote that he could have lived comfortably in a monastery. An old-fashioned bachelor, he had little in the way of a social life: he was not so much antisocial as asocial. He was an independent man who made his own lonely way, a way necessitated in part because he was a homely, small individual with bad eyesight and little physical grace. He was shy, just as one would expect, and he did not make any effort to remake himself with, say, tailored clothes or fancy eyeglasses. He lived quietly and simply—primarily to think and to write.

To understand such a person in our confessional, gaudy, and histrionic time is admittedly difficult. Most people, unless they are two-dimensional types appearing as minor characters in fiction, cannot be categorized. That was especially true of Richard Weaver, who lived more nearly in the world of images and ideas than he did in the mundane world of everyday quotidian existence.

Weaver perhaps would have been more comfortable living in the nineteenth century than in the twentieth. His intelligent and original scrutiny of the feudal system, the code of chivalry, the concept of the gentleman, and the older religiousness of the South constitutes more than just an objective analysis of a region and of a way of life that ended at Appomattox Court House and whose last vestiges were swept away by Reconstruction and industrialization. Not that he gave in to a maudlin sentimentality that idealized a past that never was. His careful study in the mind of the Confederate

South, however, did emphatically leave him with the settled conviction that the twentieth century's crisis of spirit could be treated by rediscovering timeless verities known and practiced below the Mason-Dixon line in the last century.

Although Richard Weaver's family on his father's side came from the little town of Weaverville, in the North Carolina Piedmont near Asheville, Weaver grew up in Lexington, Kentucky, where he was educated through college at the University of Kentucky. Lexington was—and is—a very sophisticated town that sits in the Kentucky bluegrass just west of coal-mining country known as Appalachia. To the east the well-heeled counties of central Kentucky—such as Fayette, Lexington's county seat—are supplanted by the rugged and impoverished part of the state, Appalachia, whose landscape is punctuated by such towns as Hazard and Harlan.

The bluegrass region, which is rolling farmland and horse country, is ideal for growing burley tobacco and producing bourbon whiskey, as everyone knows. This region has also been involved in fostering much of the middlebrow and highbrow culture in the state, with the University of Louisville, the University of Kentucky, Centre College, and Transylvania College leading the way so far as education is concerned and with symphony orchestras in Louisville and Lexington.

Lexington has long had a considerable number of Jewish families—families who deliberately came to the city as a place where tolerance was observed. During and after World War II, refugees from the Third Reich regularly appeared in Lexington, and many of them taught at the University of Kentucky, especially in the art and music departments, and at Transylvania as well.[2]

Weaver had the great good fortune of growing up and being educated in this town, and it nourished his essential liberalism as a man of good breeding and of wide-ranging tolerance and sympathy for all stripes of human beings. The region's own lack of prejudice in the bad sense of that overworked word is shown by the fact that Weaver himself was not condemned for being a socialist as a young man.

Weaver seldom had anything approaching an easy life. His father died suddenly when Richard was only five, leaving Mrs. Weaver with four children, of whom Richard was the oldest, to raise. They

went from being comfortably middle class to straitened circumstances in which they barely clung to middle-class pretensions.

During his senior year at the University of Kentucky, Weaver
enthusiastically embraced socialism. It seemed to him to provide
an explanation as well as a remedy to an America shipwrecked
on the shoals of industrial capitalism. The deep and lingering
Great Depression especially disheartened newly graduated college
students, like himself, whose employment prospects were poor
at best.

From Lexington, Kentucky, Weaver made his way to Nashville,
Tennessee, where he enrolled in Vanderbilt University to pursue a
master's degree in English. His socialist convictions had remained
intact in spite of the fact that his efforts on behalf of the Socialist
Party of America to get Norman Thomas elected president seemed
to have been fruitless. The great surprise to him at Vanderbilt was
that, although he disagreed with the Agrarians' vision of America,
he liked the men, especially John Crowe Ransom and Donald
Davidson, as individuals. Still, he was nowhere near the point of
giving up the political convictions and the view of the world that
had animated him for at least four years.

Upon completing his graduate work at Vanderbilt, Weaver
accepted a teaching position at Texas A & M University. He disliked
his job as an instructor intensely and felt trapped, although there
was plenty of time to continue a project he had perhaps begun
during his last year at Vanderbilt—reading primary accounts of
southerners who had fought in the Civil War. After two years in
College Station, Weaver resigned his teaching position and drove
to Baton Rouge, where he enrolled in Louisiana State University to
pursue a Ph.D. degree. In looking back on this experience he said
that he had begun his education over again at the age of thirty. This
was his exaggerated way of calling attention to the pivotal role his
study of the South played in the intellectual transformation that
he began to undergo while still an undergraduate at the University
of Kentucky.

In 1944, soon after successful completion of his doctoral work at
Louisiana State, Weaver was appointed to the English faculty at the
University of Chicago, partly on the recommendation of Cleanth

Brooks, who had been his dissertation advisor. He spent the rest of
his professional career there. Between his jobs at LSU and Chicago,
he taught briefly during the latter part of World War II at North
Carolina State University, a school comparable to Texas A & M,
where he was at least much closer to his family in Weaverville.

   In trying to understand Weaver's ideas one would naturally
see his association with the Agrarians as important; there can be
little doubt that they had a deep and lasting influence on him.
Conservative thinkers such as Russell Kirk and William F. Buckley
Jr., in coming to admire Weaver, saw him not as a political ally but as
a social critic with whom they shared wide areas of agreement. Yet
it would be a serious error to pigeonhole him either as a conservative
sage or as an Agrarian born a generation too late. Indeed, Weaver did
not see himself as a partisan of either cause. He had no close ties to
either group, although he did correspond fairly often with Donald
Davidson, but that association occurred years after Davidson and
the original Agrarians had distanced themselves from one another.
Russell Kirk remembers that Weaver did not attend conferences
frequented by conservatives and had few friends, conservative or
liberal, at the University of Chicago. Temperamentally a solitary
spirit, he was quite independent by nature. One of the editors
of his published dissertation remarked to me that he "wouldn't
be surprised to learn that Weaver voted for both Roosevelt and
Truman." In so doing, he would have been a New Deal democrat like
John Crowe Ransom. At a 1988 conference on Weaver sponsored
by the Liberty Fund, not one participant compared him with such
men as Buckley and Kirk.[3]
   Richard Weaver was a radical and original thinker in the etymological senses of both words. He sought root causes and meanings and scrupulously insisted that properly defining terms was
the starting point for real understanding. He jealously guarded
his privacy during his professional life and had no close friends,
exchanging letters regularly over the years with only two people—
his mother and Donald Davidson. This studied detachment and
rigorous regimen of teaching and writing were in keeping with
seeing himself as an exile. It is not going too far to say that he was
a virtual, if not an actual, hermit. E. B. White, who was far more

comfortable on a salt-water farm in Maine than at *The New Yorker,* once observed that "A writer must believe in something, obviously, but he shouldn't join a club. Letters flourish not when writers amalgamate, but when they are contemptuous of one another."[4] Weaver would have agreed.

If there was one person upon whom Weaver modeled himself more than any other, it was probably the teacher he most admired at Vanderbilt, John Crowe Ransom. He lavished praise on Ransom's *God without Thunder: An Unorthodox Defence of Orthodoxy.* His former teacher was, Weaver said, a "subtle doctor." In *Visions of Order,* dedicated to Ransom, Weaver elaborated on a certain type of individual, the "doctor of culture." Such men loved and cherished the background that had spawned them, but had come to see its flaws well enough so as to gain a certain detachment. Such a perspective enabled them to carry on a sort of lovers' quarrel with their culture. Seeing clearly what was wrong with their way of life, although deeply committed to it, they, like a physician treating a much-loved patient, did not hesitate to suggest what ought to be done about the problem. True devotion and loyalty meant telling the truth and even prescribing what might be a painful cure. The doctor of culture was not completely "in" but still very much "of" his milieu. Weaver no doubt viewed himself playing that role with regard to his beloved South. In his case the detachment was both geographical and intellectual. He chose to see himself as an exile, a term richly suggestive and freighted with meaning and historical association, as such literary historians as Malcolm Cowley and Lewis P. Simpson have observed. The Agrarians had done their best work while exiled from the South, Weaver would write. Many of the most influential figures of human history had made their greatest contributions while in self-imposed exile. And so it was that Weaver found himself, far from his beloved Weaverville, North Carolina, in cruel, heartless, philistine Chicago, where he would do his part to stem what he genuinely believed was the descent of America into barbarism by helping his students and readers write and use language correctly.

It has been said that barbarism begins with the debasement of language. Karl Kraus, the great Viennese critic and thinker who wrote about the Nazi's misuse of language for propaganda purposes during the 1930s, was rebuked by a friend who told him that he should not worry about the abuse of language when the Japanese were bombing Shanghai. Kraus retorted, "If all commas were in the right place, Shanghai would not be burning." Kraus also observed once that "Progress celebrates Pyrrhic victories over nature."[5] Both were the kind of remarks that Richard Weaver might well have made.

Weaver seldom wrote about the issues of his time. As a cultural historian he took the long view of history. The latest event of which he wrote at length was World War II, and then only in passing when he compared the total war of that vast conflict to the last vestiges of chivalry shown during the American Civil War. At the time of his death he was writing a comparative study of the mind and culture of New England and of the South, not in the twentieth century but in the nineteenth and earlier.

One of Weaver's most arresting and important rhetorical analyses involved the Scopes trial in Dayton, Tennessee, in 1925. By the time he wrote about it in his book *The Ethics of Rhetoric,* over a quarter of a century had passed. He was more comfortable in considering the Lincoln-Douglas and Hayne-Webster debates of the nineteenth century than the famous debate between Clarence Darrow and William Jennings Bryan in the twentieth.

Similarly, Weaver did not write about, say, the Holocaust, which as a monstrous fact did not impinge upon the consciousness and conscience of most intellectuals in the West until the early 1960s when Hannah Arendt, in *Eichmann in Jerusalem,* presented a concise and understandable account of the death factories. Had Weaver lived longer, he might have addressed contemporary issues, but anyone who knows how Weaver thought and worked would not argue that such a course of action on his part would have been likely. The issues that held his sustained interest were seldom contemporary, although very occasionally a contemporary event or trend might be viewed in the light he felt an earlier time might shed upon it.

By the time of Weaver's sudden death he had not been astonishingly productive, but he had written several enduring books that have made a considerable impact: on the study of southern history and literature, *The Southern Tradition at Bay* and his essays on the South (collected as *The Southern Essays of Richard M. Weaver*); on the study of rhetoric, *The Ethics of Rhetoric* and *Language Is Sermonic;* and on the study of Western civilization and culture, *Ideas Have Consequences* and *Visions of Order.* Weaver also wrote a comprehensive textbook on grammar and composition, and he had a good start on the comparative study of New England and of the South when he died in his fifty-fourth year. Such related essays as "The American as a Regenerate Being" show how wide-ranging, original, and profound Weaver's thought characteristically was.

The facts that much of his work remains in print and that he continues to be written about in such books as Fred Hobson's *Tell about the South* and Eugene Genovese's just-published book *The Southern Tradition* demonstrate the enduring quality of Weaver's thought. No fewer than eleven master's theses and eight Ph.D. dissertations have been written about him from the late seventies until as recently as 1993, most of which were completed in the 1980s.

In the pages that follow, I will be presenting the development of Weaver's intellectual life and the curve of his thought as he lived the life of the mind, becoming more remote all the while from ordinary day-to-day life in social and political senses and moving into the empyrean of thought in which something is not proven and does not take on flesh and blood until it is written down, revised, and revised once more. Although much work has been done on Richard M. Weaver over the years, no one has written an intellectual life of him, as I have now done. The result illuminates more nearly— by a long measure—the weather of his thought rather than the weather of his days.

1 A Social Bond Individualist

[HIS] WORDS NEVER SEEM TO BE PERFORMING TRICKS, NEVER SEEM TO EXIST IN AND FOR THEMSELVES. THEY ARE MERELY THE CLOTHING THAT HIS SUBJECT PUTS ON, AND WEARS AS IF IT WERE NATURAL TO THE PURPOSE. THE SUBJECT IS OBJECTIVELY THERE, SOLID AS NATURE IS SOLID, WITH NO CREVICES OUT OF WHICH A MIST . . . CAN ESCAPE.[1]

If one follows the curve of Richard M. Weaver's intellectual life, it becomes quite clear that the social context in which he was born and grew up made him the kind of thinker he was. A southern upbringing in a rural and small-town setting molded him perhaps more than he knew. While it is true that he later underwent a dramatic change that he was wont to describe by using the word *conversion,* it could be argued that he had simply returned to his roots.

However one may describe the shift that took place in Weaver's thinking prior to his return to graduate school to enter a Ph.D. program, this much is clear: He was unwavering in his commitment to traditional southern virtues, which he saw as having a timeless significance. He concluded that "One might hesitate to say that the South . . . has anything to offer our age. But there is something in its heritage, half lost, derided, betrayed by its own sons, which continues to fascinate. . . . [It] was . . . *the last non-materialist civilization in the Western World* [Weaver's emphasis]. The Old South may indeed be a hall hung with splendid tapestries in which no one would care to live; but from them we can learn something of how to live."[2] From then until the end of his life, he took those values as the point of departure for his teaching, his writing, and his speaking. Everyone works from first principles, he believed. If those were proper, lesser matters would take care of themselves.

Weaver lived an almost monastic existence for the nearly two decades of his professional career at the University of Chicago. He rigorously scheduled his work week, especially his teaching, in order to accommodate a demanding regimen of writing.

Three dimensions to Weaver's life and work stand out when one surveys it as a whole: He was a dedicated philosopher of culture, a rhetorician, and a teacher. At the time of his death, he was working on a comparative study of the South and New England that would doubtless have earned him accolades as a discerning study of the southern and New England mind and that probably would have established him as an intellectual historian.

Ideas Have Consequences and *Visions of Order* were both percep-tive critiques of culture. It is perhaps more accurate to deem Weaver a philosopher of culture rather than to deem him a cultural critic, as neither work directly dealt with surface matters or with cultural fads. Instead, he focused on the underlying beliefs that undergird a culture and that teach its members how to act. In this regard, Weaver made clear the vital role of education and insisted that the presuppositions of those in positions of authority—teachers both formal and informal—were of vital importance.

Weaver's contributions as a rhetorician—that is, one having a fundamental concern that language be taught and used properly— can best be seen in *The Ethics of Rhetoric.* It followed naturally from *Ideas Have Consequences,* in which he insisted that the study of and teaching of literature is vital to a healthy culture. He refused to yield proprietorship of the word *rhetoric* to those who were mere sophists. He recognized that such abuse of language was at least as old as Socrates. Since rhetoric dealt with human nature in all its fullness and complexity, Weaver felt compelled to inveigh against modern sophists, in whatever guise, who saw language as nothing more than a weapon or tool to make the worst appear as the better. Such prostitution of words made losers of us all, he believed.

The seriousness with which he approached his teaching respon-sibilities has been attested by Weaver's colleagues, who recall his earnestness and dedication with an admiring wonder. No doubt dissatisfied with the composition and writing textbooks available to him, he compiled his own, *Rhetoric and Composition.* He was working on a revision when he died.

At the time of his death, Richard Weaver was also working on comparative studies of representative southerners and New Englanders. One chapter, "Two Types of American Individualism," appeared in the spring 1963 issue of *Modern Age.* In it he contrasted John Randolph of Roanoke and Henry David Thoreau.

Convincing testimony to the originality and durability of Richard Weaver's thought is the fact that, three decades after his death, almost all the books he wrote are still in print: *The Southern Tradition at Bay, Ideas Have Consequences, The Ethics of Rhetoric,* and *A Rhetoric and Composition Handbook.* The staying power of *Ideas Have Consequences,* which has remained in print continuously since its first appearance in 1948, has been recently noted by Eugene D. Genovese:

> Forty years ago, Richard Weaver, in *Ideas Have Consequences,* plunged into a brave effort to rouse the faithful to struggle for something better than the moral idiocy he was excoriating. Weaver, like Tate before him and Bradford after, never succumbed to the philistinism of those, who, when confronted by long odds in defense of principles, recite the only prayer they know: "May God have mercy on me." But Weaver did warn of the ravages of what he called the "hysterical optimism" of modern man, and he felt compelled to pose an unpleasant possibility: "Whether man any longer wants to live in society at all or is willing to accept animal relationships is a question that must be raised in all seriousness." Yes, Weaver's question must be raised. And in all seriousness.[3]

A collection of essays on rhetoric entitled *Language Is Sermonic,* which originally appeared in 1970, is still available. In 1987 a collection of articles on the South, some of which had not previously appeared in print, was published as *The Southern Essays of Richard M. Weaver.*

It has happened too often that Richard Weaver has been stamped a conservative. A careful reading of the whole of his works makes it clear that this is, at best, an inadequate and partial way of seeing him. He was concerned with human nature in its totality, and therefore almost certainly would have preferred to be labeled a rhetorician. That he shared common ground with some conservatives is true, but in a speech given in 1960 Weaver took the opportunity to distance himself from the label, or at the very least tried to make it clear what kind of conservative he was: He would not abide any conservatism not undergirded by certain *principles.* He would have nothing to do with a mindless obeisance to the status quo or a timorous fear of change. The core of his conservatism was "that man in this world cannot make his will his law without any regard to limits and to the fixed nature of things."[4]

Something about this very complex man may be seen in considering the comparative study he did of Randolph of Roanoke and Thoreau.[5] A pluralistic society frequently sings the praises of individualism. Like a good rhetorician, Weaver first asked the simplest but most important of all questions necessary to understanding: What does the word *individualism* mean? Rather than going to his dictionary for guidance, which he no doubt would have excoriated as arguing from a dialectical rather than from a rhetorical stance, he posited two types of American individualism. The qualifying adjective was important. Here he implicitly appealed to his hearers' memory and experience in establishing the common ground essential if a practicing rhetorician is to get his points across. Having established that there are at least two strains of individualism in the American experience, he moved directly to his examples: Henry David Thoreau and John Randolph. There can be no denying that both men engendered not a little political controversy by the public stands they took on the issues of their day, provoking much praise as well as criticism. That they were individualists is beyond dispute.

Assuming the implicit assent of his audience by citing these examples, Weaver used that common ground as the basis for moving on to the next stage of argument. Thoreau's individualism led him to a studied withdrawal from society; Randolph's individualism moved him to political action at the local level. Weaver called the position of the latter a social-bond individualism. It recognized Aristotle's declaration that man is inescapably a political animal. Of Thoreau and Randolph, Weaver pointedly noted that the New Englander was the secessionist; he renounced society's claims on him. Randolph's spirited opposition to the centralization of political power in America underscored his individualism as one tied inextricably to his community.

Weaver's own life may be accurately compared to Randolph's, though those who do not know better might mistake Weaver's almost hermetically sealed existence in Chicago as being analogous to that of Thoreau, who, while trumpeting his independence, refusing to pay his taxes, and withdrawing from society nonetheless had to make occasional trips into Concord for supplies. While Weaver was scrupulous in fulfilling his responsibilities as a professor of English at the University of Chicago, the words *recluse* and *hermit* are the only ones appropriate to describe the kind of life he lived during his two decades in the Windy City. Was leaving his native South, whose virtues he had celebrated in his dissertation and a considerable number of articles, in itself the kind of secession of which Weaver accused Thoreau? A superficial reading of the matter might indicate that, but in fact exactly the opposite is true. He was following what he celebrated in his understanding of Randolph. He was in a real sense an exile. An exile has an identity and ties with community that become all the more precious and valued, perhaps, than they are to residents of the place where the exile finds himself. Like Randolph, Weaver knew that man was a political animal in the fundamental sense. This did not take away from the fact that *he* was virtually apolitical with regard to such matters as voting and taking part in political campaigns. What it meant, finally, was that he, like Randolph, was bound to a family and to a place that were critical in giving him both integrity and identity, enabling him to know who he was and what he was about. He prized nothing in this world more than being able to go back to North Carolina each summer to help care for his mother, visit with relatives, grow his vegetable garden, and do some of his best writing and thinking. He might live in Chicago for nine months of each year, but his true home was in Weaverville.

Had this been a study of Weaver as a southerner, with emphasis on his literary, historical, and cultural commentary of the South (especially the South from the end of the Civil War until the beginning of World War I), I would have compared Weaver with W. J. Cash. Cash, whose *The Mind of the South* remains an important study, was also a North Carolinian. His origins as one of the South's "plain people" (to use a phrase that appears in the title of a durable study by Frank L. Owsley, one of the Agrarians) are comparable to Weaver's. Cash grew up in a mill town in the North Carolina Piedmont, and his family, like Weaver's, was middle class; indeed, if one used the terms of the English, both families would probably be more properly called lower middle class. Cash's education was comparable to Weaver's until the former decided to attend graduate school and to teach, but he was more the autodidact than Weaver. Unlike Weaver, he stuck to his liberal inclinations. Soon after the publication of his one book, Cash's world turned sour, and he committed suicide in Mexico while on a Guggenheim Fellowship. At the time Cash was persuaded that he was being pursued by Nazi agents, but was in fact pursued by other demons, especially alcohol, as his biographer makes plain.[6]

Cash, had his career lasted longer and had he written more, might have proved an interesting counter to Weaver, who shared much with him in addition to a common background in the South and a fascination with its history and culture. Cash was temperamentally the same kind of loner as Weaver, but was apparently much less comfortable with his solitude and solitariness. While Weaver ultimately returned to his southern roots, Cash turned away from his, ultimately finding nothing to replace his southern piety. And so, for the purposes of this book, such figures as Perry Miller, Malcolm Cowley, and George Orwell are found worthy of comparison.

2 | The Early Years

IN THINKING OVER THE SUBJECTS ON WHICH I MIGHT BE QUALIFIED TO SPEAK, IT OCCURRED TO ME TO LOOK AT WEAVERVILLE AND THE WEAVER COMMUNITY THROUGH A PERSPECTIVE OF CHICAGO. I HAVE BEEN CONDEMNED FOR THE PAST SIX YEARS TO EARN MY LIVING IN THAT MOST BRUTAL OF CITIES, A PLACE WHERE ALL THE VICES OF URBAN AND INDUSTRIAL SOCIETY BREAK FORTH IN A KIND OF EVIL FLOWER. I SOMETIMES THINK OF THE UNIVERSITY TO WHICH I AM ATTACHED AS A MISSIONARY OUTPOST IN DARKEST CHICAGO. THERE WE LABOR WITHOUT MUCH REWARD OF SUCCESS. ANYONE WHO REMOVES TO SUCH A PLACE FROM AN OLD-FASHIONED SOCIETY LIKE OURS WITH ITS ROOTS IN THE PAST AND WITH ITS WELL-UNDERSTOOD RELATIONSHIPS, BECOMES CONSCIOUS FIRST OF ALL OF THE ABSENCE OF COMMUNITY. . . . ONE ENCOUNTERS THE CURIOUS FACT THAT THE MORE CLOSELY PEOPLE ARE CROWDED TOGETHER, THE LESS THEY KNOW ONE ANOTHER. AND I THINK THE MAN TRANSPLANTED TO SUCH A PLACE CAN SUM UP HIS PERCEPTION OF THE PEOPLE AROUND HIM UNDER TWO HEADS. (1) *THEIRS IS A CONDITION IN WHICH NOBODY KNOWS WHO HE IS,* [AND] (2) *NOBODY KNOWS WHERE HE IS FROM.* [EMPHASIS MINE][1]

In the full confidence that he knew *who* he was and *where* he was from, Richard Malcolm Weaver Jr. delivered the above remarks to the annual meeting of the Weaver family in Weaverville, North Carolina, on August 10, 1950. "The Tribe of Jacob," they called themselves: descendants of the Reverend Jacob Weaver and

Elizabeth Siler Weaver who had settled at Reems Creek, North Carolina, a decade after the Declaration of Independence had been signed. For over a century the family reunions had been held each year without fail. Richard Weaver could be a missionary in Chicago because of the "status" (as defined in his essay "Status and Function") he had as a member of his family. Status indicates "the feature of permanence" (what one is) among the inevitable changes that go along with "function" (what one does). A vitally important part of "status," in his understanding of the term, was "place," which the family was essential in defining and maintaining. Family members were valued for themselves and not necessarily for what they could do; each one was unique and had a place that no one else could fill.[2]

While he was in Chicago, Weaver purchased a home in Weaverville for his widowed mother and spent all his summers there, drawing upon the sources of what he believed to be the real and permanent things away from the rarefied atmosphere and urban artificiality he endured for the other nine months of his year and about which he wrote in *Ideas Have Consequences*. Disdaining the possibility of getting to Weaverville in a few hours by plane, he always went by train. Before he arrived, his mother would have his garden plowed and ready for him to plant. He would have reminded her to be sure to have this done by a horse or mule instead of a tractor. There he spent three happy months nourishing "what Russell Kirk calls 'affection for the proliferating variety and mystery of traditional life.' . . . There are numberless ways in which the South disappoints me; but there is something in its sultry languor and in the stubborn humanism of its people . . . which tells me that for better or worse this is my native land."[3]

His father, Richard Malcolm Weaver Sr., was born March 8, 1870. Educated at Weaverville College, he was a gregarious, outgoing man who loved music, played the violin, and had the reputation of being "the life of the party when a group of young folk met." He owned a livery stable in Asheville, North Carolina, and took great pride in his saddle, buggy, and carriage horses, many of which came away from horse shows with prize cups and ribbons. It was on one of his periodic trips to Kentucky to buy thoroughbreds that he met Carolyn Embry, whom he married in November of 1908. Richard

Malcolm Weaver Jr. was born March 3, 1910, in Asheville, the first of their four children.[4]

His sister Polly insists that Richard's precocity began when he was quite young: "When he was a child, my father used to worry about him; he'd say, 'Well, what's the matter with this boy? Why doesn't he go out and play with the others?' And there he'd be pulling a great big book out of the bookcase at three—or maybe four—years old. And he knew that he wanted to be a teacher from the time he could even think about it; mother told us that."

When Richard was five years old, his father died suddenly, probably of a cerebral hemorrhage. By this time he had two sisters, Polly and Betty, and Mrs. Weaver was expecting a fourth child. She decided to move from Asheville to Weaverville to live with relatives, and it was there that their younger brother, Embry, was born. After a two-year stay in Weaverville, Carolyn decided to move to Lexington, Kentucky, her hometown, where she became the manager of the millinery department in her brother's business, a fine women's shop that is still in business in downtown Lexington called Embry and Company. Polly Weaver Beaton recalls that her mother "always loved hats and used to make them in the old days when women wore them."

Noting that each family member was quite different, Mrs. Beaton described her brothers as "playboy" (Embry) and "scholar" (Richard). She and her sister were also counterpoints to each other, her sister, Betty, being "domestic" and she a "ragamuffin." Since Mrs. Weaver had to work full-time in order to earn a living for herself and the family, she left the children in the care of housekeepers. The connection with the Weaver side of the family was nourished and strengthened during summers spent in Weaverville at an aunt's home.[5]

The children all attended the Maxwell School in Lexington, including Richard until he was fourteen, at which time he was enrolled at Lincoln Memorial Academy in Harrogate, Tennessee, which had a college-preparatory curriculum. Richard helped pay his tuition costs by working in the kitchen at Harrogate for the three years that he was there. His sister Polly speaks of the pressures the children faced at the time: "We were not a very cohesive family since we were all sent off to different schools. Our mother's early widowhood compelled her to enter business for our support."[6]

His own experience almost surely gave Richard Weaver an appreciation for life's constraints and limitations during these adolescent years. Perhaps the source of his concern with the Spoiled Child Psychology to which he devoted a chapter in *Ideas Have Consequences* was the result of his own experience with exactly the opposite of privileged comfort. As one student of Weaver has observed, "Clearly, he did not have 'the best of everything' and he knew that the world did not exist to fill his egocentric whims, or, if it did, it was doing a precious poor job of it."[7]

Perhaps Weaver's understanding of the South during this period was his own life and experience writ large. In a passage that is surely autobiographical, he observed, "Take a fairly coherent culture: allow it to be largely displaced by a second culture of different principles; then allow the second to suffer some degeneration, and you have many a Southern community of the Twenties. People live without a frame of reference, or they cling pathetically or absurdly to different frames, which may dictate contradictory courses."[8]

The analytical bent of Weaver's mind found expression beyond the classroom at Lincoln Memorial where he founded a philosophic society and wrote its constitution. The document's preamble boldly proclaimed its purpose: "to promote the exchange of ideas, investigate theories, propagate principles, follow an argument wherever it goes, and develop ourselves." Weaver's brother-in-law Kendall Beaton commented, "Article I (obviously the most important) states 'No member shall cherish society above solitude or engage promiscuously in social activities.' They met in their dormitory every Sunday afternoon, required attendance, forbade levity of conduct, and obliged each member to present something serious and significant at each meeting."[9]

Robert Hamlin, who has written on Weaver's theory of rhetoric, perhaps went too far in writing that "The shock of his father's death had immediate and visible effects on young Richard. He became somber and serious in demeanor, and he acquired habits of detachment, reflectiveness, and solitude he never revised." Beaton more cautiously observed that "Here, certainly, is a blueprint for the life of high purpose that Dick adhered to steadfastly despite hardship and difficulty, for the remainder of his days." Charles Follette, in his study on how to interpret Weaver, also warned against trying to make too much of this document in and of itself: "Simple introspection should remind us that fifteen is an intense period in one's life during which the attraction of secret societies with passwords, rituals, and other such arcanum is virtually over-whelming. This point is reinforced through historical perspective. After all, 1925 was in many areas of the country part of a period of tremendous interest in literary societies, self-improvement groups, etc., all given to the enunciation of lofty aims in equally lofty language."[10]

That this episode represented a turning point in Weaver's life or revealed a somber personality already set in certain channels may be questioned. But it does not seem to be going too far to say that one does recognize the characteristics of the mature Weaver: a disciplined mind moving from a well thought-out premise to a plan of action.

Other extracurricular activities at Lincoln Memorial in which Richard Weaver took part were the track team and the Christian Endeavour Society. The latter organization was founded in 1881 by Francis E. Clark, a Congregational minister, as a program for young people in his denomination.[11] Here was a forum ready-made for young Weaver to try his hand at rhetoric. He had been thinking about the art of speech-making for some time, as was clear from the Socrates' quotation from Plato's *Euthydemus,* which he had carefully copied into his student notebook:

> For the composers of speeches, whenever I meet them, appear to me to be very extraordinary men, Cleinias, and their art is lofty and divine and no wonder. For their art is the part of the great art of enchantment, and hardly, if at all, inferior to it: and whereas the art of the enchanter is a mode of charming snakes and spiders and scorpions, and other monsters and pests, this art acts upon dicasts [jurors] and eccliasts [legislators] and bodies of men.[12]

Weaver, in a speech given in honor of the Christian Endeavour Society's founder, paid his tribute in language calculated, perhaps, to bring about that sort of enchantment of which Socrates spoke. He made generous use of biblical language and archaisms: "Dr. Clark is a man who has lived a good life, who has fought a good fight, who has builded a great work and now will pass from us, honored and respected by all the followers whom he has inspired." Warming to his subject, Weaver painted a portrait of Dr. Clark's contributions in the light of the Great Man theory of history. He compared him to Caesar, Alexander, and Napoleon but insisted that, although his life was "in one respect like these great characters, [he] has so excelled all others in foresight and industry that he has risen until his shadow has fallen not across a state, nor a nation, nor a continent, but a world, in the form of the Christian Endeavour Society." The wording grew even more florid as the young speaker all but got carried away trying out his rhetorical skills:

> His name will not be handed down to posterity reeking with the smell of powder and the tramp of armies: but his life may be more suitably likened to a pleasant meadow in the springtime, a house that is builded on a rock, with a character that admitted no flaws. Yet his name shall become a star in the sky of history, not shining with the ruddy, red, warlike glow of Mars and Antares, nor with the yellow opulent light of Venus, but rather emitting the clear, steady, pure white light of Vega or Rigel.

He closed out his adolescent baroque tribute with wording reminiscent of the Gettysburg Address and designed to stir the members of the society to action, charging them to be "dedicated to the proposition that men are better than brutes and consecrated to the idea that Christ is the son of God, shall not perish from the earth." This was probably Richard Weaver's first effort at a specifically rhetorical plea. Over a quarter of a century later he would write about this sort of appeal, where the speaker asks of his hearers "belief which is preliminary to action."[13]

In this same student notebook of Weaver's are four prayers, probably composed as invocations for the Christian Endeavour Society, and a speech on the importance of the church. The language of the speech is similar to that in his tribute to Dr. Clark. The prayers are thoroughly orthodox in wording and tone, while the address on the church touts it as a primarily *human* institution to be valued as an equal partner with government and education in a common venture against wrong:

> The church is that great institution that reaches down in a man, kindles that little spark of divinity and sets him upon a higher plane

of living. It would be necessary to go pretty far down into the scum
and dregs of humanity before one could be found who lacks even a
tiny spark and was utterly unresponsive.

The Church is a towering giant on the front line in that battle
against wrong which never ends. Even now it is joining forces with
the school and the government and with these three titans fighting
shoulder to shoulder it looks as if evil would soon be routed.

As a state is no better than the citizens that compose it, so is a
church no better than its members. Like all other human organizations it has its weak points and its periods of depression and needs
the stalwart backing of its supporters in order to flourish.[14]

He closed with an appeal to his auditors to do their part in what he
characterized as rather a daunting task: "Anyone who is interested
in the saving of society, who values law and custom, who wishes
to protect the good, should help the Church in its great crusade
against wrong." Reading these speeches in the light of the quotation from Plato is reminiscent of what a close friend of Weaver's
at the University of Kentucky said of him as an undergraduate:
"Dick always wanted to collect disciples; he was already a kind of
entrepreneur for his own ideas, even though they were unformed at
the time." A fellow student at Lincoln Memorial, Vadus Carmack,
recalled of Weaver that "At the time that I knew him and was
with him on a daily basis, his interests were mostly scholastic—
literature, languages, science—and he had no apparent interest in
religion at that time. He did not go to church, did not carry a Bible
or Testament as some students did, and showed no signs of religious
fervor. He did at times attend the local neighborhood revivals as an
onlooker. However, his daily life was exemplary in every respect."[15]

How does one explain the speech on the church in the light
of Weaver's personal religious life at the time? A plausible answer
is that his core beliefs were neither orthodox nor unorthodox as
the terms are usually understood; they were still unformed. Later,
it would seem that the essence of his religion found expression in
what he would characterize as the South's "older religiousness":

It was a simple acceptance of a body of belief, an innocence of
protest and schism by which religion was left one of the unquestioned
and unquestionable supports of the general settlement under which
men live. One might press the matter further and say that it was

a doctrinal innocence, for the average Southerner knew little and probably cared less about casuistical theology; what he required was the acknowledgment, the submissiveness of the will, and the general respect for order, natural and institutional, which is piety.[16]

There is general agreement by those who knew Weaver that he had a natural gravity and reserve. Perhaps he was put off by the emotional displays at revival meetings such as those he observed while a student at Lincoln Memorial Academy. Yet a close examination of what he said in these two speeches gives evidence that he regarded religion as one of civilization's essential supports. Perhaps he coined the phrase *older religiousness of the South* in order to reconcile his avoidance of orthodox formulations and his deep respect for the fundamental human and societal need that he felt only religion could fill. This wording paid the tribute that piety required but was shorn of the sharp edges of fideist specificity.

Weaver's sister recalled that whatever they had in the way of religious training as children was minor, and she related an anecdote that suggested his reticence in matters of religion began early:

We did go to Sunday school when we were little—things like that, but after that it was nothing formal that I know of. I remember one incident from when we were growing up in Lexington. I regarded him even then as the great sage—you know, the one with the brain. We were sitting on the porch one day, and I said, "Dick, do you believe in God?" He gave me the funniest look, got right up out of the swing, went into the house, and never said a word to me! Now whether it was bothering him, or whether he was thinking it all over, I don't know.[17]

Weaver's regard for religion as a support for the traditional family is evident in his later writings. His respect for the family as an institution was almost certainly heightened by the summer stays in Weaverville and the annual Weaver reunions. These gatherings each year when scores of relatives met, talked about their past, and told familiar stories may have had a special poignancy for Weaver since his immediate family was not as cohesive as he might have wished. We must remember that he was the oldest child in a family whose father had died when the children were young. That he had begun to place a premium on the institutional importance of family can be seen in a page of musings he wrote in his student notebook at Lincoln Memorial: "The family is of enormous importance to society. The decay of family life was mainly responsible for the Fall of Rome. For five hundred years after the founding of the city there was not a single divorce but as soon as woman was emancipated, sexual immorality and a disrespect for the solemnity of marriage began to prevail and this sapped at the roots of Roman civilization!" A related theme of the mature Weaver's thinking that is evident here is the holding up of classical antiquity as a model from which the present day can learn a great deal that is good.[18]

Other material in his student notebook reveals a precocious and catholic curiosity. A section entitled "Theory of Somnolism" and "Contrary Theory" bore testimony to the sort of "scientific experiment" other prep-school students no doubt had conducted before. In September 1925, Weaver began a five-week effort to get by on a minimal amount of sleep, during which time he averaged about five and a half hours per night. When this period was over, he began a four-week stint of averaging approximately seven and a half hours per night. He dutifully recorded his feelings and concluded that the only result of getting a minimal amount of sleep was an intermittent drowsiness that presented no real problem to his general alertness.

The next section manifested a just pride in his senior status and showed some alarm that the distinction between his class and that of the underclassmen was getting blurred. Taking it upon himself to do something about it, he wrote a petition to be circulated among the seniors:

> Be it resolved, by the Academy Senior Class in convention assembled that for the purpose of maintaining senior dignity and curtailing the unseemly latitude hitherto allowed Academy undergraduates, that the sole privilege of wearing black ties of any description be henceforth reserved and restricted to Academy Seniors alone. Be it resolved [that appropriate measures be taken] for the purpose of endowing girl seniors with equal exclusive rights and privileges.[19]

The outcome of this initiative is uncertain.

At Lincoln Memorial, Weaver devoted himself to his studies with a will and was graduated in three years at the top of his class. A fellow student who would achieve success and fame as a fiction writer was fellow Kentuckian Jesse Stuart. Stuart wrote to him two decades later, recalling, "I remember your being valedictorian of your class and always winning the clashes on the track team."[20]

Weaver returned to Lexington in 1928, where he enrolled in the University of Kentucky as a seventeen-year-old freshman. He continued his interest in track by going out for the university team and easily earned a letter that year. A friend recalled that he was an excellent sprinter: "He was as fast as all get-out and could outrun the bunch of us." But his interest in track waned in spite of the initial success he enjoyed; his favorite competitive endeavor was debate, and he relished the thrust and cut and parry of clashing ideas.[21]

Weaver formed close friendships at the University of Kentucky with three fellow students who were with him on the university's debate team: Sid Shell, Hugh Jackson, and Clifford Amyx. Shell, after earning a law degree, became a partner in Georgia politician Eugene Talmadge's law firm in Atlanta and for a time was an instructor in the Emory University School of Law. Jackson went on to make a career in New York City, where he became president of the Better Business Bureau. Amyx, after graduating from Kentucky, moved to San Francisco, where he became supervisor of a federal arts project. He later returned to Kentucky as a member of the university's art department, where he remained for the rest of his career. As surviving member of that group, he recalled:

> We at once formed a kind of foursome and became fairly close, except that Dick was more close-mouthed about his family and personal relations than any of the rest of us. We were state champions, and we thought we were really cocks of the walk, but Dick had by far the most incisive mind of anybody we knew except for our debate coach, who was Bill (W. R.) Sutherland. Some of the faculty referred to Sutherland as "King" because he had enormous presence.

Conducting debate as if it were a "foray into enemy camps," Sutherland "wanted us to have logic even though we couldn't study logic until we got to be sophomores; he had us boning up on Aristotle as freshmen and then he threw in Bogislavsky's *Functional Logic*." Perhaps the most influential of Weaver's undergraduate teachers, Sutherland "was fond of Teddy Roosevelt's phrase 'malefactors of great wealth.' He regarded Coolidge and Hoover with contempt, the military as the lowest of intelligence, and Bruce Barton as a fraud. Sutherland loved confrontations and took risks. He would abuse engineers for complacency while teaching them public speaking, which they were obliged to take."[22]

Sutherland, whom Amyx characterized as a willful gambler, confidently put his team up against one visiting from Great Britain that fall:

> We were crude as all get-out, but we were debating three very sophisticated young ladies from England: Nancy Sharpe, who was later a novelist; Nancy Samuel, who was the daughter of the one-time Liberal prime minister; and Lenore Lockhart, who was the granddaughter of Sir Walter Scott's biographer—and these people were from Oxford, Cambridge, and London. Now you can imagine a bunch of freshmen coming up against talent like that. Sutherland was anxious to see what would happen. Of course, Dick never took anything from anybody and the rest of us got by fairly well. The young ladies were especially complimentary, especially about Dick, saying that they hardly met anyone in America as good as he. Their debate style was all panache and grace and bitter irony and disrespect. They were commanding creatures, just overwhelming.[23]

Noting that Weaver had emphasized in the debate that no southern politician could succeed without bona-fide credentials that he was someone who was really poor, Amyx reported that Miss Sharpe took up the style and caricatured it to the point of parody, much to the delight of the audience. This debate brought campus fame to Weaver: "Dick just became a star; everybody knew that he was powerful and they were very complimentary of him. Kentucky Dean of Women Sarah Blanding, who was later president of Vassar, presided that evening and said that we had not disgraced ourselves. That helped a lot." Weaver thought that they might have been voted the winners by the audience had not courtesy dictated a nod in favor of the visitors.

Commenting on Weaver's forensic skills, Amyx remembered that he "was extraordinarily incisive in debate. He could recognize a flaw instantly. He was not large, but totally alert, quick in movement, and had a tendency to rise on tiptoe, speaking aggressively, with a somewhat strident voice." That same year Weaver represented Kentucky in a national oratorical contest sponsored by the Intercollegiate Peace Association, "the first of the left-leaning organizations with which Weaver was to be associated."[24]

It was also in 1929 that Weaver contributed to a symposium sponsored by the *Intercollegian,* a publication of the Student Christian Movement, whose December issue focused on the question of peace and stressed the importance of avoiding another European war. This was almost certainly his first published essay. In it he expressed delight with the Labour government of England and the socialist one in France, both of them "so avowedly opposed to war" and would almost certainly "have a powerful bearing on the progress of the cause of peace." Perhaps these developments in Europe would have a salutary effect on America's "jingo journals sorely pressed to keep their fires of hatred going." He was also encouraged by widespread student resistance in America to compulsory ROTC training but viewed it as superficial and questioned the motives of many of the protestors:

> Few of these uprisings have been inspired by a holy idealism or even by a conscientious objection to the performance of the duties in soldiering in war-time. Too often they are a direct result of the drafted cadet's resentment toward a hot and unbecoming uniform or of the remarks of the sergeant on the appearance of the cadet's shoes or the angle of his gun—or because a small minority, supplied with niftier uniforms and shiny sabers, cornered the glory on parade day! A student anti-war movement arising out of a knowledge of present conditions and speculation on dreadful possibilities—rather than out of trivial discontent—would doubtless be better organized than those we are familiar with. . . . But as for the outlawry of war as an international issue, there appears to be little change in the average student's indifference to anything far enough away to be international.[25]

During Weaver's undergraduate days at the University of Kentucky, he and another student whom Amyx remembered as being "a frustrated Confederate general, like Allen Tate," would get together at any football game where the visiting team was from further south in order to cheer for the "rebels to beat the Yankees—and Kentucky was the Yankees! Now that was the damnedest drunken misapprehension I ever heard of!" On one occasion, Weaver and another student almost got themselves tossed over the railing by

a couple of irate Kentucky fans. This militant and essential southernness came to the fore often.[26]

The debate team became the focus of Weaver's extracurricular interests and friendships during the four years he was in
college at Lexington. The four already mentioned "formed a kind
of core" that subsequently added a fifth member, Jim Porter (who
later became an Ohio newspaperman and a state senator), and a
sixth, a North Dakotan named Pierce. Weaver and his friends spent
their four years representing their university in meets at Harvard,
Northwestern, German International, and many others. "We had a
wonderful time," recalled Amyx. "We spent two weeks in Florida at
Rollins College, for example (on the town, practically), and having
a ball."[27]

Weaver characterized his teachers at Kentucky as having been
"social democrats." He did so in light of the fact that they were
ardent supporters of Franklin D. Roosevelt's New Deal, coupled
with their having become disenchanted with industrial capitalism.
They hoped that government might meliorate the worst effects
of the Great Depression and prevent any such catastrophes in
the future. His debate coach was without question at the top of
this list. Sutherland knew and practiced "every ploy against the
establishment even at that early date." It was perhaps from him
that Weaver picked up his animosity toward advertising to which
he devoted much of the chapter entitled "The Great Stereopticon"
in *Ideas Have Consequences*. The debaters got from Sutherland "a
constant tirade—invective, really, against advertising, against the
complete silliness of all the people that Sinclair Lewis derided."
Weaver's political-science teacher, Amry Vandenbosch, was another of Weaver's social-democrat mentors, having taught at both
Chicago and Michigan before coming to Kentucky. His specialty
was colonialism with a focus on the Dutch, and he had the later distinction of serving as a state-department consultant in 1945 when
the United Nations was holding its first meetings in San Francisco.
In those days, when the Soviet Union was seen perhaps by many
Americans as a great ally in the common fight against Nazism and
fascism, Vandenbosch confided to Amyx that he found it shocking
that the Soviet delegate Molotov was constantly accompanied by
bodyguards. Among his students, Vandenbosch was noted for his

blunt, direct style; he died in his nineties, an "unreconstructed" democrat.[28]

Although Weaver majored in English at Kentucky, he seems to have been influenced little by the most distinguished faculty member in English at the time, Grant C. Knight, who had published a number of books and had served as an editor for the *American Mercury*. More influential, perhaps, in the light of Weaver's later intellectual development was Francis Galloway, who taught eighteenth-century literature and who probably introduced Weaver to the writings of Edmund Burke. After graduation, Weaver always made a point of visiting Galloway whenever he chanced to be in Lexington.[29]

The stock market crash of 1929 was the catalyst that turned many Americans into superficial socialists or at least tended to cause them to lend a sympathetic ear to this alternative to capitalism. Frederick Lewis Allen in his book-length memoir of the 1920s wrote about the change of mood that followed the stock-market debacle:

> If the country still expected as little as ever of politics . . . it was somewhat less satisfied with *laissez-faire* for business than in the days of Calvin Coolidge. The public attitude during the depression of 1930–1931 presented an instructive contrast with that during previous depressions. The radical on the soap-box was far less terrifying than in the days of the Big Red Scare. . . . With bread lines on the streets, the Russian Five-Year Plan became a topic of anxious American interest. . . . There was no denying that the economic system had proved itself too complex, and machine production too powerful, to continue unbridled.[30]

This attitude was especially prevalent on college campuses. By 1932 Weaver had eagerly embraced socialism; he proved his commitment by becoming secretary for the campus socialist party. During the presidential campaign of Norman Thomas, he served as the state secretary for the party. His friend and fellow debater Sid Shell was also quite active in Thomas's campaign organization and activities throughout Kentucky.

Weaver's left-of-center political views had found expression before he formally joined the Socialist Party. Clifford Amyx recalls the particular emphasis on labor relations during the early thirties.

It was during a campus visit by an organizer for the League for Industrial Democracy that a university Liberal Club was formed (Weaver served as vice president, an office for which he was particularly suited by temperament). He did not want to be the most visible leader but greatly desired a position near the top. Amyx recalled that Weaver "was always willing to be hovering in the background." The two of them collaborated in writing Liberal Club pamphlets, which were passed out at basketball games and other university events, urging people not to submit to military training, to watch out for the malefactors of great wealth, and to join and be active in organizations that held to such goals. "The meetings of the Liberal Club were attended regularly by the ROTC cadet commander, and by reporters from the town papers and the campus newspaper, which hooted at the aims of the Club and suggested that we were both foolish and subversive." These activities got them in trouble with the university president, Frank L. McVay, who called in all the officers of the Liberal Club and pointedly told them that their opposition to military training was going to hurt the university in the legislature and might result in budget cuts that could permanently cripple the school. This was at a time during the Great Depression when faculty salaries had already been withheld for nearly a semester. He did not threaten them with expulsion. The upshot was that Weaver and his friends ignored McVay. Amyx remembers the president with gratitude: "I've always felt very kindly toward McVay because he didn't threaten to use any power he might have had to disrupt our lives because of our liberalism. And Dick owed a great debt to one of his 'social democrats' for that."[31]

Weaver and Clifford Amyx teamed up during the summer between their junior and senior years to write a column for the campus newspaper, the *Kentucky Kernel,* entitled "Looking over the Magazines," in which they took note of current topics of interest in magazines such as the *Nation,* the *New Republic,* the *American Mercury, Transition, Harper's, Freeman,* and others. Amyx noted that it was difficult for him to distinguish the columns he penned from the ones Weaver wrote, saying, "We were that close intellectually."[32] In the self-confident voice of rising college seniors with progressive views, "Looking over the Magazines" insisted in an August 1931 column that

The newspapers have done an incredible amount of banal moralizing over Bernard Shaw's recent trip to Russia. Some have criticized him for going, others for returning, and still others for what he did there. In the issue of August 5, *The Nation* takes time out to emit a few chuckles over the incident. Shaw, "the bad boy of the articulate world," is pictured as visiting Russia, the bad boy among the nations. They get along famously because they are audacious in about equal degrees and because they both have a sublime contempt for the world's opinion.[33]

In the same issue, Weaver paid tribute to the unconventional economist Thorstein Veblen, who wrote *The Theory of the Leisure Class:*

Thorstein Veblen is unquestionably one of the few men of genius America has produced, and yet it is doubtful if 10 per cent of the students of economics in the average college could even identify him if asked to do so on their final examination. Reasons for his failure to win recognition are easy to find. It was his misfortune to spend his life in a field where the laurels went not to the candid seeker after truth but to the glib apologist. He had not patience with the abracadabra of the traditional political economy, and his exposure of its fake problems was ofttimes brilliant. It was his great contribution to distinguish between the pecuniary and the technological aspects of industry. Mencken was the first to recognize in him an unusual gift for satire, and anyone who has read "The Engineers and the Price System" will testify to the lucidity of his prose.

Having become a convinced socialist, Weaver found much to admire in the writings of both Shaw and Veblen. No doubt he was also attracted by their fierce iconoclasm. Two years after he wrote this column, Weaver's master's thesis at Vanderbilt would reflect Veblen's cavalier dismissal of the humanities as being unscientific, elitist, and outdated.[34]

One column was perhaps as much about the intellectual ferment Weaver was experiencing as a college senior as anything else. It dealt with the proper role of

religion in the modern world and the problem of its contribution to modern life. . . . Either [the minister] may adhere to the old dogmatic religion and go down before the onslaught of skepticism and naturalism, or he may attempt to construct a new religion based on the findings of science and motivated by an ethical humanitarianism.

The clergy made its original mistake in suffering the men of science too gladly. Under solemn promises to respect all sacred things they were admitted into the temple, but they have been followed by less pious successors, so that now the temple is not only profaned but is in imminent danger of wreckage. The public that once shouted and rolled at the evangelists' camp meeting is interesting itself today in "the anatomy of faith and the psychiatry of religious behavior."[35]

This article fairly begs the question of whether religion has any validity at all in the modern world, as he put it, or, more to the point perhaps, in his own life. Weaver would later latch onto John Crowe Ransom's "unorthodox defense of orthodoxy" in fashioning the essay that would come the closest to a personal religious apologia, "The Older Religiousness of the South." This essay was accepted by the liberal editor of the *Sewanee Review,* W. S. Knickerbocker.

In an article in the August 14, 1931, issue of the *Kernel,* which took note of Edmund Wilson's trip south to look over the Tennessee Agrarians, Weaver bemoaned "the unenviable reputation for intellectual barrenness which the South has won for itself since the Civil War" and rejoiced that this stereotype was "disturbed last year when a small group centering about Nashville, Tennessee, published 'I'll Take My Stand.'" The essence of the work was, he reported, "a defense of the agrarian form of industry and the kind of society it supported." He took pleasure in Wilson's favorable impression of this group:

> As sometimes happens in the case of Northerners of the reformist turn of mind, Mr. Wilson's hostility to the yet distinctly feudal nature of Southern society was somewhat softened by actual contact with it. He frankly admits that the wage-slavery system in the North offers few improvements over the former bond-slavery system in the South. He finds that agrarian life leaves people an opportunity to remain human beings which is more than can be said of the stern regimentation imposed upon the worker hordes of our great cities.[36]

In that same issue of the *Kernel,* Weaver noted with approval eighty-year-old George F. Peabody's uniqueness among philanthropists in advocating both free trade and public ownership of railroads. Weaver's socialist perspective was evident in his endorsement of Peabody's efforts not only to "dispense liberally the wealth which a system piled into his lap," but also the way he came out "boldly for modifications in that system itself." He was less impressed with Julian Huxley's "new witches-brew to ease the wounds of the bleeding world," scientific humanism, and criticized the British thinker not for his effort to link science to some criterion of value but for the intellectual vagueness of his proposal. Quoting Huxley's assertion that "The prime task of scientific humanism is to clarify her own ideas as to the limitations of the human mind," he sarcastically concluded that "Men have been busy at such a task for a few hundred years." Huxley's pronouncement that human intelligence limits are "probably" constrained by the size of the birth canal no doubt seemed as absurd to Weaver as the thinker's amorphous ruminations on religion:

> It will need many decades before any new religion is able to organize itself; but the time ripens, and the world's dislocation of thought and the strange confusion of ephemeral and partial creeds presage a new birth now as they did before the birth of Christianity. It is not likely that any one of us will see that new birth; or, if we do, we shall very likely not recognize it for what it is. But we can to the best of our ability work towards it by clear thinking and a generous trust in the riches hidden in human nature.[37]

One can readily imagine Weaver the experienced debater trying to make sense out of the first part of that paragraph in the light of the last sentence. Where is the place in this kind of thinking for logical rigor? What are the milestones by which one can truly know anything? Is this change that Huxley exalts progress? Is it inevitable? Whatever does he mean by "clear thinking"?

The next year, Richard Weaver received his bachelor's degree. It was May 1932—the nadir of the Great Depression. College graduates—indeed, all who needed employment—were glad of any kind of work they could find. His efforts to find a job and numerous applications for graduate teaching fellowships came to naught even though he was a Phi Beta Kappa with a superior academic record. His sister remembered that he was "rather bitter" about the matter.[38]

Weaver's retrospective assessment of his undergraduate days at Kentucky was one of gloom and ran to just a few lines in his autobiographical essay. Choosing Charles Péguy's characterization of himself when he enrolled at the *École Normale* ("gloomy, ardent, stupid") as an apt account of what he was like as a freshman in Lexington, Weaver said that if the university had been *really* provincial, it would have been a better place; instead it was—"sedulously imitative of the dominant American model." Condemning it for being what a later generation would call a multiversity, the University of Kentucky, whose numbers were swelling while its campus sprouted new buildings, was "losing its character." Especially odious to him in retrospect was the "elective system" that permitted "seventeen-year-old students, often of poor previous training and narrow background, to tell the faculty (in effect) what they ought to be taught." That he yearned for the proper guidance at a time when he was expected to choose from a myriad of courses when he was unprepared to do so is evident in his introductory clause: "After many wayward choices, I managed to emerge, at the end of my undergraduate course, with a fair introduction to the history— but not the substance—of literature and philosophy." The faculty at Kentucky were

> mostly earnest souls from the Middle Western universities, and many of them—especially those in economics, political science, and philosophy—were, with or without knowing it, social democrats. They read and circulated *The Nation,* the foremost liberal journal of the time; they made sporadic efforts toward organizing liberal or progressive clubs; and of course they reflected their position in their teaching very largely. I had no defenses whatever against their doctrine, and by the time I was in my third year I had been persuaded entirely that the future was with science, liberalism, and equalitarianism, and that all opposed to these trends were people of ignorance or malevolence.[39]

This backward glance was almost certainly colored by his later philosophical rejection of the social and political philosophy he imbibed while in college at Lexington.

Like a great many others, Weaver had assumed that the Great Depression was the result of American capitalism's failures and "that some sort of political reconstruction was inevitable." Determined to do his part, he joined the American Socialist Party at the same time that he enrolled in the graduate program in English literature at Kentucky. He later held that his "disillusionment with the Left began with this first practical step." It would perhaps be more accurate to say that this was when the seeds of disillusion were sowed; it would take time for them to germinate. After all, he did spend the next two years as a party activist, serving as secretary of the socialist local and as statewide secretary for Norman Thomas's presidential campaign in 1932.[40]

The two years he spent involved in Socialist Party activities were an important arena for the struggle between two competing visions of life. The traditional view he had picked up from his family, but not in any systematic form that asserted its own rightness. The socialist vision that had been presented to him in a systematic way by nearly all his undergraduate teachers during the formative, early college years made sense to him against the backdrop of what seemed to be the unmistakable failure of capitalism. This perspective not only challenged all others but also singled out opponents as those who chose either blindness or hatred. In his later work *Visions of Order,* Weaver made some comments that apply to the struggle he was undergoing during his last year at the University of Kentucky:

> Another way of understanding this conflict of opinion is to recognize that the "optimists" have the current rhetoric on their side even while the "pessimists" have the proof. The modern world has a terrific momentum in the direction in which it is going, and many of the words of our everyday vocabulary are terms implicit with approval of modern tendencies. To describe these tendencies in the language that is used most widely is to endorse them whereas to oppose them is to bring in words that connote half-forgotten beliefs and carry disturbing resonances.[41]

After a year of graduate study at Kentucky and disillusionment with his fellow socialists as people, while still believing in the essential rightness of their vision, Weaver decided to enroll at Vanderbilt to pursue a master's degree in English. There he found the Agrarians, who, while "one of the most brilliant groups in the United States . . . held a position antithetical in almost every point to socialism and other purely economic remedies." He continued to cling to his socialist views, but was puzzled and confused by his being drawn to the group "as persons" while he was at odds with their social and political perspective. He had emphatically *not* liked many of his socialist associates, remembering them as "dry, insistent people of shallow objectives; seeing them often and sharing a common endeavor . . . did nothing to remove the disliking." Clifford Amyx bears out the point: "His detachment was not intellectual; it was personal. He kind of withdrew from distasteful, old Wobblies" and was scandalized that a country-music band was secured to attract people to a Socialist Party rally where Norman Thomas was going to be the featured speaker.[42]

Weaver's intellectual condition upon his being graduated from the University of Kentucky was probably not unlike many thoughtful college graduates at the time. A conscientious, dutiful student, he had embraced the sincerely held belief of many of his professors that free-market capitalism was in the process of being finally discredited by its inherent contradictions. The deepening depression convinced many doubters that this was an unarguable truth. But he felt deeply that man was more than just a consumer, and alongside his socialism ran Weaver's curiosity about whether religion had a role in the modern world. As a junior at Lincoln Memorial Academy, he had attended revival meetings at local churches, not as a worshiper but as a student of religion in the generic sense. Religion's visible ties with tradition in his family led him to conclude that, at the very least, it was a useful support of community. The annual family reunions he had faithfully attended since childhood were always billed as gatherings of the Rev. Jacob Siler Weaver's descendants and included not a few Methodist ministers among their number. We may be sure that Weaver knew that Methodists founded Vanderbilt, Duke, and other leading American universities.

Religion, tradition, and socialism jostled with each other in an amorphous mix in the mind of twenty-one-year-old Richard Weaver. He had strong convictions about what was wrong with the country and how socialism could right those wrongs. He had shown the courage of his convictions by taking an active role in the university's Liberal Club and had worked enthusiastically to get the socialist Norman Thomas elected to the presidency. But the strong convictions of the just-graduated college student are not necessarily settled or lasting. Weaver could not shake himself free from the image of Thomas's supporters' hiring a country-music band to attract a crowd. And he dismissed Huxley's ramblings on the future of religion as nothing really new or substantive even though they were widely heralded in academic circles at the time.

The intellectual ferment, not to say turmoil, going on in his mind would cause him to move hesitantly, tentatively, and with great caution toward an integrating principle during his graduate-school years at Vanderbilt. In Nashville, in the ideas and followers of Agrarianism, he would encounter what was from his perspective the first authentic antithesis to his socialism.

3 | Vanderbilt and the Agrarians

WHAT THE AGRARIANS, ALONG WITH PEOPLE OF THEIR PHILOSOPHIC CON-
VICTION EVERYWHERE, WERE SAYING IS THAT THERE ARE SOME THINGS
WHICH DO NOT HAVE THEIR SUBSISTENCE IN TIME, AND THAT CERTAIN
VIRTUES SHOULD BE CULTIVATED REGARDLESS OF THE ERA IN WHICH ONE
FINDS ONESELF BORN. IT IS THE MOST ARRANT PRESENTISM TO SAY THAT
A PHILOSOPHY CANNOT BE PRACTICED BECAUSE THAT PHILOSOPHY IS
FOUND IN THE PAST AND THE PAST IS NOW GONE. THE WHOLE VALUE OF
PHILOSOPHY LIES IN ITS DETACHMENT FROM ACCIDENTAL CONDITIONS
OF THIS KIND AND ITS ADHERENCE TO THE ESSENTIAL.[1]

When Richard M. Weaver enrolled at Vanderbilt University in the fall of 1933 to pursue a master's degree, he was entering not just a graduate program but rather a community in a state of creative ferment. Intellectuals at Vanderbilt had dared to take on cherished assumptions about progress and industrialization and were hammering out an apologia based on traditional values rooted in community and associated with the rural South. These Agrarians, as they styled themselves, had first come to Weaver's attention when he was a Kentucky undergraduate writing for the campus newspaper for which he wrote an enthusiastic review of their manifesto, *I'll Take My Stand*.[2]

Any account of American cultural and intellectual history of the period that began just prior to World War I and continued for the next half-century must, perforce, mark the astonishing

36

literary output of southern writers, beginning with the Fugitives and Agrarians at Vanderbilt. This was "heralded, ironically, by H. L. Mencken's provocative disparagement of the region as the 'Sahara of the Bozart.' "[3]

The roots of Agrarianism may be traced to Nashville, Tennessee, where, by 1915, a group consisting mostly of students and faculty from Vanderbilt were meeting "for some heavy philosophical discussions." After World War I, when their numbers increased, they shifted their focus to poetry and, in 1922, began publishing a periodical called the *Fugitive*. Around 1925, after the magazine ended publication and with their membership further swelled by those who shared their philosophical interests, four of the original Fugitives began to scrutinize economic and political issues as they related to the South. The published result of their thinking was the book *I'll Take My Stand,* a collection of essays by twelve southerners that launched southern Agrarianism, an intellectual movement that has been frequently called a crusade.[4]

To fully grasp what the Fugitive/Agrarian movement was about, Weaver believed, involved an understanding that this group was not a coterie of reactionary intellectuals or devotees of the moonlight-and-magnolia worship of southern culture. Critics who mistakenly labeled this group in such a fashion could only really come to grips with what this Vanderbilt school of thought involved by understanding that it combined "traditional ideals and modern potencies." They were by no means monolithic in their thinking. Paul Conkin has aptly observed that these Nashville intellectuals were no more close-knit than the New England transcendentalists had been a century earlier.[5]

Weaver's admiration of the Agrarians must take into account their Fugitive antecedents. That many of them became Agrarians did not surprise him in the least. How a speaker or writer chooses to express himself, Weaver believed, was critical to understanding that speaker or writer's values. The Fugitives' focus on poetry demonstrated to him conclusively that these were individuals for whom "values have a reality, and that [they] were capable of emotion upon the subject of value." It is no accident, Weaver insisted, that there has always been the closest association between religion and poetry.[6]

The seven original members of the Fugitives were: Donald Davidson, James Marshall Frank, Sidney Matron Hirsch, Stanley Johnson, John Crowe Ransom, Alec B. Stevenson, and Allen Tate. Those joining later included Walter Clyde Curry, Merrill Moore, William Yandell Elliott, William Frierson, Jesse Wills, Ridley Wills, Robert Penn Warren, Laura Riding Gottschalk, and Alfred Starr. The principals of the Fugitive inner circle—John Crowe Ransom, Donald Davidson, and Allen Tate—would lead the way in the transition of this group to Agrarianism.[7]

Vanderbilt University's attitude toward the Fugitives and the Agrarians was one of either "official hostility or benign neglect" during the twenties and thirties, in spite of the fact that twelve of the fifteen Fugitives and ten of the twelve writers featured in *I'll Take My Stand* were faculty members, students, or alumni of the school. "That a few brilliant young intellectuals happened to be at Vanderbilt at the same time and that they were able to join in exciting, supportive discussions, was, from the university's perspective, serendipitous. The rich intellectual harvest was in no wise contrived. Unexpected, unappreciated, and unearned, it was an academic form of unmerited grace."[8]

John Crowe Ransom, who enrolled at Vanderbilt in 1903 at the age of fifteen, eventually became "the mentor of the Fugitives, the philosopher of the Agrarians." Ransom, the son and the grandson of Methodist ministers, grew up in a home environment of refinement and gentility. Determined to provide him the best possible education, his parents taught him at home until he was ten; their expectations were high, and he did not disappoint them. After one year in public school, he entered the Bowman School in Nashville, which had a curriculum centered on the classics such that when he enrolled at Vanderbilt, his youth belied his learning. In spite of interruptions of his college studies for two years, from 1905 to 1907, to teach in two different high schools, Ransom was graduated from the university in 1909 at the top of his class. He had honed his writing skills while serving as editor of the school newspaper and the student literary journal and was honored by being elected to Phi Beta Kappa. He taught Latin and Greek for one year after graduation and then attended Oxford for three years on a Rhodes scholarship.

Ransom's familiarity with Greek and Latin served him well at Oxford, where he studied "The Greats," read philosophy, and was taken with the ideas of Kant and of Aristotle. He was somewhat dilatory in his studies, dividing his time with golf, tennis, cards, travel, and sports. This lack of discipline resulted in his barely failing to gain a first-class-honors degree. But his Oxford B.A. was enough to gain him academic respect, and he returned to America hoping for a university position in one of the better-known northern schools. None was forthcoming. Financially strapped, and having received no university offers, he took a position at the Hotchkiss School in Connecticut. There he developed his interest in English and waited hopefully for something better. The only offer that came his way was an instructorship in English at Vanderbilt beginning in September 1914. He accepted it and in time became an important and leading participant in the discussions that would lead to the publication of the *Fugitive.*

The similarities in the background and upbringing of Donald Davidson to Ransom's were such that Davidson would later characterize the two men as "de facto cousins." Davidson's father began as a public-school teacher in Tennessee and was eventually promoted to county superintendent. He chose to educate his son at home during his early years as the Ransoms had done with their son. The financial strain that accompanied his father's meager income prevented young Davidson from attending the best private schools, but he nonetheless gained important lessons in self-discipline and classical languages at those schools to which his father could afford to send him. His four years of Latin, English, and mathematics and his three years of Greek laid a solid foundation for his later studies and intellectual development. From his musically gifted mother he developed his natural talent in that area and for a time pondered whether to enter that field.[9]

In 1909 Ransom was graduated from Vanderbilt—the same year Davidson matriculated. Since he had had to borrow money to undertake his college studies, Davidson dropped out before completing his first year and spent the next four years teaching in private academies. With the help of income from a part-time teaching position at a nearby academy, he was able to reenter Vanderbilt in 1914, where he managed to fit into his schedule the early Fugitive meetings, and he was the one who invited Ransom—his Shakespeare professor—to join them.[10]

By dint of sheer discipline, Davidson in three years had earned almost enough credits for his bachelor's degree by 1916, but penury again stopped him just short of his goal. He took a teaching job in a Pulaski prep school to make ends meet. While there he met Theresa Shearer, a Latin teacher and an Oberlin graduate whom he would later marry. Military-science credits he had picked up because he had volunteered for the service in 1917 added to those hours already on his record at Vanderbilt and gave him the requisite number for graduation; he received his B.A. degree that year.[11]

One might have expected that the Calumet Club, a Vanderbilt honorary society and the usual campus setting for literary discussions, would have served a similar purpose for the group that became the Fugitives. Sidney Matron Hirsch was perhaps the most important reason that did not happen. Hirsch's half brother and sister, both of whom attended Vanderbilt, frequently brought fellow students to their home "to the delight of Sidney, who liked nothing more than presiding over brilliant conversation." Davidson and Ransom soon became regulars along with others who would later become Fugitives.[12]

Hirsch was the catalyst vital to the group's intellectual growth and development, even though he was unlike those to whom he played host in a remarkable number of ways. Undisciplined in his thinking, he nonetheless possessed a creative imagination that seemed to be in a constant state of ferment. For Hirsch, the obvious meaning always masked subtle and hidden significances that only those properly initiated could understand. He believed that poetry and philology were the keys that often unlocked such mysteries. His "walk[ing] over philology on high stilts" entranced, provoked, and stimulated the gatherings. That this discussion group lasted as long as it did can be at least partially attributed to the point/counterpoint of Hirsch and John Crowe Ransom: "Hirsch, half guru and half clown, always ready to find great truths in any youthful comment, provided the needed stimulus toward originality; Ransom, with his dry detachment, set the standard for rigor and for intellectual self-discipline."[13]

The initial focus of the group was not on poetry; there were long, rambling discussions on philosophy and the theory of art. The readings at the Calumet Club and in Ransom's course on Shakespeare, as well as Professor Edwin Mims's class on English literature, gave opportunity to the circle to further probe ideas discussed in the Hirsch household. It was at about this time that Davidson and Ransom had begun to write poetry in private. The latter went to Davidson first with some verse he had written, seeking his friend's comments. One result of Davidson's approval and encouragement was that Ransom was able to get *Poems about God* published in England in 1919. Although the small volume attracted little attention, it did give Ransom "a professional reputation, a degree of eminence not enjoyed by his students or young colleagues."[14]

With the entry of the United States in the Great War, Davidson and Ransom went off to Fort Oglethorpe, Georgia, to officers' training school and were subsequently shipped out to join the other Americans in Europe. It is a mistake to view World War I as nothing more than a parenthesis in the dynamic of these men, or as just a change of setting for the group as one writer has suggested. While it is true that they saw little combat and that none was wounded in battle or suffered any of the various illnesses associated with trench warfare, ten Vanderbilt men who had been regulars in the Fugitive discussion group met often at the officers' field artillery training base at Samur, France, where Ransom was first a student, then an instructor. After the armistice, Ransom took courses at Grenoble, and others studied at the Sorbonne and at the University of Clermont.[15]

When the Fugitives returned to Nashville they learned that Hirsch's sister had married Nashville businessman James Frank and that Hirsch had moved in with the Franks. The group gradually reassembled, and with it came discussions in the Franks's home, where poetry soon became the topic central to their round table. Others became attached to the group as "the two men [Ransom and Hirsch] once again worked their magic with the growing number of newcomers."[16]

In 1921 Davidson began to bring with him to the meetings a Vanderbilt junior named John Orley Allen Tate. He was "an *enfant terrible,* a slim, wiry, intense, large-headed prodigy out of Kentucky.

To Hirsch the mystic, and Ransom the disciplined professor, Tate added an entirely new intellectual ingredient: youthful rebellion joined with a sympathy for poetic experimentation. As yet he was a rebel with too many causes, a somewhat obscure high priest of poetry as contrasted to Ransom's role as lucid philosopher." An enthusiastic admirer of T. S. Eliot, Tate added to the group just the right amount of irritant often crucial to creativity.[17]

A milestone was reached by the circle with the appearance in April 1922 of the first issue of the *Fugitive*. Begun with the barest of financial backing, those at the struggling little periodical often saw that shoestring reduced to a thread in imminent danger of breaking. Ransom and Tate continued to be the leading figures who "helped insure that the *The Fugitive* would exemplify careful crafts-manship." The majority, perhaps, of the university community and not a few of the periodical's regular readers found the poetry difficult, even opaque. Nonetheless, Vanderbilt and Nashville took pride in the reputation this new journal was gaining in critical circles. Interesting in the light of what would come later was the swipe taken by the first issue of the *Fugitive* at the moonlight-and-magnolia version of the South: "*The Fugitive* flees from nothing faster than from the high caste Brahmins of the Old South. Without raising the question of whether the blood in the veins of its editors runs red, they at any rate are not advertising it as blue; indeed, as to pedigree, they cheerfully invite the most unfavorable inference from the circumstances of their anonymity."[18]

Robert Penn Warren, an undergraduate from Guthrie, Kentucky, located on the border near Tennessee, had a poem published in 1923 and was subsequently invited to become a member of the *Fugitive*'s editorial board. Even though the group began to break up that same year, they had "guided the final maturation of Ransom as a poet, forced Tate to the brink of his poetic efforts, offered a rich apprenticeship to Warren, and pulled a somewhat reluctant Davidson into some critically acclaimed experimentation."[19]

The year 1930 marked a watershed that divided Fugitives from Agrarians. The former had focused on poetry and literary topics that, perforce, pushed ideology to the background or at least held it at bay during their discussions. "A Fugitive meeting was a poetry seminar, not a place to plot Agrarian conspiracies." A case could even be made for seeing the Fugitives as a study in contrast to the later Agrarians. Their poetry did not center on the lost cause or any other specifically southern ideas and the plaudits they earned were for the most part from north of the Mason-Dixon line. Nonetheless, hints of their later Agrarianism began to appear in the correspondence of Ransom, Davidson, and Tate in the early twenties; there were occasional references to southern issues, but they were anything but wedded to the region if one takes their professional lives as a measure. Tate went off to New York City in 1924, exulting in his escape from the South, happy to be in a place "where no one asked if you were a virgin or drank liquor." Ransom wanted very much to leave Vanderbilt and would have eagerly accepted an offer from any well-known northern school. Davidson's public avowal of his southern roots while in uniform during World War I may have been little more than a homesick soldier's lament, especially given that he later "married a Yankee, sought a newspaper job in Cleveland, and long contemplated a job in Ohio."

Both Ransom and Davidson were caught up in the ferment that resulted from the heady brew of the Scopes trial and from H. L. Mencken's many pointed barbs aimed at the South. The controversy boiled over onto the Vanderbilt campus and engaged the two men, provoking them to consider "possibly for the first time in their lives . . . the problems of an impoverished South and to explore the southern component of their own identity."[20] Since the "Fugitives [were] proud of their sophistication and freedom from provinciality," one would have thought that they would have sided "with the journalists and laughed at the yokels. But the descriptions of the Tennessee people, the stories filed by reporters savage with hangovers and heat, and the cartoons in the northern papers were so offensive that there could be no passing them off with a tolerant smile." When Professor Edwin Mims of the English department approached Ransom about having the Vanderbilt faculty publicly repudiate what had happened at Dayton, Ransom angrily told him no and defended the fundamentalists. Davidson, for the first time in his life, seemed to become aware of "the apparent contempt, often joined to an implacable hostility" that many Americans felt for the South. Writing to Richard Weaver a quarter of a century

later, he focused on the Dayton trial as a pivotal event that helped
transform the Fugitives into Agrarians. These men, as "poets and
literary critics . . . knew their limitations as political agitators and
organizers, but they felt compelled to take a stand." Allen Tate,
who was still in New York City, began an intellectual odyssey that
would eventually lead him to come to terms with his self-identity
by the indirect route of grappling with the meaning of the South.[21]

By 1927 the three of them were working together on how best
to defend the region and pondered the idea of a collection of essays
to help them toward their goal. This was the embryonic stage of
I'll Take My Stand, which would be published in 1930. By 1933, in
large part as a result of the book, the fledgling Agrarian movement
was on its way.[22] Davidson's description of the metamorphosis of
the circle from Fugitives to Agrarians is to the point:

> Our Fugitive meetings were rather staid, sometimes a little stilted,
> affairs (largely because of "Dr." Hirsch's constant insistence on trac-
> ing questionable etymologies and expounding mysticism). But from
> 1925 on—when we forsook Dr. Hirsch—our intimate discussions
> were much more informal, more frequent, and intense; and when
> "members" were absent, there was constant correspondence. We also
> widened our company, steadily, and broadened the range of argument.
> The year that preceded publication of *I'll Take My Stand* was a year
> of exceedingly intensive, almost furiously urgent discussion. I have
> never known anything like it. And in addition to our intimate per-
> sonal meetings we "sounded out" a considerable number of persons,
> through visits and letters.[23]

John Crowe Ransom wrote the introductory essay in *I'll Take
My Stand.* His choice of a title, "Reconstructed but Unregenerate,"
is pregnant with meaning. Reconstruction was more than just a
verbal shorthand for what he and his fellow writers believed was a
painful part of southern history. The word is redolent of invading
carpetbaggers and traitorous southern scalawags eager to curry
favor with Yankees for the basest of reasons—money and power.

Reconstruction was carried out under the watchful eye of
Union soldiers who took their orders from their Radical Republican
bosses in Washington. Former slaves were enfranchised in short
order while whites lost their right to vote and hold office under the
Wade-Davis Bill, brainchild of that most radical of all Republicans—

Thaddeus Stevens. Leaving aside the question of whether this was an oversimplification and a tissue of muddles, as some have suggested, it was the version of Reconstruction that Ransom and the other Agrarians had taken in with their mothers' milk.

It is helpful to remember that Ransom was the first of the original Fugitives to write poetry. Economy of language has always been characteristic of that mode of expression. A word or phrase may—indeed, must—have more than just surface meaning. Hence, *reconstruction* in this title served to define not only a period of American history and the southern understanding of it but also an implied aversion to the notion of reconstruction per se. The word by itself and without the above referents denotes a rebuilding. This is an entirely appropriate metaphor for the kind of rebuilding done by those who are *merely* builders: they make things; they are able to rebuild an exact physical replica of what has been destroyed so that an untutored eye can not tell the difference. But how can one rebuild the broken human spirit? Or reconstruct a civilization irretrievably lost? When the Union troops were withdrawn from the South in 1877, the South was in one sense reconstructed. Cities were growing, and thousands of miles of new railway tracks crisscrossed what had been the Confederacy. Evident signs of the war's destruction were gone and smoke was belching from the smokestacks of newly sprouted factories.

But what about the unseen? The antebellum South had a way of life, a culture all its own. Had that also been "reconstructed"? What about the unique qualities of the southern spirit? According to Ransom, that part of the South was not only not reconstructed, but it was "unregenerate" as well. The unregenerate, of course, remain implacably what they are apart from a radical change or conversion, which is usually understood to result from the action of an outside, or even divine, agent. Ransom concluded that the South was gloriously unregenerate in spite of losing a devastating four-year-long war and being superficially reconstructed. It clung stubbornly to its "European principles of culture," and, more specifically, to what he called the tradition of the English countryside. By this he meant his readers to understand:

> The human life of the English provinces long ago came to terms with nature, fixed its roots somewhere in the spaces between the rocks and

in the shade of the trees, founded its comfortable institutions, secured its modest prosperity—and then willed the whole in perpetuity to the generations which should come after, in the ingenuous confidence that it would afford them all the essential human satisfactions. For it is the character of a seasoned provincial life that it is realistic, or successfully adapted to its natural environment, and that as a consequence it is stable, or hereditable.[24]

Industrial America, by way of contrast, was at war with nature and nature's rhythms and worshiping the gospel of progress. The wonder of technology was not what it could do but that it was mindless and created its own momentum. Noting that "the old Southern life was of course not so fine as some of the traditionalists like to believe" and that "slavery was a feature monstrous enough in theory," Ransom appealed to the South to "be industrialized—but to a certain extent only, in moderation." The section had to hang on to its historic identity for its own sake as well as for that of the nation. The refusal to be regenerated by the gospel of progress, the unhurried way of doing things, and not seeing nature as something to conquer were lessons that all of America desperately needed, he concluded.[25]

Richard Weaver first read and reviewed the Agrarian manifesto while on the staff of the student newspaper at the University of Kentucky. He was delighted when *I'll Take My Stand* was reprinted as a Harper Torchbook in 1962. It is significant that he twice referred to it as a great work of American social criticism. In order to grasp how this work influenced his thinking, we must take a look at the last essay to be published during his lifetime. The title of his essay "The Southern Phoenix" underlined his belief in the work's endurance and continuing relevance. Those who cavalierly tried to dismiss it as merely controversial were only admitting, he believed, that a nerve had been touched: this book dealt with values, a realm reviewers more often than not preferred to ignore.[26]

We live in an era that celebrates pluralism and diversity. This usually translates to a belief that attaches equal merit to all ideas and practices and ultimacy to none; questions of real moment often go unasked as being simply irrelevant. Interestingly enough, Weaver lauded *I'll Take My Stand* as a place a reader might go "to learn something of the pluralism of American culture." He of course meant that America, in spite of industrialism, had not become a monolith.

Three things gave this book its enduring quality, Weaver believed. The contributors, gifted men all, had spent hundreds of hours in discussion together over a long period of years so that the whole of their written wisdom and insights was greater than the sum of the group's individual members. Additionally, they were all legatees of the southern tradition and intuitively understood and agreed on many fundamental presuppositions as givens that did not need to be set forth in any formal way. Finally, they shared a belief that they could together defend against all comers the tradition that they loved and that had been under attack for over a century.

It was of little wonder that one of the causes of *I'll Take My Stand*'s unpopularity was its hostility to both socialism and capitalism. The book first appeared just at the time when capitalism seemed to be permanently on the rocks and shortly before the beginning of the New Deal, which had at least some features of socialism and would be offered as a solution to America's woes. Agrarianism had a venerable ancestry that antedated both. Thomas Jefferson had insisted that farmers were God's chosen and extolled their way of life as superior to that of city dwellers and tradesmen. "Socialism is by definition anti-conservative," Weaver wrote, "and capitalism cannot be conservative in the true sense as long as its reliance is upon industrialism, whose very nature is to unsettle any establishment and initiate the endless innovation of technological 'progress.' "[27]

What influenced Weaver most in this southern manifesto was its ready juxtaposition with his southernness that, although it had retreated to the background of his thinking, remained intact and responded favorably to the Agrarians under whom he was studying in Nashville, especially John Crowe Ransom. The "social democrats" at Kentucky, whom he remembered as being midwesterners, had dealt telling blows to the commonly accepted summary of the antebellum myth with which he had grown up of a southern golden age destroyed forever by war and reconstruction. The Agrarians at Vanderbilt rekindled his interest in the myth. He had developed enough of a critical attitude at that point to question the northern myth of a nation going forth simply to save the Union and free the slaves. "Southern history, as the Agrarians interpreted it, represented a moral alternative to national myths of innocence, omnipotence, and invincibility." Underneath the commonly accepted southern version, Weaver believed that he had found a core of truth that the force of war and legislation could never change. The endurance of *I'll Take My Stand* as a work of social criticism could easily be explained, Weaver said, writing over thirty years after it first appeared. The southern characteristics that he most admired had stubbornly refused to yield to military defeat, occupation, and the passage of time for the very simple reason that they were timeless. What were they? A society that retained some of the characteristics of feudalism, a resistance to scientism, and a reverence for Scripture.[28] Those enduring qualities he would explore at length in his doctoral dissertation at Louisiana State University; no doubt the seed was planted in his mind while he was at Vanderbilt.

Donald Davidson's essay in *I'll Take My Stand,* "A Mirror for Artists," also caught Weaver's attention. In it, Davidson lamented the effects of industrialism on the arts. The frenetic pace of work in such an order took away the leisure necessary to creativity. All great art is necessarily provincial; indeed, Davidson believed, it must be anchored to a time and place and culture in order for it to speak to the larger world outside. To protect the integrity of their calling, American artists ought to "flee the infection of our times, to stand for decentralization in the arts" and "resist with every atom of . . . strength the false gospels of art as a luxury which can be sold in commercial quantities or which can be hallowed by segregation in discreet shrines."[29]

Frank Lawrence Owsley's essay in this symposium emphasized that the North had imposed its version of American history on several generations of southern schoolchildren. This point was one with which Weaver was in hearty agreement: that the South was being robbed of its history. "In short, the South either had no history, or its history was tainted with slavery and rebellion and must be abjured."[30]

It is a fact that the Agrarians assumed that whites should exercise political authority over blacks in the South. Taken at face value, this would seem to be simply nothing more than racism.

Allen Tate, who did believe that blacks were culturally—if not racially—inferior to whites, in a letter asked his correspondent to imagine a biracial southern society made up of caucasians and Chinese. The Chinese were racially superior to the caucasians, of course. But the latter would have to deal with the Chinese in more or less the same way that they had been dealing with the blacks. "Racial dictatorship [did not] rest on claims to self-anointed racial superiority." The real issue was how to maintain the culture so that the community as such could continue and prosper. This "theoretical point retains its chilling force" notwithstanding Tate's lamentably limited and narrow perspective that blinded him to blacks' many contributions to southern culture and to recognizing them as a vital component of that culture.[31]

It was not Weaver's purpose in "The Southern Phoenix" to comment directly on every essay in this symposium but rather to focus on *I'll Take My Stand*'s unique qualities. The Agrarianism it set forth stood in stark contrast to the other "isms" jostling for attention at the time—humanism, Marxism, technology as savior, and the New Deal—in one critical way. Agrarianism offered a multifaceted prescription for the nation's ills instead of a simplistic cure-all:

> There is nothing of the narrowness of a cult about it. . . . Humanism was very much a cult. . . . Marxism was fatally flawed by its assumption that economics is the prime determinant of social organization. Technocracy was nothing more than an engineering approach to the problems of economic dislocation. New Dealism, though socialistic in tendency, hardly enjoyed the benefits of a theory at all; it was a hand-to-mouth dealing with problems created by the Great Depression, a set of improvisations which became more politicized as time went on.

All who contributed to this symposium, Weaver insisted, believed that ideas that are true will have consequences. The Agrarians were undaunted by the odds they faced; they believed in their heart of hearts that the order they were proposing was achievable, even though the circumstances under which they published their manifesto seemed to point to *I'll Take My Stand* as doomed from the outset, a pathetic exercise in futility.[32]

Although he was Richard M. Weaver's thesis advisor at Vanderbilt, it would be some time before the extent of Ransom's influence would be evident. Weaver would one day praise *God without Thunder* as the most profound work produced by any Agrarian writer. He did not shrink from criticizing the South for its paucity of this sort of work. With the exceptions of the writings of Jefferson, John Taylor, and Calhoun, the South had produced no significant works of a philosophic bent. H. L. Mencken's "Sahara of the Bozart" might even have been an understatement: The South was a cultural wasteland and specifically a place of "philosophical barrenness." Writing in 1950, Weaver noted, "Though the modern South has become prolific in a literary way . . . there is still hardly a trickle of analytical writing, apart from the stuffy treatises of social science which emerge from university presses. Reporters of the local scene have appeared in swarms, novelists in shoals; poetry and drama have their following, but philosophy does not. . . . The bane of Southern writing has been an infatuation with surfaces."[33] Here is the kind of penetrating and independent criticism that characterizes Weaver's thought; he was no neo-Confederate or card-carrying conservative.

God without Thunder was anything but a superficial work. Subtitled *An Unorthodox Defence of Orthodoxy,* the book was an extended philosophical critique of "an amiable and understandable God . . . who wouldn't hurt us; who would let us understand him; who would agree to scrap all the thunderbolts of his armament. . . . The new religion reduces the God of the Old Testament to a minor figure in the Godhead, or even now and then expels him altogether."[34]

Ransom's work can best be understand as an extensive and biting critique of the theological liberalism that arose in the late nineteenth century. It began with Adolf von Harnack's series of lectures given at Tübingen University in Germany in 1899 entitled *Das Wesen des Christentums (The Essence of Christianity).* It was Harnack's purpose to make Christianity acceptable to the men of his day. He lay stress on the ethical teachings of Jesus and downplayed the miraculous. This way of understanding seemed to critics to make of God a learned professor who, if given time, would rationally explain all of his acts in a gentlemanly fashion. Such a deity was also most anxious not to offend scientific sensibilities by interfering with nature.[35]

Ransom's critique shared some characteristics of another reaction in the English-speaking world against liberal theology—neorthodoxy. Neorthodoxy was self-consciously grounded in the Protestant Reformation tradition and held that the Bible contained the word of God, although it was not inerrant. Narrative secular history, or *Geschichte,* this movement claimed, ran parallel to *Heilsgeschichte,* or sacred history: both could be found in Scripture. It was the latter that was most important. The critical responsibility of individuals was to bow before the Christ of faith rather than the Jesus of history since each person was a sinful rebel against a holy God.[36]

Ransom principally differed from the neorthodox understanding of God in three ways. First, he refused to recognize the *Geschichte* understanding of history. Instead, he insisted that the Bible be seen as an Eastern book, and be understood primarily as myth. Myths, in his calculus, were not historical events but stories nonetheless pregnant with meaning. Secondly, he saw the Bible as primarily an Oriental, rather than an Occidental, work. And, finally, God was the source of both good *and* evil.

The religion that flowed naturally from nineteenth-century theological liberalism's concept of the deity proceeded on two assumptions, Ransom wrote: "that God as the ruler of the universe governs it in such a manner as to make it accommodate itself to the welfare of man. The earth is for man's abode and God 'developed it'; this phrase suggests that his instrument was an evolutionary or scientific process. Thus God is a scientist; the universe is his workshop; but among his productions he has produced man, and all the other productions are for man's benefit." The second assumption of this new faith defined man: "God is the great and original scientist; but man himself is a little scientist. For he can understand God's scientific technique, and he can in considerable degree apply it in the human sphere, anticipating God, and hastening the course of his good work. . . . [This] God . . . we are given to understand is a God who serves. The beneficiary, of course, is man." This benevolent deity would not dream of interfering with man's technological progress since "now that it is God's will that mankind be served, it becomes holy living if mankind proceeds to serve itself as hard as possible." In summary,

> The God of the new religion is anthropomorphic. So doubtless, are the gods of most other religions. But the present anthropomorphism is peculiarly tame and ingenuous. When God was pictured in the likeness of a fabulously Great Man, of marvelous technique and uncertain favor, it was fairly difficult for one to be at ease in Zion; for his fiat was unaccountable and unpredictable; and man worshipping him was necessarily humble, and for the time being neglectful of the ordinary routine of practical life as a very vain thing. But the new religion represents God as a Great Man with the uncertainties left out: a Great Man whose ways are scientific and knowable and whose intention is amiable and constant. The net result of holding by this religion is just to be encouraged in attending to one's own human concerns, secured of God's favour and finding no propriety in burnt offering and sacrifice.[37]

It was only a short step, Ransom wrote, from man's dismay and humility engendered by the displacement of the Ptolemaic cosmology with that of Copernicus, to his aiming "perhaps, slyly and half-consciously at first, and then greedily and openly as soon as they can, at reducing them [natural phenomena] to human prediction and control." Such thinking ineluctably resulted in "the triumph of the God of Science over the God of Israel."[38]

Evil as well as good originated with the God of Israel, Ransom said. One must come to terms with evil in the world; the "new religionists" simply ignored evil out of existence, becoming de facto Christian Scientists. They turned away from the "Oriental" God of the Old Testament and became "militant Occidentals [who] acknowledge no limits to their power."[39]

Ransom himself was anything but orthodox when measured by the historic creeds of Christianity, and the theology of his book is Unitarian. But while he did not accept the biblical record as literal and historic, he nonetheless saw essential truth expressed there as myth. He prefaced his treatment of myth with a blunt assertion: "Myths are construed very simply by the hard Occidental mind: they are lies." Granting to the higher critics of Scripture their premises, he insisted that "their [the Scriptures'] unhistorical and unscientific character is not their vice but their excellence."

Myth rounds out history and gives meaning to brute fact. And it makes demands on its hearers. In Ransom's words, *"The myth is not descriptive but prescriptive"* [Ransom's emphasis].[40]

Weaver noted that Ransom's critique of technology in *God without Thunder* would play a pivotal role in the Agrarian movement. This work, Weaver wrote, "employed all the means of modern dialectic to show two things: what happens to religion when it is deprived of its sternness and is reduced to a mild humanitarianism; and what happens to the individual man when he sacrifices a certain free aesthetic impulse to the tyrannous demands of efficiency."[41]

God without Thunder, according to Weaver's interpretation, explicated the basic dichotomy between a "poetic or aesthetic" view of the world as over against one that was strictly "technical" or "utilitarian," with Ransom coming down on the side of the former. This work, Weaver insisted, had thrown down the gauntlet before modernism and directly confronted its presuppositions. The tame God of theological liberalism had been displaced with the righteous judge whose mighty acts could not be explained away because they were embarrassing to modern readers of Scripture. Weaver's greatest admiration was for Ransom's insistence that "myth is a form of cognition not displaced by rationalism." And he admired the work's "suave language" as much as its fighting spirit. He did wonder why the book had not attracted much critical attention.[42]

Weaver was also indebted to Ransom for his critique of what he called "modernism." This is not to be confused with the movement that Daniel J. Singal treats in *The War Within: From Victorianism to Modernist Thought in the South, 1919–1945.* Weaver saw this phenomenon as "the breakdown of cultural forms . . . [an] urgency, impatience, truculence . . . [a] determination to strip aside all concealing veils and see what is behind them." In order not to confuse the two, it would have been better if he had used the word *modernity,* whose origins Weaver pushed back to William of Occam and the birth of nominalism in the fourteenth century. A recent essay by Samuel Francis comments on modernity and notes with appreciation Weaver's incisive commentary on the phenomenon as understood by Ransom.[43]

It is commonplace that the impact of a seminal work is sometimes inversely proportional to the number of those who first read and understand it. That Weaver admired the work and was attracted to Ransom's diagnosis of modernity we have seen from his own words. Charles K. Follette has observed that it was perhaps Ransom's subtitle that caught Weaver's eye and fired his imagination. "It is 'catchy' in the same way as a popular melody or lyric that 'runs through one's head,' and one might suppose that Weaver spent some time reflecting on what it meant." For Ransom to have written precisely about the subtitle's message would have been to give away the game and put him at cross-purposes with the general tone of the work. It is to be remembered that the book was self-consciously written to enable the reader to understand the "Oriental" view of religion (mystical, mythic, indirect, and transcendent) as opposed to the "Occidental" (scientific, demythologized, direct, and immanent).[44]

Rather than taking the pose of a crusader planting the flag with sword at the ready, Ransom seemed to be saying that the best approach in defending truth is the indirect one. "New tactics" could mean a number of things, but if the battles are fought primarily in the arena of ideas, the indirect approach might meet with more success than a frontal assault. Myths, Ransom held, were powerful weapons in this particular fray.

While it would appear that Weaver cannot say too much in praise of *God without Thunder*, he lavished even more admiration on its author as the teacher par excellence. Musing on Ransom's style, Weaver averred that it was difficult to explain exactly *how* he managed to have so much influence on his students:

> If one judged solely by outward motions and immediate results, he seemed neither to work very hard at teaching nor to achieve much success. Long after the date of a lecture—a week, a month, a year—you would find some remark of his troubling you with its pregnancy, and you would set about your own reflections on it, often wishing that you had the master at hand to give another piece of insight. The idea of Ransom which chiefly took possession of me at this time was that of the "unorthodox defense of orthodoxy," which he had developed in his brilliant book, *God without Thunder.*

Weaver's emphasis, it must be noted, was not on the book but on the man.[45] As is often the case with admirers, Weaver focused more on the person than on what he had written.

Ransom's unorthodox defense of orthodoxy did not practice a strategy of confrontation by insisting that he was holding out for truth against error. Instead, he used the same sort of approach as that taken by the demythologizers—pragmatism. Putting aside the question of whether the great religious stories of the Bible are historically or scientifically verifiable, he sought to persuade his readers that the kind of truth they embodied was of great practical value in giving people meaning and purpose in life.

It was while he was under the tutelage of Ransom and other Agrarians at Vanderbilt that it began to dawn on Weaver that "many traditional positions in our world had suffered not so much because of inherent defect as because of the stupidity, ineptness, and intellectual sloth of those who for one reason or another were presumed to have their defense in charge."[46]

Troubled by that premonition, Weaver tried to make sense of it over the course of the next two years in the light of the stresses that the Great Depression was putting on America. During the thirties, when thoughtful Americans were asking hard questions about basic national assumptions, many had despaired not only of free-market capitalism but also of democracy itself. Unemployment lines in the country's cities were swelled by farmers who had lost their land and given up hope of ever being able to make a living tilling the soil again. Having found credible the socialist critique he had learned at the University of Kentucky, Weaver had it reinforced by the undeniable economic realities of the Great Depression. It was clear to him that "nearly all of the traditional American ideologies were in retreat," but he had not even "suspected that this retreat might be owing to a kind of default." As much out of curiosity as anything else, he wondered whether there could be a legitimate defense of that tradition. Might the problem be that their advocates failed because they were too lazy to learn how "to speak a modern idiom or even to acquire essential knowledge"? What if his own ignoring of time-honored ways of seeing might be owing to nothing more than chronological snobbery, a sort of unthinking assumption that the latest is always the best, and a predisposition to put everything into a modern context? He would later declare flatly: "It is the most arrant presentism to say that philosophy cannot be practiced because that philosophy is found in the past and the past is now gone. The whole value of a philosophy lies in its detachment from accidental conditions of this kind and its adherence to the essential."[47] But that kind of bold certainty would be many years in coming.

While he was drawn to the Agrarians at Vanderbilt as persons with individuality and genius, Weaver was not one to abandon hastily what he felt were carefully thought-out premises about himself and the world; he also admitted to a "reluctance over giving up a position once publicly espoused, made somewhat greater by a young man's vanity." He had been a foot soldier for socialism and was loath to lower his weapon much less to join the other side, in spite of the fact that both socialists and Agrarians shared common ground in insisting that industrial capitalism was a dismal failure. In spite of that, what continued to draw him powerfully toward the Agrarians' orbit was their "ideal of the individual in contact with the rhythms of nature, of the small-property holding, and of the society of pluralistic organization."[48]

Weaver's M.A. thesis at Vanderbilt, written under the direction of John Crowe Ransom, was entitled "The Revolt against Humanism." Irving Babbitt and Paul Elmer More were the chief spokesmen for this movement in American literary criticism, which was most influential from 1915 through 1933. They insisted on the existence of universal criteria to which both ethics and aesthetics ought to conform. While they were greatly influenced by Christian tradition, they shied away from creedal formulations of any sort. Man's emotions, they believed, ought to be subordinated to his will and reason and were not to be allowed to run riot. During the time that Weaver was writing his thesis, the critical issues over which the humanists and their opponents clashed included: "the extent of the artist's freedom to create without restriction [and] the relationship between the absolute and the relative."[49]

The new humanists offered a penetrating diagnosis of the intellectual mood of early-twentieth-century America that they felt had "a sterile obsession with the unique, the individual, the immediate, and the changing," and a consequent unhealthy fascination "with the pluralistic diversity of an 'open universe.'" The naturalism and pragmatism of the late nineteenth century, they believed, had fostered the view that human beings were little more than the playthings of their impulses, emotions, and environment. Determinism had pushed aside free will, which in the view of the naturalists and pragmatists was little more than a quaint philosophical notion that had no basis in reality.[50]

Weaver argued in his thesis that Babbitt and More were engaged in a quixotic quest that was doomed. He also left little doubt that his respect for his mentor did not extend to embracing Ransom's ideas. John Dewey, the target of much criticism in Weaver's later writings, came in for kind words. He especially appreciated that thinker's antisupernaturalism: "Dewey has . . . [shown] that any of those things which are consequences of intelligent action may be termed enjoyments. He has also spiked some guns by proving that values exist—since they have a naturalistic basis—before any need is felt to 'validate' them: in other words that we do not have to prove the existence of what is [exists] inevitably. Supernatural sanctions come after the fact is already established, and are at any time superfluous."[51] He goes on to quote with approval Henry Hazlitt's harsh assessment of the literary humanists as "a small clique of the self-appointed [who have] arrogated to themselves a name that stood, in the fifteenth century, for a genuinely liberating attitude, and degraded it to a synonym for tight academicism. The whole doctrine has become little more than a rationalization for neo-phobia and a piece of special pleading for the genteel tradition." Besides Ransom, the only other Agrarian mentioned in his thesis is Allen Tate, whose observation that "the religious unity of intellect and emotion, of reason and instinct, is the sole technique for the realization of values" was gleefully quoted by Weaver to buttress his point that the literary humanists could not even agree among themselves about the function of religion.[52]

In the conclusion of his thesis, Weaver used strong language that might have come from either William James or John Dewey: "Beliefs," he flatly asserted, "also must undergo the *pragmatic* [emphasis mine] test, for the man who wins a convert to his side is thereby confirmed in the conviction of his own rightness, and to be [a] solitary cherisher of a principle is a thing intolerable to all but a few whom the world would call cranks and fanatics." Thus, humanism had failed in America. Not only that, but the Great

Depression made a mockery of the notion that what really matters is an integrated worldview based on timeless verities that would keep one serene among the vicissitudes of daily life. The economic throes that much of the country was in had shattered the new humanists' vision beyond repair. In a kind of implied determinism that he would later self-consciously reject, Weaver added: "Surely the course of history has been unkind to them."[53]

Excoriating this group for what he believed was a dogged obscurantism, Weaver scorned the humanists for their dogmatic and hostile stance toward their enemies. Their fatal flaw was an insistence on an "unscientific" reliance on intuition:

> Although absolutely no worse off than mystics, idealistic philosophers and evangelists, they were in a time when objectivity in all things was cultivated as a virtue. Science, being the most abstract and the most general type of systematized knowledge, has the highest communicability. It has, moreover, methods of proof which purposefully rule out the 'personal equation,' treating it as something untrustworthy. The validity of its laws depends on the number of instances outwardly visible. Against truths of this sort, based on objects of common perception, the Humanists could bring only a mythical psychology and a spirit of exhortation.

Weaver thus concluded that literary humanism not only had failed but also was doomed from its outset. His grappling with the question of why that had happened was the first effort he made in studying lost causes. He struggled with whether there even existed such a thing as free will. If responsible choice were demanded of human beings, he wondered, then there must be some enduring standard by which right and proper choices can and should be made. Otherwise, "it becomes nonsensical to evaluate those circumstances unless we are willing to empty 'good' of all its meaning by making it equivalent to success."[54] Here we can discern Weaver's mental anguish reaching a kind of crescendo. If he were to abandon his socialism, then it too would be simply another lost cause rather than a source of the enduring standards he greatly desired. Still, he continued to shun Agrarianism as a valid alternative. At this point in his life what he principally shared with the Agrarians was a scorn for the new humanists, especially Paul Elmer More and Irving Babbitt.

Looking back on this group some two decades after he had studied under them at Vanderbilt, Weaver placed heavy emphasis on the point that many of the Agrarians were poets. Ransom wrote, "Poetry is the kind of knowledge by which we must know what we have arranged so that we shall not know otherwise." Weaver was saying the same thing when he wrote, "The very acceptance of poetry commits one to the realm of value, and this meant that their judgments were to be in part ethical and aesthetic." Their apologia for the South and Agrarianism was thus not a political or legal defense, but rather one built on "ethical and aesthetic considerations [which] cannot be ignored at any time." *I'll Take My Stand* was a real departure since it put the South on the offensive against such critics as H. L. Mencken. As an undergraduate at the University of Kentucky, Weaver had greatly admired Mencken and had commented favorably on him in an article he wrote for the student newspaper, the *Kentucky Kernel*. Resorting to martial language and metaphor, as he often did, Weaver described the Agrarian manifesto as "a general offensive against the enemy positions, with some excellent results."[55]

Weaver's friend and fellow debater during his undergraduate days at the University of Kentucky, Clifford Amyx, stopped by Nashville for a brief visit while Weaver was a graduate student there. Amyx was somewhat surprised to discover that his socialist friend had fallen under the spell of the Agrarians. Weaver insisted with a kind of evangelistic fervor that the two of them sit in on John Crowe Ransom's poetry class, even though Amyx had a train layover of only a few hours; he was on his way to San Francisco and a job. "He promised me a treat," Amyx remembered, "and indeed I have never heard a more luminous session on poetry. Ransom was a man of indelible charm and perhaps the least aggressive among the Agrarians and the attraction of the men of Vanderbilt was manifest that day." Amyx recalled further that the Agrarians "had just a kind of compelling kind of southern charm that Dick Weaver could never resist."[56]

Of the fact that *I'll Take My Stand* had a powerful impact on him, there can be little doubt. The combined effect of the Fugitive/Agrarian circle in Nashville on Weaver, as a graduate student in some of his most formative years, is clear in the words he wrote about how the book affected thoughtful readers at the time of its publication: "Penetrations were made and flanks were threatened; and the enemy was alerted to a degree he had not experienced in decades."[57] His own mental fortress was undermined by Agrarianism, although it would take some time for him to admit it. His admiration for poetry and respect for the poets as those who speak about ultimate truths further weakened his socialist convictions. Like many under such an attack, he fought all the harder—for the time being. And so he left Vanderbilt in 1936, having earned his M.A. degree in English, but still torn between the leftist vision he had committed himself to during his undergraduate days in Lexington and that of the Agrarians whom he had come to know and respect while at Vanderbilt.

4 | The Poetical and Ethical Vision of Life

[THE AGRARIANS] UNDERSTOOD FROM THE BEGINNING . . . THROUGH THEIR REVERENCE FOR THE OFFICE OF POET, THAT MAN REQUIRES SOME CONCEPTION OF THE ABSOLUTE TO MAINTAIN HIS HUMANITY. ACCORDINGLY WE HAVE RANSOM'S SEARCHING CRITIQUE OF HUMANIZED RELIGION; TATE'S PREMISE THAT MAN IS BY NATURE INCURABLY RELIGIOUS; AND WARREN'S SUBTLE STUDIES, IN VERSE AND PROSE, OF ORIGINAL SIN AND THE PROBLEM OF REDEMPTION. . . . THEY HAD THE COURAGE OF THEIR COMMITMENTS, AND . . . THEIR HUMANISM IS A WAY INTO SOMETHING DEEPER AND MORE MEANINGFUL, WHERE THERE IS NO EVADING THE QUESTION OF WHETHER MAN HAS A FINAL CAUSE.[1]

Having left Vanderbilt with his socialism intact, although shaken by his encounter with the Agrarians, Richard M. Weaver accepted a teaching position at Texas A & M University in College Station in 1937, thus beginning a miserable chapter in his life. To the careful student of Weaver, his seemingly neutral characterization of the university as "a large technical college in Texas" is freighted with meaning. He was put off by bigness and numbers as measures of success, and he found the wide-open spaces of east Texas depressing. In his later life, backward glances at those three years in the Lone Star State always awakened distasteful memories. In language as strong as he used anywhere, Weaver characterized what he found there as "a rampant philistinism, abetted by technology, large-scale organization, and a complacent acceptance of success as the goal of life." The experiences of those

61

years joined the issue of his halting between two opinions. "I was here forced to see that the lion of applied science and the lamb of the humanities were not going to lie down together in peace, but that the lion was going to devour the lamb unless there was a very stern keeper of order," he wrote. Viewing the matter from the perspective gained from more than twenty intervening years, he concluded that his "conversion to the poetic and ethical vision of life dates from this contact with its sterile opposite."[2]

Weaver was not, however, the lone critic or dissenter at A & M. He found a colleague in the English department, Frank W. Powell, who was asking the same kind of hard questions. In a long letter to Weaver that he wrote partly by way of response to *Ideas Have Consequences* shortly after it was published in 1948, Powell reminisced about the good discussions the two had had at "the Yellow Dog, located, as you will remember, on the periphery of Bryan, where to escape the local bourgeoisie, we did oft repair to mix and mingle with the underprivileged, the 'divine average.'" Lambasting materialism and progress with a vigor that no doubt warmed Weaver's heart, he wrote:

> I think it was James Truslow Adams who said that we moderns identify progress with change and that this explains our worship of machines, which change things. I also acknowledge with deep sorrow that our materialistic scale of values is leading us away from the eternal verities, to which we must return if we are to think of man's destiny as moral rather than economic. To the Scriptural pronouncements that "The love of money is the root of all evil" and that "It is more blessed to give than to receive," the Modern says "Pure Nonsense!" I believe, too, that selfishness (egotism, you call it) is at the root of our troubled world.[3]

Gently chiding his friend for an imprecise use of the word *conservatism* in *Ideas Have Consequences*, Powell ended with fulsome praise of the work as a whole and promised to elaborate at length on his favorite chapters in later correspondence. Weaver's standing as one who enjoyed intellectual sparring over a drink with one friend or just a few was buttressed by Powell's closing sentence: "Would that we might discuss the fate of the world over a cold glass of lager beer!"[4]

Even though his misgivings about the socialist vision may have been growing while he was teaching in Texas, Weaver did the politically correct thing in contributing to the socialist cause célèbre of the mid-1930s by sending a check to the Spanish loyalists who opposed General Franco during the Spanish civil war. He received a certificate from the headquarters of the Clothing and Leather Workers Union in Paris expressing their official thanks for his "donating a pair of combat boots for an antifascist soldier at the front fighting for the Spanish Republic."[5] The one thing that American socialists of every stripe could agree on at this time—whether they were old-line campaigners who had tried to get Eugene V. Debs elected president, or those who had broken with the American Communist Party—was that the Spanish civil war provided a laboratory in which Marx and Engels might be vindicated.[6] Jeffrey Hart has written about the Spanish civil war as a watershed between an old and a new style of conflict— the internationalized civil war. "The first such war . . . began in Spain in 1936 when the forces of General Franco rebelled against the Republic." Here was a struggle that divided not only Spain but Europe and the United States as well. "To the battlefields of Iberia came men from Germany, Italy, France, Britain, Russia, and America. The Spanish Civil War was the prototype of the transnational ideological war between Left and Right; the same 'cleavage of opinion' had recurred ever since: over Yugoslavia, over Greece, Cuba and Vietnam. Spain, to borrow a phrase from Allen Guttmann, opened a 'wound in the heart.' "[7]

The Spanish civil war ended, of course, with the triumph of General Franco and the defeat of the loyalists. Brute force decided the contest: Franco won largely because Hitler and Mussolini sent military hardware that was more advanced and plentiful than what the loyalists received from the Soviet Union and elsewhere. His socialist idealism and convictions had led Weaver to contribute to the side that he no doubt felt deserved to win. But might had defeated right. Weaver must have experienced the same kind of disillusionment that George Orwell poignantly wrote about in *Homage to Catalonia*.[8] Orwell, who had been a communist sympathizer like Weaver and many other intellectuals in the 1930s, had trekked off to Spain and spent the better part of a year fighting against Franco until he was hit in the throat by a bullet and nearly died. In observing the brutality of the communist forces, Orwell saw firsthand what Weaver and many other Party members, fellow travelers, and communist sympathizers such as Malcolm Cowley had to find out in slower and more subtle ways—that communism was a failed dream. Orwell's experience in Spain, like Edmund Wilson's travels a little earlier in Russia, turned him immediately and totally away from communism. Cowley and others, hearing such reports, were slower to act. The result was that Cowley was investigated by the Dies Committee in 1942 when he worked for the Office of Facts and Figures in Washington and wrote, with E. B. White and others, about the Four Freedoms.[9] Weaver, had he not had wretched eyesight and other physical disabilities, might have volunteered for the Lincoln Brigade and gone to Spain; on the other hand, had he been a little older and more advanced in his career, and stayed with socialism longer, he might have undergone the kind of investigation and opprobrium that Cowley suffered. But Weaver, like Cowley, in responding to his own frustrating experiences with the communist form of socialism, gave up garden-variety politics altogether, and was not thereafter associated with a political party. Shortly before he died, Cowley set forth his political philosophy in words that could well have been written by Weaver if one were to substitute North Carolina place-names. "I am a little American. I am and always have been a patriotic native of some American neighborhood: at first it was Blacklick Township in Cambria County, Pennsylvania, then later—and for fifty years—it has been Sherman, Connecticut (present population about 2,300, which I think is too many). . . . Perhaps the America I love best is the country of my boyhood, with open fields to run barefoot in and never a chainlink fence in days of travel over dirt roads."[10]

It is almost certainly the case that pondering this doomed crusade in Spain led to Weaver's intense study of another lost cause, that of the American South defeated in the Civil War. Concerning that struggle, he wrote: "The American Civil War, because it was a civil struggle, with an elaborate ideology on both sides, left a rich store of material on the subject." One of the prime reasons for the North's military victory was its industrial might. Factories in the United States churned out the implements of war in amazing numbers and at an astonishing pace. The Confederacy simply could not compete industrially. Why the South went to war in the first place and why it continued to fight in the face of overwhelming military odds were two questions to which Weaver had begun to give increasing attention while living in College Station.[11] He was especially interested in primary sources, an aspect of his intellectual interests and procedures that he followed as a singularly independent thinker throughout his career. What others said in secondary works about his subjects held considerably less interest for Weaver, who seldom cited such sources.

During his trip back to Texas in the fall of 1939 to begin his third year teaching at A & M, Weaver brooded over the gloomy prospect of being yet another two semesters in a place he loathed. What happened to him then is best described in his own words:

> I recall very sharply how, in the autumn of 1939, as I was driving one afternoon across the monotonous prairies of Texas to begin my third year in this post, it came to me *like a revelation* [emphasis mine] that I did not have to go back to this job, which had become distasteful, and that I did not have to go on professing the clichés of liberalism, which were becoming meaningless to me. I saw that my opinions had been formed out of a timorous regard for what was supposed to be intellectually respectable, and that I had always been looking over my shoulder to find out what certain others, whose concern with truth I was beginning to believe to be not very intense, were doing or thinking. It is a great experience to wake up at a critical juncture to the fact that one does have a free will, and that giving up the worship of false idols is a quite practicable proceeding. . . . At the end of that year I chucked the uncongenial job and went off to start my education over, being now arrived at the age of thirty.[12]

Weaver apparently never discussed this pivotal experience in his intellectual odyssey with anyone and devoted a bare two paragraphs to it in his autobiographical memoir. This presents some difficulty in trying to explain and understand exactly how and why the change occurred. To be sure, his new way of seeing things was not an isolated revelation that Weaver had experienced while on his way back to College Station. We must remember that he left Vanderbilt still "poised between the two alternatives" of Socialism and Agrarianism. The contextual framework of this change also included his extensive reading of primary sources of the Civil War. During his years in Texas, Weaver had also become more and more critical of the *way* he had been schooled. That he had been taught factual knowledge, gained critical skills, and could reason logically he did not dispute. But something vital was lacking. With regard to history, for example, Weaver felt that he had learned its form without really understanding it. Recalling a line from one of his Agrarian mentors at Vanderbilt, Allen Tate, who wrote, "There's more to killing than commentary," Weaver said:

> The wisdom of this will be seen also by those who study the killings in which whole nations are the killers and the killed, namely, wars. To put this in a prose statement: the mere commentary of a historian will never get you inside the feeling of a war or any great revolutionary process. For that, one has to read the testimonials of those who participated in it on both sides and in all connections; and often the best insight will appear in the casual remark of an obscure warrior or field nurse or in the effort of some ill-educated person to articulate a feeling.[13]

To use religious language, we would say that Weaver underwent the secular equivalent of a religious conversion. William James in *The Varieties of Religious Experience* defines conversion as the process by which, gradually or suddenly, "a self hitherto divided . . . becomes unified . . . in consequence of its firmer hold upon religious realities." Weaver knew this book, for he quoted it in an essay.[14]

Another useful way to describe Weaver's experience is to call it a "paradigm shift" as described by Thomas Kuhn in *The Structure of Scientific Revolutions*. To be sure, Kuhn's phrase makes sense only after we study his laborious explanations, but it applies nicely to the change that Weaver experienced. Kuhn noted that professionals usually accept what their mentors and peers say about the proper interpretive framework for understanding the "givens." Such explanations make sense of the preponderance of the data or "save the appearances."[15] But, at a certain point, some individual or group in the profession begins to question the commonly accepted paradigm in the light of newer data or of questions inadequately answered by the "official" understanding. Weaver's gradual turning from socialism can be said to have begun at Vanderbilt when he studied under the Agrarians, especially John Crowe Ransom who directed his thesis on humanism. It was pressed still further during his first two years at Texas A & M and was completed while he was reading extensively about the "lost cause" of the South near the end of his three years there.

In 1940 Weaver moved from College Station to Baton Rouge where he enrolled in Louisiana State University's graduate school to pursue his Ph.D. Awarded a graduate teaching assistantship, he continued to extensively read primary Civil War sources. Weaver began his study under Arlin Turner, a distinguished literary historian who went on to teach at Duke University and to write well-received biographies of Nathaniel Hawthorne and George Washington Cable. When Turner was called up for service in the U.S. Navy, Weaver asked Cleanth Brooks, a founding editor of the *Southern Review,* to direct his dissertation, which in time he would dedicate to another Agrarian—John Crowe Ransom. Brooks remembered that, while Weaver's dissertation was all but finished when he agreed to become his advisor, he thought highly of the work and was sympathetic "with many of his ideas and purposes." The dissertation was entitled "The Confederate South, 1865–1910: A Study in the Survival of a Mind and a Culture"; slightly revised, it would become *The Southern Tradition at Bay,* which would not be published until after Weaver's death.[16] He earned his Ph.D. in English in 1943.

In the same connection, Weaver was writing a series of essays that would be published in such quarterlies as the *Sewanee Review* at the University of the South, the *South Atlantic Quarterly* at Duke University, and, later, the *Georgia Review* at the University of Georgia. I refer especially to "The South and the Revolution of Nihilism" and "Southern Chivalry and Total War," both of which appeared in the *South Atlantic Quarterly* under the editorship of W. B. Hamilton. In both essays Weaver compared the South and its code of chivalry to the totalitarian regimes of Franco, Hitler, Mussolini, and Stalin. Here, from a southern perspective, he would anticipate such distinguished writers as Thomas Molnar, Jean François Revel, and Hannah Arendt in their philosophical and cultural studies of totalitarianism.

Weaver's appearance belied the incisiveness and originality of his mind. Robert B. Heilman, another distinguished literary historian and critic at LSU, remembers Weaver's hayseed appearance in those days.

> Dick looked rather ill put together; his black hair seemed not to yield to the comb but to pop out in various awkward tufts here and there. He wore thick glasses, and he was not an elegant dresser. My recollection is that he was somewhat of a loner. He was very independent, but not in a 1960s aggressive, personally aggrandizing way. He was instinctively the gentleman. You could differ with him, and never feel that the atmosphere was hostile or even difficult.

An especially vivid memory of Heilman's is that while both of them enjoyed football, Weaver could not bring himself to go to the game between the LSU Tigers and the A & M Aggies for fear the Tigers would lose. Moving to Baton Rouge obviously had done nothing to temper Weaver's implacable dislike for Texas A & M.[17]

The politically charged atmosphere of America from the depression through the fifties—the years encompassing Weaver's undergraduate, graduate, and professional careers—was brilliantly summarized by Heilman in his article "Baton Rouge and LSU Forty Years After":

> In the 1930s to think was to think politically, and if one was traveling anywhere, with or without fellows, the right turn to make was to the left. By the time the more perceptive converts were finding that the left was not right after all, the right was becoming sinister, so that by the '40s there was no choice: one had to live with the world's left in the hope that the center would remain a possibility. Historical pendulums of sensibility being what they are, it might have been predicted that by the '50s the left would become generally sinister, if not that it would spawn excesses of exorcism by a right fallen into gross manipulating hands.[18]

Louisiana State University from the mid-1930s onward was not as politicized as were some campuses in America. Those who did not know better might be tempted to conclude that it was an intellectual desert in a poverty-stricken southern state where people were unconcerned about trying to alleviate the misery of the world. This was belied by the fact that the university faculty boasted such men as Cleanth Brooks, Arlin Turner, and Robert Penn Warren; indeed, "most of the talented junior faculty . . . made LSU a better-than-average place to be." This group enjoyed a remarkable diversity and plurality of opinions:

> There were many conventional "liberals," of course, and there were "conservatives" of different hues. . . . There was a wide spectrum of ideas as to what the South meant and where it should go: agrarianism, regionalism, modernization, industrialization, internationalism all attracted capable voices. There were men and women with religious convictions, and most secularists were not fanatical evangelizers. There were several Communists, whether party-members or just emotional kinfolk I do not know.[19]

To this point when one looks at Richard Weaver's academic life beginning with his undergraduate days at the University of Kentucky and continuing through his Ph.D. program at Louisiana State University, there had been three primary intellectual influences: the socialist views he took up as an undergraduate living in Lexington, Kentucky, while attending the University of Kentucky; the diverse views of the Agrarians as a group and, in particular, of John Crowe Ransom; and the new way of seeing which occurred in conjunction with Weaver's immersion in the primary sources on the southern mind.

It is clear that even though Weaver wrote under John Crowe Ransom's direction at Vanderbilt, he was anything but his teacher's acolyte at that juncture; indeed, his thesis took aim at some cherished Agrarian beliefs.[20] New humanists such as Paul Elmer Moore and Irving Babbitt came under fire from Weaver in his thesis in language that is almost precisely the opposite of what one finds in Weaver's later work. Scoring the new humanists for their lack of courage, he said, "They were practicing a kind of resurrected Calvinism in the hope of shutting out an augmented sea of troubles. Their defeat is a sign that life is more complex than any statement of it yet made can convey. That is what the empiricists and the pragmatists recognize." Weaver found them to be pitiable for not seeking "certainty [by means of] a rational science" and concluded with advice to novelists and poets to come to terms with modernity. The former were counseled to give up "a certain intellectual flabbiness to retain the attention of more scientific-minded readers . . . [and to] make practical recognition of the fact of specialization in modern life." Observing that "literature has

probably never had a strictly didactic purpose," Weaver blandly
concluded, "it is plainer today than ever before that the poet cannot
hope to be an oracle."[21] Thus it is plain from Weaver's M.A. thesis
that at the time he did not believe that poetry might somehow
serve as a window into truth and was a superior form of communication.

If one applies what Kuhn holds ("a paradigm crisis simultaneously loosens the stereotypes [of the old paradigm] and provides
the incremental data necessary for a fundamental paradigm shift")
to Weaver's experience, then we can say that his crisis began shortly
after he joined the American Socialist Party. Looking back on that
act with a perspective gained with the passage of two decades, he
felt that becoming an active socialist was the first step toward his
ultimate disillusionment with it and all leftist movements,[22] indeed
with garden-variety politics of any kind—right, center, or left.

From the outset Weaver puzzled over the fact that the Socialist
Party's faithful were of two types. There were the academic sorts
who were committed to socialism and understood how it was
supposed to work but were political novices with an aversion to
politics. Yet there were an equal number of "people who cannot be
described for the good reason that they were nondescripts. They
were eccentrics, novelty-seekers, victims of restlessness; and most
of them were hopelessly confused about the nature and purpose of
socialism."[23]

Active for two years, even serving as secretary of his socialist
local, Weaver remained loyal to the party program since it "had
a certain intellectual appeal." But he developed a growing aversion to his fellow party members: "They seemed dry, insistent
people, of shallow objectives; seeing them often and sharing a
common endeavor, moreover, did nothing to remove the disliking.
I am afraid that I performed my duties with decreasing enthusiasm, and at the end of the period I had intimations, which I
did not then face, that this was not the kind of thing in which
I could find permanent satisfaction."[24] On the theoretical level,
at least, this ad hominem argument perhaps ought not to have
mattered in his assessment of socialism as a philosophy. On the
practical level, that individual is indeed rare who is able to separate others' ideas from their personalities and characters. Weaver

would later write that both status (who one was) and function (what one did) were of equal importance in defining individuals' identity to themselves and others. What is clear from his own words—that his personal dislike of the socialists he worked with in the party caused him to question the movement itself—is buttressed by college-friend Clifford Amyx's testimony that Weaver "just sort of withdrew from distasteful old Wobblies."[25] His withdrawal at this point did not cause him to question the assumptions of socialism as a movement. Indeed, it was probably the case that his loyalty to the movement made him more of a purist with regard to its theoretical base. Pandering to the electorate or trying to draw its members to a meeting by hiring a country-music band was a crass and vulgar approach to important matters that ought to be taken seriously by all concerned. To Weaver, the country was in the grip of a continuing and deep depression that even the simplest of minds ought to see was caused by intellectually bankrupt and economically failed industrial capitalism.

Weaver's intellectual struggles during the two years that came on the heels of his graduation from the University of Kentucky parallel what Kuhn says about those in the midst of a paradigm crisis: "Though they may begin to lose faith and then to consider alternatives, they do not renounce the paradigm that has led them into crisis. They do not, that is, treat anomalies as counterinstances . . . though . . . that is what they are. . . . Once it has achieved the status of paradigm, a . . . theory is declared invalid only if an alternate candidate is available to take its place."[26]

Weaver had brought with him to Nashville all the criticisms of Agrarianism that had been leveled by its detractors, some of whom had seen the phenomenon as nothing more than a mindless antiquarianism. Others, he wrote, had scored the movement as "fascist, since it rejected science and rationalism as the supreme sanctions, accepted large parts of the regional tradition, and even found some justification for social classes." Reading *I'll Take My Stand* had convinced him that the Agrarians were "one of the most brilliant groups in the United States," and he simply found it impossible to ignore the fact that the only thing their stance had in common with socialism was a hostility toward industrial capitalism. But, beyond that, the Agrarians rejected a strictly economic solution to the nation's woes.[27]

Kuhn's observation that "The decision to reject one paradigm is always simultaneously the decision to accept another, and the judgment leading to that decision involves the comparison of both paradigms with nature *and* with each other" is implicit in what William James said about the kind of spiritual or intellectual crisis leading to a religious conversion, when "the divided self" is "a series of zig-zags, as now one tendency and now another gets the upper hand."[28] Both provide interpretive grids that help explain Weaver's growing dissatisfaction with socialism that resulted from his regular interchange with the Agrarians while still in graduate school in Nashville. Of his experiences with them at Vanderbilt, he later wrote:

> But here, to my great surprise and growing confusion, I found that although I disagreed with these men on matters of social and political doctrine, I liked them all as persons. They seemed to me more humane, more generous, and considerably less dogmatic than those with whom I had been associated under the opposing banner. It began to dawn upon me uneasily that perhaps the right way to judge a movement was by the persons who made it up rather than by its rationalistic perfection and by the promises it held out. Perhaps, after all, the proof of social schemes was meant to be a posteriori rather than a priori. It would be a poor trade to give up a non-rational world in which you liked everybody for a rational one in which you liked nobody. I did not then see it as quite so sharp an issue; but the intellectual maturity and personal charm of the Agrarians were very unsettling to my then-professed allegiance.[29]

It may appear that Weaver's first consideration was the personal and not the intellectual: His paradigm shift or conversion secondarily involved a change in ideas and was primarily motivated by his personal aversion to socialists and by his affinity for the Agrarians. But it must be understood that, from Weaver's perspective, the person could not be separated from his deeply held tenets. For years he clung to his socialist convictions and refused to yield to a personal dislike of fellow party members for the simple reason that he believed the cause ought to be above such considerations.

Kuhn's explication of what happens to the individual in a paradigm crisis sheds additional light on Weaver's odyssey: It is not a cumulative process that builds on the earlier paradigm or simply modifies it.

> Rather, it is a reconstruction . . . of . . . elementary theoretical generalizations. . . . Others have emphasized its similarity to a change in visual gestalt: the marks on paper that were first seen as a bird are now seen as an antelope or vice-versa. . . . The switch of gestalt, particularly because it is today so familiar, is a useful elementary prototype for what occurs in a full-scale paradigm shift.[30]

The incipient paradigm takes shape, Kuhn insists, often before a crisis has developed; here one is reminded of Weaver's confusion at finding the company of the Agrarians preferable to that of his socialist friends. This occurred in spite of the fact that he was no less committed to that political vision as the solution to depression America's problems.[31]

Weaver's debt to John Crowe Ransom has already been discussed in a previous chapter, especially with regard to his "unorthodox defense of orthodoxy" of which Ransom's *God without Thunder* was an extended treatment. In trying to understand the reasons why his mentor had so influenced his students, he "doubted whether any could tell how he worked his effects." Weaver went on to say, "If one judged solely by outward motions and immediate results, he seemed neither to work very hard at teaching nor to achieve much success. But he had the gift of dropping living seeds into minds." Notice that Weaver began with language appropriate to the socialist vision of society and politics—"outward motions and immediate results." But in the very next sentence, he took up a metaphor from farming; and the sowing of seeds, ever a risky undertaking, was a richly evocative phrase particularly apt for Agrarians. Planting seeds was only the first step in a process that did not always yield happy results; the exigencies of weather, disease, and insects underlined Andrew Lytle's insight that "A farm is not a place to grow wealthy; it is a place to grow corn."[32] Here was a vivid illustration of the two visions vying for Weaver's loyalty. One was dedicated to progress understood as activity that yielded quantifiable results and the other to the proposition that making a living was not the same as making a life.

Kuhn, in treating the conflict between competing paradigms, noted that there is no possibility of a kind of Hegelian synthesis;

the "debate is about premises, and its recourse is to persuasion as a *prelude* to the possibility of proof." By their very nature, paradigms "provide . . . not only . . . a map but also . . . some of the directions for essential map-making." He further explained that "the competition between paradigms is not the sort of battle that can be resolved by proofs. . . . Just because it is a transition between incommensurables, the transition between competing paradigms cannot be made a step at a time, forced by logic and neutral experience. Like a gestalt switch, it must occur all at once or not at all."[33] To sum up: The crisis may build over a relatively long period of time, but the switch to a new way of seeing sometimes occurs with dramatic suddenness.

While he was a student of Ransom, Weaver first posed the question of why traditional answers to the basic questions seemed to be in retreat and disrepute during the thirties. The possibility that perhaps those time-honored premises were being ignored owing to the lack of someone to properly articulate them piqued Weaver's curiosity. Here was a challenge he could take up. But not yet. He had left Vanderbilt keenly aware of Agrarianism's antiquarian aspect, which seemed to suggest to some that the whole movement was an embarrassing irrelevancy. Weaver admitted that pride also played no small part in his continuing to espouse socialism: "There was . . . reluctance over giving up a position once publicly espoused, made somewhat greater by a young man's vanity." This would seem to dovetail almost exactly with Kuhn's observation regarding those suffering a paradigm crisis: "Though they may begin to lose faith and then to consider alternatives, they do not renounce the paradigm that has led them into crisis."[34] It took two years at Texas A & M to bring Weaver's paradigm crisis, or Divided Self, to a head.

The radical turnaround that the word *conversion* implies means that the person involved will experience a new way of seeing and understanding all that had happened before. This is what Kuhn says when he observes that such a change "emerges all at once, sometimes in the middle of the night, in the mind of a man deeply immersed in crisis." Those who undergo this experience "often speak of the 'scales falling from the eyes' or of the 'lightning flash' that 'inundates' a previously obscure puzzle, enabling its components to be seen in a new way. . . . No ordinary sense of the term 'interpretation' fits these flashes of intuition through which a new paradigm is born." Such changes often are preceded, Kuhn explained, "by a period of pronounced professional insecurity." Weaver's change was congruent with Kuhn's picture of what this experience entails. Note that Kuhn used religious language to describe such a change: "The conversion experience that I have likened to a gestalt switch remains, therefore, at the heart of the revolutionary process. Good reasons for choice provide motives for conversion and a climate in which it is more likely to occur." Why does this happen? "There simply remains an element of mystery about the whole process."[35]

Perry Miller, the great intellectual historian of the American Puritans, in the preface to *Errand into the Wilderness*, told how he came to have a passion for explaining this group to his fellow countrymen. In some important ways, Miller's experience is analogous to Weaver's. Having missed out on the adventures some friends of his had had in the Great War, Perry Miller volunteered for military service in World War II and was posted to central Africa, where he was given the task of supervising the unloading of oil drums imported from the United States. Dissatisfied, bored, and almost overcome by tropical heat, he experienced a "sudden epiphany (if the word be not too strong) of the pressing necessity for expounding my America to the twentieth century." This "mission" was "thrust" upon him, he wrote. "However it came about, the vision demanded . . . that I . . . had to commence with the Puritan migration." Miller's work on an unpleasant task paralleled Weaver's plight at Texas A & M University. Since both were reflective men, they sought consolation in pondering matters beyond and larger than the unhappy circumstances in which they found themselves. Miller wrote that he had an "epiphany" thrust upon him while sitting disconsolately on the edge of the jungle far from his home; Weaver recalled his gloom at the prospect of an endless succession of tomorrows in what was to him a barbarous environment, only to be relieved by an experience that came to him "like a revelation." It was like "waking up" and realizing that he had "free will" and could give up "the worship of false idols."[36] Common to both men's experiences were the elements of mystery about what had happened, although they were equally adamant that whatever it was took on some of the qualities of a religious experience. It was as if they were under a compulsion to use religious language in discussing what had occurred even though they apologized in advance for doing so. But, if the element of mystery remained about the "epiphany" or "revelation," both Miller and Weaver were convinced that they had practical tasks to accomplish. (Both were wont to use the word *mission* in describing their life's work.)[37] Late in his life Weaver himself would write about New England and Puritanism.

It is fundamentally important to our understanding of the intellectual transformation Weaver underwent when he abandoned socialism by focusing on the word he chose to characterize his new way of seeing: it was a *conversion*, "a conversion to the poetic and ethical vision of life." No doubt he chose the term for its religious resonance. It would not be accurate, strictly speaking, to say that he was converted to Agrarianism from socialism. Of course, no one is utterly original in his thinking, but Weaver did not derive his ideas from Ransom, Tate, and Warren in any direct or slavish fashion. It would be more to the point to say that they mediated an important lesson to him that was the centerpiece of Weaver's conversion and that informed all he wrote and taught and said for the rest of his life. And that lesson is this: Absolutes do exist, and they are inextricably intertwined with "theism."[38] It is certainly an open question as to whether he used theism in the ordinary Judeo-Christian understanding of it. But there can be no denying that Weaver became convinced that new humanists such as Irving Babbitt and Paul Elmer More who both believed that man is the measure of all things—whom Weaver had fulsomely praised in his master's thesis—lacked this vital dimension. They contended that man could scrutinize the finest human achievements of the past and find his proper fulfillment in studying them. This was at best a worthy, but partial, endeavor. From the Agrarians, Weaver had learned that the central role played by poetry in a civilized society meant that it could never be simply the handmaiden of politics.[39] With their heavy emphasis on poetry, they had taught him an undeniable and deeper truth understood by those who take a sacramental view of the world: Being human and exercising one's humanity fully make belief in God a necessity.

5 | The Southern Tradition in Weaverian Perspective

[THE SOUTH IS] THE LAST NON-MATERIALIST CIVILIZATION IN THE WEST-ERN WORLD. IT IS THIS REFUGE OF SENTIMENTS AND VALUES, OF SPIRITUAL CONGENIALITY, OF BELIEF IN THE WORD, OF REVERENCE FOR SYMBOLISM, WHOSE EXISTENCE HAUNTS THE NATION. . . . THE OLD SOUTH MAY IN-DEED BE A HALL HUNG WITH SPLENDID TAPESTRIES IN WHICH NO ONE WOULD CARE TO LIVE; BUT FROM THEM WE CAN LEARN SOMETHING OF HOW TO LIVE.[1]

The implications of the intellectual shift or conversion that Weaver experienced just prior to his third and last year of teaching at Texas A & M took some time for him to work out. The principal means by which he would complete that conversion can be seen in two works. The first of these was his doctoral dissertation at Louisiana State University, "The Confederate South, 1865–1910: A Study in the Survival of a Mind and a Culture," and the second was the book *Ideas Have Consequences,* which was published in 1948. Throughout his professional career, he never wavered from the essential arguments he made in his work on the South and elaborated on them in some fourteen articles, the first of which was published in 1944 and the last in 1964, one year after his death.[2]

In 1958 when he wrote that he had started his education over again at the age of thirty, Weaver was stressing the point that the intellectual framework through which he would understand and write about the world for the rest of his life was initially presented while he was a graduate student at Louisiana State University pursuing his Ph.D. in English under the direction of Arlin Turner.

Weaver was in the final stages of writing his dissertation when Turner left LSU to take a position at Duke University; Cleanth Brooks became his advisor at that point and oversaw the work to its conclusion. Weaver's dissertation is more than an historical investigation: It is an apologia. It was published five years after his death exactly as he wrote it and was entitled *The Southern Tradition at Bay: A History of Postbellum Thought*. Weaver began this work by identifying four persistent characteristics of the southern mind: a feudal theory of society, the code of chivalry, "the ancient concept of the gentleman," and a noncreedal faith.[3]

Taking each in turn, he insisted that the feudal system was transplanted into the virgin soil of the American South after the original European stock had passed its prime. He did qualify the generalization by pointing out that land, climate, and slavery made the American variant differ in some important ways from the parent plant. The primary motives of those who came to settle the southern colonies were economic. Daniel J. Boorstin has noted that while New England was peopled by those anxious to avoid the worst features of seventeenth-century English society, those persons who settled the southern colonies aimed at an ideal modeled on societal arrangements in England. There the burgess or country gentleman presided over a well-ordered estate of respectable size and acquired management and leadership skills essential to a self-confident ruling class. Eugene D. Genovese has recently written about the religious underpinnings of the Old South, a society that "grew out of people who settled Virginia and the Carolinas not to build a City on a Hill but to acquire freeholds and, with them, the status and self-respect appropriate to Englishmen." What bound them together as a people was what has been characterized by Weaver as "social bond individualism." His editor, M. E. Bradford, pushed this concept back to classical Roman and Christian roots to make clear that Weaver was not thinking either of the Renaissance or of the Enlightenment as antecedents.[4]

That relatively small numbers of men achieved this ideal was, in Weaver's view, not evidence that there was not an aristocracy: "It is never the number alone of the dominant element which makes its presence decisive; it is rather the economic, the political, and especially the moral influence it is able to exert. An oligarchy always tended to communicate its attitudes and habits to the lower groups, just as in a monarchy the court sets the fashions for the nation." Jackson Turner Main, who has done extensive work on the colonial social structure, concluded of the South that "some ten per cent of the whites at the top, consisting principally of large landowners . . . owned nearly half of the wealth of the country, including perhaps one-seventh of the country's people." Two essential pillars of this system, Weaver noted, were structure and hierarchy. The "typical plantation was a little cosmos in which things were arranged by a well-understood principle giving coherence to the whole."[5]

The notion of place was reinforced by the paternalism that governed the plantation and perpetuated an almost impervious provincialism. If "our people" seemed little more than a euphemism for slavery, it at least suggested a more humane assumption than a later era in which people spoke of "manpower." Weaver believed that the novelist John Pendleton Kennedy, in *Swallow Barn,* was on the mark when he singled out the steamboat as a threat to that secure world: "With the protection of this seclusion, the hierarchy stood firm. From the owner of the estate at the top, down to the field workers, bond or indentured, who, if not bound to the soil, were at least under some constraint to work on it, the ranks were plain."[6]

While leaving no doubt to anyone who reads him that he felt that slavery was a great and unacceptable evil, Weaver knew that it would "seem anomalous that a slaveholding society like the South should be presented as ethically superior. Yet the endeavor to grade men by their moral and intellectual worth may suggest a more sensitive conscience than proscription of individual differences." When one recalls that Weaver was a politically active socialist for a period of time, it is not surprising that George Fitzhugh's socialist defense of the South appealed to him as a "remarkable foreshadowing of the modern corporate state" where workers' sweat only adds to "the vulgar pomp and pageantry of ignorant millionaires."[7]

Weaver's view of the South as "a type of corporative society, held together by sentiments which do not survive a money-economy" no doubt owed much to what he had learned during his undergraduate days in Lexington. His debate coach loved to quote

Theodore Roosevelt's stinging rebuke against "malefactors of great wealth" and had trained and rehearsed his team to debate economic matters raised during the depression years, an era that has been called the heyday of American communism. While Weaver came to loathe communism and became closely associated in the minds of some with modern American conservatism, he retained a certain hostility to capitalism all his life. It showed up in *Ideas Have Consequences,* where, in the chapter entitled "The Last Metaphysical Right" (to own private property), he made it abundantly clear that he was not defending the sort of property he associated with corporate capitalism: "For the abstract property of stocks and bonds, the legal ownership of enterprises never seen, actually destroys the connection between man and his substance. . . . Property in this sense becomes a fiction useful for exploitation and makes impossible the sanctification of work." Here again is an instance of Weaver's independence of thought and kinship to Henry David Thoreau, about whom he would write late in his career.[8]

The slave master's authority was not a legal office conferred by an electorate to whom he was accountable and to whom he must periodically turn for approval or rejection. Naturally the temptation to abuse such power was great, as Weaver readily conceded, but the master "ordinarily acknowledged a responsibility for the welfare of his dependents which proceeded from moral obligation." The hierarchy continued down from master to overseer to driver; the latter was ordinarily chosen by the slaves from among their own.[9]

But who could really be trusted with such a measure of authority over others? In the abstract, the question could seem to allow only one answer. Weaver agreed that there were many slave owners who emphatically did *not* have the moral quality essential to the proper exercise of the office. Yet he went on to aver that although perhaps too much has been made of the slave owner's noblesse oblige, the primary sources indicate that most of the great planters followed its demands. George Washington, as exemplar of that tradition, was never too busy with his many duties at Mount Vernon to call on or even treat ailing slaves. This sense of obligation of the landowner for his tenants survived the Civil War and the Thirteenth Amendment. But Weaver was not naïve about the adverse impact this system had on the character of even the best masters: "It made them arrogant and impatient, and it filled them with boundless self-assurance. Even the children, noting the deference paid to their elders by the servants, began at an early age to take on the airs of command."[10] The classic statement on the dark side of this system is in Jefferson's *Notes on the State of Virginia*:

> The whole commerce between master and slave is a perpetual exercise of the most boisterous passions, the most unremitting despotism on the one part, and degrading submissions on the other. Our children see this, and learn to imitate it. . . . This quality is the germ of all education in him. . . . The parent storms, the child looks on, catches the lineaments of wrath, puts on the same airs in the circle of smaller slaves, gives a loose to his worst of passions, and thus nursed, educated, and daily exercised in tyranny, cannot but be stamped by it with odious peculiarities. The man must be a prodigy who can retain his manners and morals undepraved by such circumstances.[11]

Weaver also pointed to another trait that, while not peculiar to the American South, took on particular importance in the region: the desire to link the family name with a particular piece of land. This was at the outset the self-conscious imitation of the English ruling classes in the seventeenth century. The determination to wed family to soil found ready expression in the works of such southern writers as Thomas Nelson Page and George Washington Cable. On this point, Weaver concluded that the great planter's sense of noblesse oblige, his rootedness in the soil, and the hierarchical social structure were the foundations of a

> Southern feudalism, which outlasted every feudal system of Europe except the Russian, until it was destroyed by war and revolution. It possessed stability, an indispensable condition for positive values: it maintained society in the only true sense of the term, for it had structure and articulation, and it made possible a personal world in which people were known by their names and their histories. It was a rooted culture which viewed with dismay the anonymity and the social indifference of urban man.[12]

Surviving along with this mutant strain of feudalism, Weaver wrote, was the code of chivalry, yet another European transplant that throve in the South even though it was frequently recognized only in the breach. The associated sense of personal honor was exaggerated in the southern planter. In 1858 the governor of South Carolina published a dueling code in the hope that this might restrain and diminish the practice. Such a premium on honor suggested that material rewards were to be regarded with disdain or indifference—at least publicly. "Such views, combined with the inveterate Southern habit of extravagance, created a type not far removed from the aristocratic wastrels of Europe, incapable of making money by personal effort, but unable to see why it should not be forthcoming to support their elegant mode of life." Other components of the code that were pervasive in the South included the importance of truth-telling to the point of making "a fetish of the pledged word." Some southern juries felt that killing someone who called a man a liar was justifiable homicide. The most important aspect of the code, however, had to do with how one fought a war: "The Southern people as a whole possessed a highly romanticized picture of the ordeal, which the business-like methods of Grant and Sherman only partly effaced. They regarded it as an elaborate ceremonial, to be conducted strictly according to rules, and with maximum display, color, and daring—in other words, as a gigantic tournament with the Lord of Hosts for umpire and judge." Weaver admitted that while the southerner's perception of the Civil War—as a struggle between those who fought as gentlemen punctiliously observing the rules and taking special pains to spare civilians whereas the materialistic and barbarian Yankee foe could not have cared less about either—contained elements of exaggeration, it was nonetheless a valid generalization. The two southern commanders who "were hard, self-made men, who believed simply that 'war means fighting and fighting means killing' "—Stonewall Jackson and Nathan Bedford Forrest—were the exceptions that, in Weaver's calculus, tested and sustained the rule.[13]

Another trait of the southern aristocracy that Weaver dwelled on at some length was its indifference to belles lettres. Comparison with the English nobleman was apt. "The Restoration wits were gentlemen first, and authors only by way of divertissement." As education commonly took the form prescribed by society's dominant class, in the South, then, the great planters set the standards. Such an education was to be a general, humane curriculum that would inculcate "magnificence, magnanimity, and liberality." Universities would produce gentlemen by teaching "propriety, rather than . . . cleverness or ingenuity." A student at the College of William and Mary gave voice to the ideal in 1699 by criticizing its opposite: "For in such a retired corner of the world, far from business and action, if we make scholars, they are in danger of proving mere scholars, which make a very ridiculous figure, made up of pedantry, disputatiousness, positiveness, and a great many other ill qualities which render them not fit for action and conversation." The idea that mere scholars were useless dilettantes found expression in the *Southern Literary Messenger* six generations later: a writer insisted that those "who are endowed in any extraordinary manner with one talent, are generally unfit for any other pursuit in life. . . . It is well . . . that society is not made up of such men—but that it consists of those who have no very great capacity for one pursuit more than another—and who possess all the faculties in a moderate degree."[14] Such a self-confident class of gentlemen simply assumed their right to rule. That articulate southerners such as Patrick Henry, John Taylor, John Randolph, and Thomas Jefferson had learned governance while growing up—as naturally and easily as all human beings learn their native tongue—went a long way toward explaining why southern writings of the antebellum era focused on law and politics rather than on fiction or philosophical treatises characteristic of New England writing during the same period.[15]

According to Weaver, it was not until that great sectional watershed in American history, the Missouri Compromise, that the South began a belated foray into literary and cultural matters expressive of the region. A number of scholarly journals were planned. Some were stillborn; others did not survive beyond a few issues. Charleston's *Southern Review* was the exception. A journal of high quality, it lasted only four years. The *Southern Literary Messenger* made its appearance in 1834 and endured for three decades, enjoying modest success in spite of the fact that it engaged in a constant battle "with much apathy and indifference in its regional constituency." An additional drawback was that the particularly gifted southern writers felt compelled to devote much of their energies to the political struggle.[16]

Three burning issues occupied the minds of most southern writers during this period: the tariff, nullification, and radical abolitionism. There was an important intellectual shift, Weaver contended, during the period 1829–1835. Jefferson, Madison, and John Taylor had earlier turned out works "philosophic in a real sense of the word." That is, they grappled with those universal questions men living together in society have always faced:

> After the South had been warned to look for destructive attacks on her institutions, both temper and point of view shifted. Her writings became devoted . . . to an exposition of propositions already crystallized into laws . . . [and] to a demonstration of the humanitarian aspects of slavery. The real question was begged; it was now not how might the South best define the legal status of the African for the benefit of the general polity, but what would be the most effective propaganda to counter the stream flowing from the North.[17]

Weaver pointed to John C. Calhoun as the transitional figure whose thought manifested aspects of both the old and the new in southern political theory. While few could deny the brilliance or even originality of his thinking on the concurrent majority as a way to protect minorities from a tyrannical majority, this effort was finally neither more, nor less—nor other—than a defense of slavery.[18]

The fourth sectional characteristic that Weaver paid particular attention to in this work was what he termed the "older religiousness" of the South. Free of theological speculation and doctrinal sophistication, it was characterized by a respect for traditional arrangements and a humility before the limitations of one's own will and the exigencies of nature. The nearest it came to controversy was not about metaphysics but on the proper view of the church as an institution: "The Southerner did not want a reasoned belief, but a satisfying dogma, and the innumerable divisions which occurred on the Western frontiers are ascribable to a religious intensity together with an absence of discipline rather than a desire to effect a philosophic synthesis, as was elsewhere the case."[19]

New England offered a marked contrast to the South in this area. A recent study points out that northern abolitionism's anti-Catholicism and anti-Semitism have yet to be fully studied, although the issue has been pointedly raised by Louis Filler.[20] The first two Jewish United States senators were elected from slave states, and Judah P. Benjamin was offered a seat on the Supreme Court, although he refused it. Both Catholics and Jews found southern slaveholders more hospitable than the general public in the North.

The descendants of the Puritans had retained the unbending attitudes of their forefathers while rejecting the veracity of the Scriptures that had kept the reins on sinful man's propensity for power and pride. These offspring became simply "puritans." Enamored with "the right to criticize and even to reject the dogmas of Christianity," they lost the

> will to believe them. . . . Instead of insisting upon a simple grammar of assent, which a proper regard for the mysteries would dictate, they conceived it their duty to explore principles, and when the exploration was complete they came out, not with a secured faith, but with an ethical philosophy, which illuminated much but which had none of the binding power of the older creeds. There followed as characteristic results Unitarianism and Christian Science, two intellectual substitutes for a more rigorous religious faith.[21]

Propagating the gospel was high on the list of stated reasons for the establishment of both the New England and southern colonies. Over time, the sections diverged in how they understood their faith in relation to their society. In the South it became a "crystallized popular sentiment," while the faith of New England, more sensitive to European currents of thought, "gave way to rational inquiry." The two best-known groups of dissenters in Virginia—the Quakers and the Baptists—were persecuted not for heterodoxy but for the corroding effects that pacifism, refusal to pay taxes, and unstructured meetings had exerted on the commonwealth's body politic. Unitarianism likewise found the South stony soil for its arcane vision of truth since "the Southerner clung stubbornly to the belief that a certain portion of life must remain inscrutable, and that religion offers the only means of meeting it, since reason cannot here be a standard of interpretation."[22]

Weaver was careful to distinguish the established church (Anglican/Episcopal) in the South from the evangelicals—the former aiming at "the exposition of a revealed ethic" and the latter at "the conversion of the inner man." He insisted that both shied away from using their position for any political platform, only resorting to such matters when defending the ramparts. They could never be political reformers; rather, they were content with being "custodians of the mysteries."[23]

Central to the older religiousness of the South, Weaver believed, was reverence for the written word. In their insular, rural world with so much that was unpredictable—crops might be damaged or destroyed at every stage during the growing season each year by the caprice of weather, insects, and disease—southerners clung to the Bible as an anchor that would hold them. Scripture would stand through "the welter of earthly change" when nothing else would. Commenting on the Scopes trial, Weaver averred that those who knew the South were not really surprised at the trial's outcome, since in that region, "science had not usurped the seats of the prophets." And, indeed, the epithet *backward* that was repeatedly flung at the South during this controversy was in one sense entirely fitting: "It may therefore be proper to describe the South as 'backward' if one employs the word not in some vaguely prejudicial sense, but with reference to the continuum of history." The extent to which the religious bent in the southern mind had leavened their thinking may be illustrated by the fact that many had chosen to see the sectional quarrel in religious terms. One well-known southern religious leader insisted that abolitionism itself was no more than the hoary heresy of Socinianism dressed up in new garb.[24] The intellectual currents that helped bring about and later emanated from the French Revolution spread to England and thence to New England and the rest of America. These new ways of thinking piqued the interest of but a few southerners, however. "It was . . . a transient phase, confined while it lasted to small cultivated groups, and it disappeared so completely in the antebellum years that it can be properly ignored in any account of the molding of the Confederate South." There were short-lived flirtations with what was then called free-thinking at the College of William and Mary, Transylvania University, the University of North Carolina, and the University of Georgia during the early nineteenth century, but after 1830 interest waned. The University of South Carolina went so far as to oust a president who questioned the Pentateuch's authority. When the war came, this traditional piety was a vital characteristic of most southern soldiers. It can hardly be an accident that there were large-scale religious revivals with thousands of conversions reported during the four-year ordeal.[25]

In the chapter entitled "Writing the Apologia," Weaver quoted Yeats's line that "things reveal themselves passing away," and, after pointing to Hobbes, Burke, and Clarendon as examples, he insisted that the same could be said of the South. The war and Reconstruction wrought a social revolution of far-reaching consequences. Just how radical the changes were became clear only in retrospect. A cri de coeur that was perhaps autobiographical bears quoting at length:

> War is a destroyer of patterns, and those who have grown up in one order, familiar with its assumptions and customs, and feeling that the rules of its collective life somehow emanate from themselves, are likely to be seized with nostalgia when struggling with a new pattern. The alteration which came over the whole country after the triumph of the nationalist party was one of a worldwide tendency. It was modernism, with its urgency, impatience, truculence, and its determination to strip aside all concealing veils and see what is behind them. When the men of the new order did strip aside these veils and found that there was nothing behind them, but that the reality had existed somehow in the willed belief, or the myth, they marked the beginning of modern frustration.[26]

After the South's surrender at Appomattox, the *Southern Review,* a periodical edited by Albert Taylor Bledsoe, made its appearance. Its main purpose was to come to the South's defense in light of northern histories of the conflict. The point of view presented in its pages was that because the North had made a revolution by military means, it consequently bore much of the guilt for bringing on the late war. It had repudiated the common heritage left by the Founding Fathers in favor of an aggressive centralism based on force. This periodical provided a forum for such men as Bledsoe and Robert Louis Dabney to defend the South, although "in the political field its victories were victories in debate only, and its religious theory of the social order went unheard amid the crude materialism of the Gilded Age, but it remains the last repository of the views of the unreconciled Southerner."[27]

Weaver called attention to a vital part of the South's argument that had been all but ignored, or at least had received scant attention when compared to critiques of the South's legal case—something he termed "The Attack upon Secular Democracy." Among the innovations of the French Revolution was a pervasive secularism by which the state became nothing more than the means used by the majority to impose its will without reference to any transcendent order. The restraining power or counterforce of the church was swept away.[28]

One southern spokesman who took great pains to rebut this view at his every opportunity was Robert Louis Dabney, a Presbyterian minister from Virginia who spent the war years on Stonewall Jackson's staff and who wrote a biography of the general that was published in 1883. Like many southerners, Dabney had opposed secession at the outset but came to the later conviction that the conflict was between an essentially Christian South and a North opposed to Christianity. Carrying out what he clearly felt was his duty as a true southerner, Dabney wrote what Weaver labeled "the bitterest and the most eloquent" of the major apologias: *A Defence of Virginia and through Her of the South in Recent and Pending Contests against the Sectional Party,* which appeared in 1867.[29]

Insisting that hierarchy was essential to any functioning society, Dabney attacked Locke and Hobbes for what he saw as their false presuppositions about man and society. No one could or did *choose* to live in society: Man, a fallen creature with a bent will, has been divinely ordained to live under authority. Man was free, he agreed, but his freedom was not of the kind propounded by such "infidel democrats" as Danton and Robespierre. True liberty was not a licentious freedom for the individual to do whatever he might wish, but rather to do what "he has a moral right to do." This was reminiscent of John Winthrop's distinction between "liberty to evil as well as to good" and "civil or federal . . . liberty to that only which is good, just and honest" that individuals exercised in submission to proper authority.[30]

Albert Taylor Bledsoe focused more narrowly on what Dabney had dealt with as an unspoken assumption: the imperfection of human nature. Any government that began with the notion that man was by nature good was doomed, he insisted, and faulted the Founding Fathers' work in 1787 on that score.

That southerners and Yankees were fundamentally different was another premise underlying the postwar apologias. Almost all the defenders of the South ignored the Declaration of Independence's egalitarian implications but were fond of quoting the document's unequivocal proclamation of the right of an aggrieved people "to *dissolve* the political bands which have connected them with another" [emphasis mine].

How Yankees differed was a matter of some debate; that they differed was an idea that had an all but universal currency among the southern people. This did not mean that southerners viewed themselves with uncritical adulation. E. A. Pollard zeroed in on the South's undue emphasis on physical courage and "animal combativeness" and deplored its provincialism as a people "who pass over their lives in local neighborhoods, and who, having but little knowledge of how large and various the world is, easily take conceit of their own powers and virtues." This same writer also took note of the constant bickering that all too often characterized the Confederate Congress's closed sessions and saw the desertion and conscription laws as incontrovertible evidence that patriotism had waned in the South after the initial burst of enthusiasm.[31]

The southern whites' most vexing questions at the end of the war had to do with the freed slaves. Four million blacks (fully a third of the southern population) were granted equality before the law—a truly frightening prospect for those who believed that they were unfit by nature, temperament, and training for political equality with the white man. While the North had been trumpeting for two generations that the institution of slavery had reduced naturally good men to a bestial existence, the same proponents of an abstract view of human nature held that the Thirteenth Amendment had transmuted the freedmen into political adepts and obliterated any historical baggage they might have brought with them.[32]

Southern opinion was not unanimous on the question. Some believed that in time the blacks might excel in the arts, but the political arena was one in which they could never hope to match the whites because of their congenital lack of self-control, combined with an uncritical adulation of power in whatever form it might take. Others even went so far as to say that the only solution to the dilemma would be to keep the blacks "in a condition approximating slavery." A careful perusal of the periodical literature, speeches, and editorials of the southern writers in the Gilded Age led Weaver to conclude that southern whites clung to the idea that blacks were the white's inferiors with the same tenacity exhibited by their fathers and grandfathers.[33]

The southern apologias that were turned out for three decades had mixed results, at best. A triumphant cosmopolitanism became a part of conventional wisdom on both sides of the Atlantic as Europeans and most Americans bowed down before the gods of secular democracy. The one facet of the apologia that endured was the notion of white supremacy, which, by 1900, gave vent to a widespread campaign to deprive the black man of the franchise. This, Weaver admitted, using mild language, was more often than not done by means "more effective than honest."

In his chapter on the southern soldier, Weaver observed that Appomattox did not seem to have affected the South's stubborn persistence in looking to her military captains for advice and leadership. This is not to be wondered at since the South had offered her best to the nation during the Revolutionary War, the War of 1812, and the Mexican War. The brilliance of Washington, Jackson, and Zachary Taylor seemed beyond dispute. Most southerners on the eve of the Civil War simply assumed that the region's superior statesmen and soldiers would carry the day. The shock and dismay at the loss on the battlefield brought forth a flood of memoirs whose numbers only began to recede a half century after the swords had been sheathed.

The basic question any soldier about to go into combat poses is a simple one: "Why am I fighting?" Weaver's close scrutiny of the written records led him to conclude that the Confederate soldiers saw themselves as "the upholders of a particularism which had been present in 1787, and which had greatly increased by 1860. . . . Thus the Civil War becomes a version of the argument between universalists and particularists, with the Southern soldiers choosing to defend the past, made dear by nativity and association." The same point has been made in simpler terms by Bruce Catton and Bell Wiley: Typically, a Confederate would say he was fighting to defend his home and family against invaders, while his Union counterpart believed he was fighting to save the Union. At this juncture, Weaver wrote in a manner characteristic of his way of thinking when he generalized from *this* particular to a broad platonic summary:

> There are those who maintain that the true principle of history is a dynamic universalism, so that all true development is a sloughing off of particularities and individualities in an approach to the typical. There are others who believe that life consists in the richness of diversity and that conformity to a universal pattern is a kind of death. The opinion that the world cannot be one half one thing and half another is an extremely bold statement of the first view. On the level of everyday politics it takes the form of democratic resentment against exclusiveness, just as the second expresses itself in a distaste for incorporation into something felt to be alien or inferior. The backwoods politicians of the mid-nineteenth century America were unknowingly entangled in the great debate of the Schoolmen, with the Southern separatists playing the part of the Nominalists, and the Northern democrats and equalitarians that of Realists. This view of the conflict, though unfamiliar, is not farfetched, and if all questions resolve themselves ultimately into metaphysical problems, as is not impossible, it becomes the philosophical description of the event.

It is doubtful whether more than a few Confederate soldiers would have understood what they were about in the context of classical philosophy's debate about the one and the many. Nonetheless, a particularly striking theme of the Confederate soldiers' memoirs was the centrality of the war to their thinking. By that experience they judged all others: It gave them integrity in the truest sense of the word. This should come as no surprise, Weaver insisted, when seen against the backdrop of a pervasive provincialism that caused southerners "to regard their country as the world, and because of a lack of comparisons to form exaggerated notions of their own merits. The peculiar type of blindness which results from being thus cut off is an affliction which will visit any people so circumstanced. . . . It was inevitable, therefore, that the war should bring to many of them the one intense experience of their lives beside which all that happened before or after seemed commonplace."

The suffering and destruction that came during the four blood-soaked years changed the rebel soldier's mind not a whit about the rightness of what he was doing. He remained unshaken in his conviction that some things were worse than war and "spent the next thirty years trying to imagine not how war might be banished from the earth, but how the South might have won this war."[34]

In keeping with an essential component of the feudal tradition, the leaders of the southern fighting men believed they were Christian warriors, Weaver held, which was consistent with the older religiousness of the region. They were not systematic theologians and often spoke and wrote of their faith with a certain reticence; yet, men are often reluctant to speak about things they hold most dear. Robert E. Lee might be said to have epitomized this ideal of the Christian warrior; his fellow officers shared it to greater or lesser degree. This faith steeled them in defeat and protected them from bitterness after Appomattox. Quite simply, they believed, "God had foreseen all, and our suffering and our defeats in this world were part of a discipline whose final fruit it was not given to mortal minds to perceive. . . . Great calamities had to be regarded as part of the design of an inscrutable providence."[35] Lee's long view of history, jotted down shortly prior to his death, is quoted with approbation by Weaver precisely because its alloy of hope and caution so well mirrored his own:

> My experience of men has neither disposed me to think worse of them, nor indisposed me to serve them; nor, in spite of failures, which I lament, of errors, which I now see and acknowledge, or of the present state of affairs, do I despair of the future. The march of Providence is so slow, and our desires so impatient, the work of progress is so immense, and our means of aiding it so feeble, the life of humanity is so long, and that of the individual so brief, that we often see only the ebb of the advancing wave, and are thus discouraged. It is history that teaches us to hope.[36]

The Confederate soldier was often horrified at the methods of his enemy and in particular at the deliberate blurring of the distinction between combatants and noncombatants. Civilization understood as a refined blend of tradition, custom, and practice fell by the wayside as new seeds were sowed that yielded a bitter crop. Commenting on Sherman's march through Georgia, a Confederate officer later observed that the tactics employed were "excused on the ground that 'War is Hell.' It depends somewhat upon the warrior." It was not surprising that the methods of Sherman,

Sheridan, and Grant were seen as the natural playing out of northern civilization's gross "materialism, equalitarianism, and irreligion."[37] Weaver buttressed his position by pointing to the contemporary assessment of Richard Taylor, son of a former president, brother-in-law of Jefferson Davis, and himself a Confederate lieutenant-general. During a visit to the North after the war, Taylor concluded that a crass materialism had triumphed everywhere:

> For two or three years I was much in the North, and especially in New York, where I had dear friends. The war had afforded opportunity and stimulated appetite for reckless speculation. Vast fortunes had been acquired by new men, destitute of manners, taste, or principles. The vulgar insolence of wealth held complete possession of public places and carried by storm the citadels of society. Indeed, society disappeared. As in the Middle Ages, to escape pollution, honorable men and refined women (and there are many such in the North) fled to sanctuary and desert, or, like early Christians in the catacombs, met secretly and in fear. The masses . . . lost all power of discrimination.[38]

The shock of being propelled from the eighteenth to the nineteenth century found ample expression in the writings of postbellum southerners. Their "French Revolution" had come with a vengeance, Weaver insisted. He saw Burke's assessment of that turbulent event and era as analogous to what happened to the South after the Civil War. While World War I initially made clear how frayed the fabric of Western culture had become, the second produced an unmistakable showdown between civilization and barbarism.[39]

Weaver's painstaking scrutiny of a great number of memoirs of the "second American Revolution" led him to conclude that the women diarists recorded the drama with a particularly keen discernment. It would really not be going too far, he believed, to say that the South became a matriarchy during the postbellum era. The general portrait he painted of the southern women who "turned lionesses, took over direction of their own households, in many instances supported their men, and taught their children what they wanted believed about the Southern Confederacy" almost certainly owed a great deal to his perception of his own mother.[40]

The studied avoidance of, and aversion to, detail on the part of southern leaders generally—attributable, perhaps, to a mind-set determined on being a counterpoint to what was seen to be typically Yankee—resulted in a kind of cavalier attitude toward the basic necessities of war or, at least, toward modern warfare. In a masterly understatement, Weaver noted that "at the beginning of the war it was not fully appreciated that courage and determination by themselves could fail." The Confederate Congress spent hours discussing the color and design of the proposed flag while urgent questions of military moment went begging.

Weaver was convinced that the determined effort of northern propagandists to break up the southern social order was a failure. Instead, the different classes of whites were driven closer together by their common effort to ward off the invader. The planting and slaveholding aristocracy produced leaders who proved themselves in battle. That there was a chasm between them and the backwoods farmers Weaver did not deny. The latter group knew how to contend against nature in the struggle to extract a living from the soil, but had little talent for or inclination to the scramble for position that goes on in every complex community. Nonetheless, both groups were part and parcel of an ordered society where each had a place that guaranteed a measure of respect and security. Weaver reflected that the fall of France in 1940 provided a vivid example of what happened when a people cynically concluded "that ideas are illusions and self-sacrifice is only foolishness."

Just as the published diaries and reminiscences of the Civil War were apologias for the lost cause, much southern fiction that appeared from 1865 to 1910 had as its primary motive, Weaver believed, the vindication of the region. Very different writers, with other motives to be sure, still labored under that burden. Over time, however, the uncritical adulation of Thomas Nelson Page gave way to the perspective of writers such as George Washington Cable, who was able to criticize what he nonetheless loved and cherished. A satirical vein entered a bit later with Opie Read's *A Kentucky Colonel,* illustrating the point that an artistic detachment gave a perspective not often seen by the impassioned partisan. The novels of Ellen Glasgow completed the bridge that Weaver said fiction built across the chasm divide from Reconstruction to the twentieth century: Both the old southerners and the new southerners have their places in her works. "Her Virginia nobility is a true nobility, firm in its virtues but limited in its sympathies, and its shortcomings are held up to full view. But it is especially significant that her new men too are real . . . the offspring of the vital lower orders who will not be denied their entrance upon the stage of the world." Weaver commended that spirit and saw in it reason to hope that his era's "political zeal which . . . manifests itself in sociological caricatures" would itself finally yield to the artist Time. He concluded that a genuine apologia would require no less: "Only when the impulse to justify is replaced by the impulse to see a thing in the round does something like an enduring justification become possible." Southern fiction by the early twentieth century, while not turning its back on a cherished past, had come to terms with inevitable change.

In the final chapter of *The Southern Tradition at Bay,* Weaver insisted that the universal human temptation to prostrate oneself before the bitch goddess "Success" was all the more reason for lost causes to be studied. The South, he averred, "is in the curious position of having been right without realizing the grounds for its rightness." What was needed was a theorist such as Burke or Hegel to articulate its vision, rather than the multitude of lawyers and journalists that it produced. The second error of the region followed perhaps as a consequence of the first: Having lost on the battlefield, the South went on to capitulate in other areas as well. For example, it had only been willing to buy and read books and magazines published in the North.[41]

Any effort to put Weaver's work in the context of southern scholarship from the mid-thirties to the early forties in order to explore intellectual currents of the day and how they may have affected him must take into account the kind of person he was. Shy by nature and several years older than many of his fellow students at LSU, he spent little time socializing with them.[42] Because he was older than the other students, he no doubt felt impelled by a special sense of urgency to get on with his research and writing.

One work that loomed large as an analysis of the region was W. J. Cash's *The Mind of the South,* which was published in 1941.[43] Although Weaver did not quote it in his dissertation (Cash's book came out after Weaver had finished writing his dissertation), *The Mind of the South* is listed in his bibliography.

Cash's work drew rave reviews not only from writers and journalists but also from historians such as Clement Eaton and C. Vann Woodward. The latter lauded Cash's "literary and imaginative, rather than scholarly approach," as well as his "brilliant analysis" and "penetrating observations."[44] Exactly the same compliments could have been paid to Weaver's book with one important addition: Taking a scholarly approach, he *combined* the literary and the imaginative in *The Southern Tradition at Bay.*

Far from ignoring the colonial history of the South, Weaver properly set the stage for what was to follow in his section entitled "The Heritage." There he developed at length from the primary sources the four characteristics of that heritage that have already been discussed. His preference for primary sources is characteristic of all Weaver wrote. Rather than giving slavery and the race issue little more than a passing nod, he devotes a chapter to the institution and does not shrink from looking at it from every facet in his chapters on "The Theory of Race" and "The Negroes in Transition."

The southern women that Weaver wrote about and whose diaries and reminiscences were a vital primary source in his research were anything but "totemic objects of southern mythology." Weaver wrote in a way that leaves absolutely no doubt about the importance of women in southern life:

> In sober truth the history of the women in Reconstruction makes better reading than that of men. Dismayed by failure and left idle by want of opportunity, the men in some cases became poseurs or fribbles [triflers]. But the women for the most part turned lionesses, took over the direction of their households, in many instances supported their men, and taught their children what they wanted believed. . . . It is no small part of the truth to say that after the Civil War the South became a matriarchy, and the decisive hand of its women was seen not only in social life, but also in letters. They produced some of the best of the older type of writing, and they were the first with the new. Consequently, whoever wishes to know the tenor of the Southern mind from 1865 to 1900 and beyond must pay considerable attention to their testimonials.

Southern women's impressive contributions in every area naturally included politics, Weaver noted. How could it have been otherwise when they grew up in homes where politics were constantly discussed?

While Cash has been criticized for his provincialism in focusing on the North Carolina Piedmont as typical of the South, Weaver gave due attention to the differences of Coastal, Tidewater, and Piedmont South and its antebellum class system in his chapters on "The Particularism of Peoples," "Southern Leadership," and "The Class System." If *The Mind of the South* betrayed a lack of understanding of southern intellectuals, *The Southern Tradition at Bay* devoted almost half of its pages to them in the sections on "Writing the Apologia," "Fiction across the Chasm," and "The Tradition and Its Critics."

Michael O'Brien's characterization of Cash's assessment of Reconstruction as "primitive" is in stark contrast to Weaver's clear-eyed assessment of that vexed era's problems and challenges that has no truck with the simplistic views of how much worse things became after emancipation, or how all the newly freed blacks wanted was a steady job and decent wages. Nor does he turn the whole episode into a morality play with either white southerners or Yankee occupiers playing caricatured roles as villains or heroes. White supremacy's ill effects were deplored by Weaver and he especially singled out the effort to disenfranchise blacks.[45]

The immediate success of *The Mind of the South* was due in large part to the attention focused on the South as the poorest part of the nation during a time when the country was mired in the Great Depression. Margaret Bourke-White's haunting photographs etched graphic images on the minds of many Americans of a South they had before only heard about or imagined. It is no small achievement for any book that it remained at the top of the recommended-reading list of a majority of historians, "a profession not known for coddling its young nor deferring to its elders." Richard H. King believes that the enduring quality of Cash is that his primary burden was one shared with the Agrarians: explaining the South by getting inside the southern tradition, keeping the best and forgetting the rest.[46]

Michael O'Brien, while lauding Cash's prose and saying that perhaps some isolated aspects of his analysis are valid, severely criticizes the book overall:

It . . . ignores the colonial history of the South, scants the Old South, and misunderstands the New South. It barely mentions slavery and is more or less racist in its characterization of blacks. It neglects women, except as totemic objects of Southern mythology. . . . It misunderstands the nature of aristocracy. It overstresses both the unity and the continuity of Southern history. It has very little grasp of political history and has no coherent explanation for the Civil War. It is provincial in its emphasis both upon white males and upon the Piedmont of North Carolina as the archetypal South. It exaggerates the guilt of Southerners over slavery. It shows little understanding of the formal ideas of generations of Southern intellectuals. Its view of Reconstruction is primitive.

"So the corpse [of the book] is riddled," O'Brien concludes, "and it would require a necromancer to piece together the shattered bones, torn sinews, and spilled blood."[47] The weaknesses in Cash's work of which O'Brien and others have taken note mark *The Mind of the South*'s contrast with Weaver's *The Southern Tradition at Bay*.

Weaver's section in his dissertation on the South's heritage with its emphasis on the transplantation of the feudal system and the code of chivalry in Virginia would seem to be very much at odds with Cash's ironic evaluation of that image of the Old South:

It was a sort of stage piece out of the eighteenth century, wherein gesturing gentlemen move soft-spokenly against a background of rose gardens and dueling grounds, through always gallant deeds, and lovely ladies, in farthingales, never for a moment lost that exquisite remoteness which had been the dream of all men and the possession of none. Its social pattern was manorial, its civilization was that of the Cavalier, its ruling class an aristocracy coextensive with the planter group . . . men in every case descended from the old gentlefolk who for many centuries had made up the ruling classes of Europe.[48]

Weaver, it should be noted, did not maintain that the Old South's ruling classes traced their *bloodlines* to English gentry; instead, he insisted that they learned their *ideals* from them.

Donald Davidson, who had been one of Weaver's teachers at Vanderbilt, and who became a friend and admirer of Weaver during his years at the University of Chicago, took issue with Cash's picture of the antebellum South in a lengthy review. Davidson scored Cash for claiming to have interpreted "*the* Southern mind, not *a* Southern mind or *some* Southern minds." He also criticized the book's scanty documentation and fairly bristled at Cash's comparison of the southern mind to some elements of communism and fascism. It is interesting to note, however, that, near the end of his dissertation, Weaver wrote: "It is undeniable that there are numerous resemblances between the Southern agrarian mind and the mind of modern fascism." Here one is tempted to conclude he had picked up on Cash's analysis on the point that had so infuriated Davidson. At any rate, Weaver calmly observed that the only common theme to both southern Agrarianism and Fascism was hostility to a strictly materialist understanding of history and society and the central role played by the human spirit.[49]

The only reference to *The Mind of the South* in Weaver's works is in an essay entitled "The Southern Tradition," which was published in 1964, a year after his death. Weaver might have intended it to be a counterpoint to Cash's famous book, which had continued to be widely read and extensively quoted. He wrote: "I agree with Mr. W. J. Cash that the Southern mind is one of the most intransigent on earth; that is, it is one of the hardest minds to change. Ridiculing its beliefs has no more effect, as far as I have been able to observe, than ridiculing a person's religious beliefs—and the Southerner's beliefs have been a kind of secular religion with him: that only serves to convince him further that he is right and that you are damned." The South, Weaver held, had much to teach the North if only the North would listen. The region had served as the flywheel that had stabilized American society. The purpose of such a device is to speed up or slow down a machine, whatever the need of the moment happens to require. He reminded those focused on the region's conservatism that the South had proved important to the success of the New Deal, provided the needed votes to pass the Conscription Act of 1941, and had always been for free trade.[50] While he deplored what he believed were the excesses of Reconstruction and the humiliation endured by the defeated whites, he took note of the cynical racism characteristic of the Bourbons, by observing that "it is unfortunate but it is true that the Negro was forced to pay a large part of the bill for the follies of Reconstruction."[51]

Weaver concluded his study of the South on an upbeat note about a regional characteristic that many continued to find attractive. It was what he called the "last non-materialist civilization in the Western World." A technology that had been touted as a cure for all the world's ills had also come up with fearful weapons of mass destruction. Not a few have commented on the phenomenon that technology seems to create its own momentum; if something *can* be done, it eventually *will* be done.[52] There must be, Weaver concluded, a return to the words of "poets, artists, intellectuals: workers in the timeless . . . these unacknowledged legislators of mankind." Turning to the language of religion, he said that the "image of man in a morally designed world, ennobled by a conception of the transcendent" was the only hope. "The creation of a religious moral world will bring an end to the downward conversion which today threatens institutions and culture. . . . By restoring the moral and aesthetic medium . . . we can will our world, and retrieve our defeat by an upward conversion." Distinctions thoughtlessly cast aside must be rediscovered and restored. The truth that structure and hierarchy were the essential foundations upon which any society must rest must be acknowledged and acted upon. Reestablishment of the life of the Old South was emphatically not what he wanted, Weaver said, but a careful study of that culture could give us hints on how we might salvage our own.[53]

When one looks at Richard Weaver's study of the South (from Appomattox Court House to the sinking of the *Lusitania*) as a whole, it is vital to focus on his understanding of Reconstruction. His close study of primary sources revealed that those who lived through this era felt themselves the victims of a sort of cultural imperialism; the values cherished by the South were being purposely destroyed. Destruction and Reconstruction were going on simultaneously. The tearing down had not stopped when the guns fell silent. It began in earnest with congressional Reconstruction under the Radical Republicans whose hope for egalitarian order turned out to be an impossible dream. No doubt Weaver was reading his own experience into this interpretation of southern history. He had put his faith in that ideal when he became a socialist and had concluded that the pursuit of this chimera in the political realm led not to equality but ultimately to a loss of freedom. The government bureaucracy necessary to create a classless society would itself become the ruling class. Take away class distinctions, Weaver said, and you remove what makes life bearable and sometimes even enjoyable.

The antebellum South's attenuated feudalism, code of chivalry, concept of the gentleman, and older religiousness were vital not just for themselves alone but for what lay behind them. To worship them as such would be *traditionalism,* what Jaroslav Pelikan has called "the dead faith of the living." What Weaver focused on were the timeless truths found in the *tradition,* which Pelikan defines as "the living faith of the dead." Weaver was very careful to distinguish between "respect for tradition because it is tradition and respect for it because it expresses a spreading mystery too great for our knowledge to compass."[54] This southern tradition he extolled provided the means by which an ordered and refined civilization brought relative peace and order to the daily lives of people and built a wall against barbarism. No doubt one species of barbarism that Weaver especially loathed was the frenetic pursuit of wealth that he had witnessed from his early adolescence through his undergraduate college years. The Roaring Twenties had culminated in the Crash of 1929 and the Great Depression. These catastrophic events were the catalyst for his becoming a socialist. When he received his B.A. degree in the depths of the depression, he was no doubt convinced that an America economically devastated owed its ruin to industrial capitalism and the never-ending chase for material wealth.

Where had America gone wrong? How had that sorry state of affairs come about? Was there a time and place in the country's past when there was a different way of seeing and doing, a different life, another culture? These were the kinds of questions that dogged Weaver from his last years at the University of Kentucky through his time at Vanderbilt and Texas A & M. By the time he got to Louisiana State University, he had already immersed himself in the primary sources of the South from the end of the Civil War to the beginning of World War I. At that point he was beginning to feel that he had found a vanished culture. He emphatically did not believe it could or ought to be replicated in twentieth-century America, but that its essence was timeless, which was another way of saying it was true.

Weaver had seen that social mobility in a capitalist system was based upon the ability to amass wealth and knew that any society that did not provide for upward movement invited discontent and even revolution. He was emphatically not plumping for a reactionary, ossified society. Instead, in the South of which he wrote, the code of chivalry and concept of the gentleman provided the examples and set the standards for those who wished to move up. These nonmaterial measures, Weaver believed, were much to be preferred to a yardstick that only measured success in terms of wealth. One wonders what he would have made of the ability to shock as a measure of success in the entertainment field in this age of MTV.

Organized religion played a small role in Weaver's life if one goes by church attendance. All the record tells us is that he attended church irregularly as a youth, went to a revivalist meeting while he was in prep school only because it was a curiosity that interested him, and attended an Episcopal service once a year while he was on the faculty at the University of Chicago. This did not mean that he was irreligious; rather, it is perfectly congruent with what he characterized as the South's older religiousness. It was a faith that, perforce, must always have an element of mystery. And the science and technology that accompanied an urban, industrial country such as the United States had become by the 1940s was not congenial to that notion. A reductionist and rationalist belief that scoffed at mystery and purported to explain everything was automatically suspect since to explain everything is to explain nothing.

At the time that he completed his dissertation and was graduated from Louisiana State University with a Ph.D. degree in 1943, Richard Weaver had reached the point in his intellectual odyssey of being virtually apolitical. Like many other thoughtful people during the 1930s he had embraced the Left because of his idealism and disenchantment with capitalism. But he had gone a step further by becoming active in local party activities as well as a national political campaign. His study of the South from the end of the Civil War to World War I convinced him that purely political solutions were always suspect. All such nostrums focused on particular aspects of the general problem: a crisis of spirit that could not be cured by humanism or socialism or New Dealism or any other such "ism." Prescriptions of that sort were doomed because they were reductionist and did not consider the whole man. The Old South had a culture that was comprehensive and coherent, taking into account the unpredictability, recalcitrance, and quirkiness of the whole person in all his "givenness." Richard Weaver's challenge as he left Louisiana State University was to work out how the best of that culture might be applied to a twentieth-century America weary of panaceas and having to fight yet another world war.

6 The Potency of Belief

I RECALL SITTING IN MY OFFICE IN INGLESIDE HALL AT THE UNIVERSITY OF CHICAGO ONE FALL MORNING IN 1945 AND WONDERING WHETHER IT WOULD NOT BE POSSIBLE TO DEDUCE, FROM FUNDAMENTAL CAUSES, THE FALLACIES OF MODERN LIFE AND THINKING THAT HAD PRODUCED THIS HOLOCAUST AND WOULD INSURE OTHERS. IN ABOUT TWENTY MINUTES I JOTTED DOWN A SERIES OF CHAPTER HEADINGS, AND THIS WAS THE INCEPTION OF A BOOK ENTITLED *IDEAS HAVE CONSEQUENCES.*[1]

Thinking through the lessons he derived from his study of the post-Confederate South from 1865 to 1914, Richard Weaver constructed a model for criticizing the America of the mid-twentieth century in his book *Ideas Have Consequences*. It was his first published book, appearing in 1948. There Weaver set forth basic themes and ideas that he would later develop at some length in other works, although he adhered to the basic arguments he made in this book for the rest of his life. Paul Tillich described it as "brilliantly written, daring and radical. . . . It will shock, and philosophical shock is the beginning of wisdom."[2]

Weaver began with the startling declaration "that modern man has become a moral idiot. . . . For four centuries every man has been not only his own priest but his own professor of ethics, and the consequence is an anarchy which threatens even that minimum consensus of value necessary to the political state." Standing squarely on the lessons he had learned from the Agrarians, Weaver "was openly attacking capitalism and modern bourgeois society, as well as socialism and communism." Marxist historian

104

Eugene D. Genovese finds "eerily echoed" in this book both "Marx's *Capital* and Lenin's *Imperialism: The Highest Stage of Capitalism.*"[3]

The seedbed from which this book grew was Weaver's disillusionment not only with World War II itself but also with how it was prosecuted. He had at one time found the doctrine of original sin "archaically funny" until the events from 1941 to 1945 hammered home to him that original sin was a basic and undeniable truth. While he was writing his dissertation, he became aware that war carries its own dynamic. The real as well as the stated purposes of such conflicts often change with the passage of time and the vicissitudes of battle.

Convinced of the rightness of the Allies' cause at the outset, Weaver was appalled and disillusioned by what he perceived to be the betrayal of Finland by America and Great Britain. When Roosevelt broached the subject of Finland with Stalin at the Teheran Conference, the Soviet dictator responded that while he had no plans to annex Finland, he would insist that it meet certain conditions. Finland would be required to retreat to her 1940 border with the Soviet Union, drive the Germans completely out of the country, and be willing to pay hefty reparations to Stalin after the war. Although American diplomats pressed the Finns to accept this proposal, they formally turned the offer down in April 1944. Stalin immediately began making plans that called for Finland to be crushed in his 1944 summer offensive. It took less than a week for the Red Army to crush the Finns, who immediately turned to the Germans for weapons and supplies. Aid from that quarter enabled them to hold on for a couple of months before yielding to overwhelming military force and accepting Soviet terms on September 4, 1944. Retreating to her 1940 border with the Soviet Union, Finland gave up the Petsamo area, agreed to pay substantial reparations, broke diplomatic relations with Germany, and promised to take into custody any German troops still in the country two weeks after the signing of the agreement. Finland also had to agree to pursue a foreign policy that would not be in any way hostile to the U.S.S.R. The whole matter might have seemed to some at the time to be of little consequence, but the later entry of the word *Finlandization* into the vocabulary bespeaks the importance of what was at stake. A half century of hindsight does allow one to argue that this agreement enabled Finland to retain her sovereignty and independence during the Cold War. In the heat of the moment, however, Weaver recoiled from American attempts to press Finland to accept any accommodation with Stalin. "What does a small country count for," he asked, "in a world where everything is decided by a Big Four or a Big Three or a Big Something?"[4]

The abandonment of this small and valiant country was bad enough in Weaver's eyes, but what stung him perhaps even more was the fact that the Office of War Information, with the collusion of a willing press and most public officials, downplayed the matter. This same troika never came to grips with a reasonable explanation of what were the real issues at stake; instead they indulged in sloganeering. One that particularly galled him was to be told that once again Americans were fighting a "war to end all wars." He feared that infelicitous phrase could help lead to future conflict since it turned a blind eye and deaf ear to the givenness of evil in a fallen world.[5]

It was from such disillusionment that Weaver took his inspiration for *Ideas Have Consequences.* But if that was the negative element that drove him to write the book, the positive was his belief that the ideal of chivalry had at one time held men back from the worst sorts of evil deeds. Indeed, that was one of the reasons the code had developed in the first place and, throughout its long history, had helped to mitigate the worst features of warfare. Fresh on his mind was his study of the South; he expanded the section in his dissertation on chivalry to produce an article entitled "Southern Chivalry and Total War," which first appeared in the *Sewanee Review* in 1945. The code, which was spiritual in nature, was above conflict and made claims on combatants on both sides. This ideal did not encourage its adherents to engage in simplistic sloganeering; instead, it recognized the intransigence of human nature and the almost certain truth that wars will occur, but that rules might be followed that could control them in some measure. Even mortal combat did not excuse the casting off of all restraints in order to kill one's enemies.[6]

Ideas Have Consequences was, without question, a seminal work in which Weaver probed for what one writer called the *"vrai vérité des choses."* Eschewing the label *philosophy,* he insisted instead that what he had penned was a diagnosis of Western civilization's malaise that might properly be labeled "an intuition of a situation." The book was indeed indisputably more than a bloodless philosophical treatise or a landscape of the twentieth century painted from intuition. In a letter to his friend and former teacher Donald Davidson, Weaver displayed some of the passion and sense of urgency that lay behind the book: "I wrote it with the feeling that the important thing was to hit hard. . . . I felt from the beginning that there must be many persons in this country who are eager to hear the truth about these matters, and to hear it said in words as hard as cannon balls."[7] *Ideas Have Consequences,* then, was a challenge flung at those enamored of modernity who seemed to be equating change with progress and at those who were rushing pell-mell toward doom while gleefully cutting themselves off from their past.

Weaver's point of departure in this book was the nominalist philosophy of William of Occam, who insisted in the fourteenth century that universals are not real, only particulars. Ernst Troeltsch made the same point, saying that Occam and his followers had "severed the connection between Reason and Revelation" as well as "intensified psychological self-analysis." Universals had thus become only a kind of shorthand: useful for description, but of no value in describing something that has any *intrinsic* meaning. One *knows* individual things directly through the senses and not, as Plato insisted, through the instrument of ideas.[8]

In an essay written at about the same time as *Ideas Have Consequences,* Marshall McLuhan weighs in against nominalism and lauds southern writers for refusing to surrender to its claims. He contrasts New England with the South: "The New England mind . . . perceiv[es] its own roots in . . . Abelard and Occam (striving to settle the problems of metaphysics, theology, and politics as though they were problems of logic); . . . the South has been able to feel and to focus its own forensic tradition of Ciceronian humanism."[9]

The logical outcome of nominalism, Weaver believed, was a solipsism that made each person his own arbiter of truth since no other measure was available. Those who adhered to this position logically tended "to banish the reality which is perceived by the intellect and to posit as reality that which is perceived by the senses." To those who might argue that he was setting up a straw man, Weaver averred that nothing was more important about an individual than his presuppositions. Triumphant nominalism had yielded a series of disastrous consequences. First came despair of finding objective truth; it was no accident that one Renaissance theme was "Man, the measure of all things." A new model of nature also emerged. Earlier understood as a fallen creature though still good in essence and reflecting the Creator's handiwork, nature during the Renaissance came to be regarded instead as a closed system impervious to any divine interference, containing and setting its own standards. The practical results of this new paradigm were two: Nature was more thoroughly studied by men who were not disinterested learners, but partisans. As Bacon said in the *New Atlantis,* what they had on their mind was controlling nature in order to make it serve their personal ends. One Renaissance scholar has observed that magic and science were intertwined: "The serious magical endeavour and the serious scientific endeavour were twins: one was sickly and died, the other strong and throve. But they were twins. They were born of the same impulse." The second result of a triumphant nominalism, Weaver said, was the abandonment of Augustine as well as Aristotle: "The expulsion of the element of unintelligibility in nature was followed by the abandonment of the doctrine of original sin." If one dwells in a universe that is a closed system and man is a part of that universe, his failures and imperfections must finally yield to education or proper environment, or some other panacea. If man is in fact an *unfallen* creature, it follows that he is *naturally* good.[10]

The tree of nominalism continued to yield poisonous fruit, Weaver complained, with the worship of a false goddess—eighteenth-century rationalism as exemplified by Hobbes and Locke. The "why" of the cosmos became meaningless or at least took second place to the "how" of it. Since the why is an unambiguously religious question, Weaver went on, religion had to make a truce with eighteenth-century rationalism and science. One answer was the anthropomorphic god of deism who might have had a hand in the making of the universe but would not have the temerity and bad manners to interfere directly with its regularity. Such a faith was impotent in affecting human behavior, however; it made no moral or ethical claims on its adherents since it was arrived at through the senses. Darwin's *Origin of Species* in 1859 was itself not so much a seminal scientific treatise, since others had independently reached the same conclusions before him, but rather was the result of a philosophical need "to explain man by his environment." Thus human motivation came to be understood, he concluded, as nothing more, nor less, nor other, than biological determinism. "Weaver scored . . . heavily when he charged that the outcome of modern thought has been a denial of all objective truth and that denial has generated social atomization and personal alienation from God and one's fellow men."[11]

As the nineteenth century moved toward its conclusion, thinkers such as Marx and Darwin took environmentalism as their starting point and reduced the drama of human history to a desiccated model that understood man as nothing but the tool of his largely unconscious desire for wealth. He consequently found himself in the pathetic state that Weaver terms "abysmality." Living, if it may be properly called that, a life of "practice without theory," modern Western man is trapped. He still yearns for the truth and makes some effort to deal with the vicissitudes of existence but with no comprehensive worldview:

> He struggles with the paradox that total immersion in matter unfits him to deal with the problems of matter. His decline can be represented as a long series of abdications. He has found less and less ground for authority at the same time he thought he was setting himself up as the center of authority in the universe; indeed there seems to exist here a dialectic process which takes away his power in proportion as he demonstrates that his independence entitles him to power.[12]

Education was one of the first victims to fall prey to nominalism by shifting its focus from the idea of truth apprehended by the intellect to experiences subsumed under what has been called brute factuality. Weaver would write in a later book about the apotheosis of the very word *fact.* It was among those terms that could be used as a sort of incantation designed to settle arguments;

almost any statement prefaced with "the facts tell us" became an ex cathedra pronouncement beyond dispute and greeted by some hearers with a credulity once reserved only for papal bulls. An excessive emphasis on words' historical context fed the notion that they could not be used to describe objective reality, and thus encouraged those with a solipsist bent to use them as they pleased. It followed that those who viewed language as a window to truth were disillusioned.[13]

Nominalism had far-reaching consequences not only on educational method but also on what was taught. The Renaissance aimed at training men to be successful in the modern sense of the term, though there was enough inherited capital to spend to educate men in the older way for a long time. Nonetheless, the trend had been set and the legatees' offspring became prodigals. Two nineteenth-century developments sped up the pace of decline in Weaver's view: "The first was a patent increase in man's dominion over nature which dazzled all but the most thoughtful; and the second was the growing mandate for popular education." The push for education in and of itself could have been a blessing, he felt, had it not foundered on the rock of "equalitarian democracy's unsolvable problem of authority: no one was in a position to say what the hungering multitudes were to be fed." Hard on the heels of these two trends came "a carnival of specialism, professionalism, and vocationalism" encouraged and hedged about by government and many universities that joined this parade of folly by exalting *Homo faber* at the expense of Homo sapiens.[14]

What could be done about such a malaise? Weaver insisted that modern Western man must first come to terms with the fact that there is a problem. Until that happened, "hysterical optimism will prevail." A proper distinction between right and wrong had to be made so that eyes bleary with looking at particulars could be refocused on universals. This would require an important act of the will since, from the time of Francis Bacon in the seventeenth century, the West had for the most part been doggedly distancing itself from first principles, chanting the word "empiricism" in a kind of crazy mantra, all the while hoping that "experience will tell [them] what [they] are experiencing." Many thoughtful moderns are drowning in particulars of which there are more all the time;

they have no organizing vision that could integrate a blizzard of facts into a whole that makes sense.[15]

In his chapter entitled "The Unsentimental Sentiment," Weaver discussed three levels of reflection common to humanity: specific knowledge of particulars, a set of convictions, and a "metaphysical dream of the world." It is impossible, he wrote, to live at the first level for any length of time without falling prey to "disharmony and conflict." This result is so obvious that men move to the second level by "defin[ing] a few rudimentary conceptions about the world which they repeatedly apply as choices present themselves." But, he went on to insist, the third level is the most important of all. It is a "metaphysical dream" and "an intuitive feeling about the immanent nature of reality" that orders and gives meaning to the particulars and the intermediate set of convictions. "We must admit this when we realize that logical processes rest ultimately on classification, that classification is by identification, and that identification is intuitive." Some medieval scholars' strenuous efforts to preserve their overall scheme made sense, Weaver maintained, of ventures that were otherwise simply amusing or absurd.

> The Schoolmen understood that the question of how many angels can stand on the point of a needle, so often cited as examples of Scholastic futility, had incalculable ramifications, so that, unless there was agreement upon these questions, unity in practical matters was impossible. For the answer supplied that which bound up their world; the ground of this answer was the fount of understanding and evaluation. . . . It made one's sentiment toward the world rational, with the result that it could be applied to situations without plunging man into sentimentality on the one hand or brutality on the other.

The acceptance of an arbitrary and abstract standard gave man freedom and self-control, Weaver went on, since he did not have to resort to an ad hoc pragmatism to justify everything he did. The idea that it did not really matter what one believed was anathema to Weaver, who wondered "how men who disagree about what the world is for" could "agree about any of the minutiae of daily conduct." Weaver believed this was another example of the decline of language, since such a declaration really meant that anyone could believe whatever one chose as long as the beliefs were not taken seriously.[16]

Only barbarians, Weaver insisted, were driven by the lust to see all things "as they really are." That sort of reductionism was a fearful phenomenon that tried to relate things to themselves and other things while ignoring the vital role that imagination plays. This mind-set wants to tear away all veils and coverings and inhibitions; it is obscene in the etymological sense of that "which should be enacted off-stage because it is unfit for public exhibition." Lest some think he was plumping for a sort of neopuritanism at this juncture, Weaver illustrated his point from both Greek and Elizabethan drama: The former proscribed scenes of excessive physical and psychological violence as did the latter, which was nonetheless replete with earthy references without being obscene. The outstanding example of this systematic stripping away of the robes of decency, Weaver believed, was sensational journalism that justified its actions by stridently claiming that it was simply giving its readers "the real world" or "life as it is." This, he said, "begs the most important question of all," since "the raw stuff of life is precisely what civilized man desires to have refined, or presented in a humane framework, for which sentiment alone can afford support." By sentiment, he meant a metaphysical vision or world view that orders and organizes a culture. He was convinced that this was the only alternative to "sentimentality, with its emotions lavished upon the trivial and the absurd" and "brutality, which can make no distinctions in the application of its violence."[17]

Equally as execrable to Weaver as the reductionist mind-set, which wanted to rip aside all veils in order to see "the real world," was an uncritical adulation of egalitarianism. He scored the notion of equality as a concept that undermined order, a pernicious doctrine that yielded predictable results. Equality before the law—well and good. But any other kind creates chaos, since "there can be no equality of condition between youth and age or between the sexes; there cannot be equality even between friends. . . . The assignment of identical roles produces first confusion and then alienation. . . . Not only is this disorganizing heresy busily confounding the most natural social groupings, it is also creating a reservoir of poisonous envy." What is the antidote to this deadly draught? A recovery of the belief that this is a hierarchical world whether one likes it or not. Here Weaver appealed to Shakespeare, Milton, and Saint Paul in pleading for a recovery of social amiability based not upon equality but upon fraternity. A family recognized and cherished the peculiar and distinctive traits and roles of each member. "It demands patience with little brother, and it may sternly exact duty of big brother. It places people in a network of sentiment, not of rights." Here, one suspects, is another instance of Weaver's drawing upon his own experience in order to make the larger generalization. As the oldest child of his family, he took upon himself the responsibility of caring for his widowed mother, buying her a house in Weaverville as soon as he could scrape together the money after taking the teaching job at the University of Chicago in 1945.[18]

This hankering after a mindless egalitarianism also began with nominalism, Weaver insisted. If categories describing nature are only *façons de parler* then such must also be the case with societal arrangements. Twentieth-century man still yearned for a metaphysic to order his world and, in many instances, had opted for progress. But this term had come to be a measure for material goods only, a rubber yardstick that was constantly being stretched as new wants were created by the multiplicity of new *things* available. Some intelligent or perspicuous individuals who had despaired of progress as a satisfying vision succumbed to another type of sentimentality, an existentialism that in the face of a world felt to have no meaning pathetically asserts that it does.[19]

Modern man lived, Weaver felt, in a shattered world. Since there was no metaphysical vision making sense of the whole, "this fragmentation leads directly to an obsession with isolated parts." Those like himself who argued for absolute values were sneeringly dismissed by some with such phrases as "you can't turn the clock back." The language was revealing. Behind this jibe lay the presupposition that all are locked in the prison of the present for which there can never be a key. But truth by its very nature must be timeless. And what Weaver was calling for here was not a reactionary infatuation with the past, he insisted, but rather a return to some sort of metaphysical or theological integrating vision. A quest for that which is timeless could very simply be described as the pursuit of truth. What he was affirming, Weaver said, was simply "that there is a center of things, and . . . that every feature of modern disintegration is a flight from this toward periphery."[20]

The philosophic doctor of the Middle Ages and the gentleman of the eighteenth century had one trait in common, Weaver noted: They both distrusted specialization. "For them the highest knowledge concerned, respectively, the relation of men to God and the relation of men to men." Their vision of what was ultimately important was not obscured by a welter of facts. Moderns are engaged in an increasingly frantic scramble for factual information. Those who have rejected (perhaps not consciously so) the possibility of knowing the truth have tried to put in its place a mountain of data. Weaver buttressed his point by calling attention to the phenomenon of the quiz shows and games that tested not knowledge but memory of particulars. "The acquisition of unrelated details becomes an end in itself and takes the place of the true idea of education." To "let the facts speak for themselves" is to ask the impossible, Weaver insisted. There has developed as a corollary to this false doctrine an unhealthy fear of generalization. In another work, he deplored this development by insisting, "It is useless to argue against generalization; a world without generalization would be a world without knowledge." He would have heartily agreed with C. S. Lewis, who wrote, "Generalities are the lenses with which our intellects have to make do."[21]

This fragmentation characteristic of modern man has spawned an exorbitant egotism in his work and art, according to Weaver. Workers and artists who think of themselves first and their tasks second make an egregious error by "denying the reality of forms imperfectly realized. The reality then is merely the actuality which his desire or whim cares to produce." One is reminded here of what Picasso said about his own work: "A picture used to be a sum of additions. In my case a picture is a sum of destructions."[22] In art, the shift to egotism has resulted in an obsession with technique, a predictable outcome of those who ignore the larger philosophical questions. Nominalism began in painting, Weaver believed, with impressionism, which rejected form and concentrated exclusively on substance and color. Monet, for example, focused on the concept of change when he painted an identical haystack at different times on the same day. Music's similar plunge could be sketched, Weaver said, in three stages. "In its highest form this music was architectural; it then became thematic; and finally . . . textural. It hardly needs pointing out that this is a movement away from the autonomous and integrated ideal toward a collection of fragments which afford maximum opportunity for subjective and egotistic expression."[23]

The egotism that has become pervasive in the twentieth century, Weaver asserted, is the natural fruit of a noxious weed, a false view of man's nature and destiny. Such a person lived only to please himself and did not need to serve others or worry about some theoretical eternal destiny. Apprehensive about the effects of rampant self-centeredness on man's political destiny, Weaver held that this sort of egotism was characteristic of those people to whom the whole notion of self-discipline was anathema. The real danger was that those who sneered at such a concept were flirting with tyranny. If they would not control their own actions, some sort of external restraints would become necessary. He would have agreed with Franklin's warning to the Philadelphia Convention just after they had signed the Constitution:

> I agree to this Constitution, with all its faults, if they are such, because I think a General Government necessary for us, and there is no form of government but what may be a blessing to the people if well administered; and believe further, that this is likely to be well administered for a course of years, and can only end in despotism, as other forms have done before it, when the people shall become so corrupted as to need despotic government, being incapable of any other.[24]

Some of Weaver's sharpest barbs were aimed at what has come to be referred to simply as "the media." He called it "a wonderful machine . . . the Great Stereopticon," whose purpose is "to project selected pictures of life in the hope that what is seen will be imitated. All of us in the West who are within the long reach of technology are sitting in the audience. We are told the time to laugh and the time to cry, and signs are not wanting that the audience grows ever more responsive to its cues." The typical newspaper reader, Weaver believed, accepted without question what he found on the printed page. "He no more thinks of examining [the presuppositions behind what is printed there] than did his pious forbears of the thirteenth century—whom he pities for sitting in medieval darkness—think of questioning the cosmology."[25]

Taking each one of the Great Stereopticon's parts in turn, Weaver first scored the newspaper by noting the dubious circumstances of its birth. Modern journalism, the "spawn of the machine," has served as a tool of exploitation and special interest. The yellow press of the late nineteenth century served as an obvious example. In the larger cities, two or three editions every day from the never-sleeping newspapers bombarded their readers with information. Weaver would have agreed with novelist Dick Francis's definition of the newspapers' creed: "Today is important, tomorrow more so, but yesterday is nothing." The insidious effects of the medium included the layout and arrangement of stories, not a neutral endeavor by any means: What was on the first page was by implication more important than what one found on the second and so on. But perhaps more impact was made on the reader by the repetition of certain phrases that "are carefully chosen not to stimulate reflection but to evoke stock responses of approbation or disapprobation." They encoded a point of view that could be accepted by the reader without so much as a thought. The well-known British journalist Malcolm Muggeridge commented at length on the latter phenomenon while recalling his days with the *Manchester Guardian* and the following phrases that appeared repeatedly in each edition:

> No thinking man will underestimate the. . . .
> While there are many circumstances which. . . .
> There are solid grounds for hoping that. . . .
> It is surely incumbent upon all of us to. . . .
> While recognising the reality of. . . .
> No mere conflict of interest should. . . .
> The immeasurable strides that Science has. . . .
> Such is the choice that at present confronts. . . .
> It is idle to think that politicians can. . . .

Muggeridge labeled such phrases "non-language; these drooling non-sentences conveying non-thoughts propounding non-fears and offering non-hopes."[26]

An even worse feature of journalism, in Weaver's calculus, was its propensity to report the bizarre and exacerbate conflict gratuitously. The old adage "When a dog bites a man, that's not news; when a man bites a dog, that's news" comes to mind. While the Soviet Union was making no bones about controlling news, public-relations officials and agencies in the United States performed a quite similar function in restricting and shading information about themselves, all in the guise of better informing the public.

In treating the cinema, the second leg of the Great Stereopticon tripod, Weaver took note of the artistic license that movie producers enjoyed; they had at their disposal the means to completely change a literary work beyond all recognition of what it had been on the printed page. He hastened to point out that those who deplored the deleterious effect of this medium on morals were missing the point in calling for a particular kind of censorship. "The thing that needs to be censored is not the length of the kisses but the egotistic, selfish, and self-flaunting hero; not the relative proportion of undraped breast but the flippant, vacuous-minded, and . . . egotistic heroine. Let us not worry about the jokes of dubious propriety; let us rather object to the whole story, with its complacent assertion of the virtues of materialist society."

Weaver believed that radio, the third component of the Great Stereopticon, was perhaps the most mischievous of all. No doubt he would have made the same statements about television, which of course was a relatively new phenomenon in the late 1940s. Subscribers might selectively read a newspaper or magazine; no one was under compulsion to go to a cinema. But radio was ubiquitously present. Public places abounded with them, and those blaring from nearly every home violated the silence of their neighbors. Human beings, perforce, listened and became used to hearing "the weirdest of juxtapositions: the serious and the trivial, the comic and the tragic, follow one another in mechanical sequence without real transition. During the recent war what person of feeling was not struck by the insanity of hearing advertisements for laxatives between announcements of the destruction of famous cities by aerial bombardment?"

The practiced monotone of those reporting the news on radio was that of "the cheerful liar," Weaver asserted, the natural voice of those who have sedulously avoided sentiment, until they are dead to it. And they infect their viewers and listeners with the same sickness because human beings are affected willy-nilly "by the continued assertion of cynicism and brutality." But he refused to yield to despair, because he saw in many people a healthy skepticism of the media that he attributed to the disillusionment born of World War II. It was a visceral rather than a reasoned distrust, but nonetheless salutary.

The special pleading of the Great Stereopticon about "the peoples' right to know" simply would not wash, Weaver concluded, because what was being spoken of was not knowledge but sensation and brute factuality. The result was further fragmentation. He endorsed Henry James's assessment of journalism as particularly apt: "It is criticism of the moment at the moment."[27] There were no proper referents to put what was being reported into a proper context.

From his discussion of the media, Weaver moved on to a scrutiny of urban man in a chapter on the "spoiled child psychology," which was, as he believed, yet another logical result of nominalism. Shorn of a transcendent metaphysic that might demand self-discipline, modern city man seeks no other salvation than that which the further conquest of nature can provide. Conditioned by the Great Stereopticon, he is impatient of restraint and difficulty of any sort; in short, he is a spoiled child who will tolerate nothing less than the gratification of his immediate wants. "He wants things, but he regards payment as an imposition or as an expression of malice by those who withhold for it. His solution . . . is to abuse those who do not gratify him."

The contrived environment of the city had helped this process along, Weaver believed. Behind the walls of his air-conditioned and heated apartment, the city dweller had concluded that he is freed from the limitations nature normally imposes with the changing seasons, and the march of science would make a world where work would be obsolete. Having no historical perspective, such people concluded that those who had more were the enemies. This attitude frequently manifested itself in the slogan that property rights must always give way to human rights. More often than not,

Weaver wryly observed, this meant comfort or convenience. The real problem was that the connection between rights and duties had been severed. Once that happened, the next leap in logic by mass man was that work, an unpleasant enough task in most cases anyway, was irrelevant to getting things; such people then moved by whatever means available to take what they wanted.

A vital ingredient of Weaver's prescription for modern Western man's resuscitation was private property, which he called "the last metaphysical right." Although his soul had been ravaged by nominalism, modern man retained his humanity in being able to know and will. What was required was to put him in front of a mirror to make him see his condition and recognize the truth "that there is a world of ought," and "that the apparent does not exhaust the real." Put another way, it is a call for those floating in the sea of relativism to consider "living again in a world of metaphysical certitude." That was possible because private property is the one institution that makes it so.

The metaphysical dimension of this right was simply that its existence was not based on *any* utilitarian premise. "Property rests upon the idea of the *hisness of his,* . . . the very words assert an identification of owner and owned." It has continued to be a "self-justifying right" not subject to the vicissitudes of public opinion. Weaver hastened to add at this juncture that what he was talking about was real property in contrast to stocks and bonds. The latter he denigrated as "abstract property" because it "actually de-stroy[ed] the connection between man and his substance without which metaphysical right becomes meaningless." Weaver chided those who thoughtlessly applied the label private enterprise to com-panies since the corporation by its very nature could be private in no real sense. What he would have liked to see was the "distributive ownership of small properties. These take the form of independent farms, of local business, of homes owned by occupants, where indi-vidual responsibility gives significance to prerogative over property. Such ownership provides a range of volition through which one can be a complete person, and it is the abridgement of this volition for which monopoly capitalism must be condemned along with com-munism." This kind of "sanctuary against pagan statism" Weaver compared with the catacombs where the early Christians could take refuge from persecution. Freed from meddlesome bureaucrats and the press of public opinion, men may exercise choice and learn the value of *self*-discipline. If he should fail, there is no one on whom to fix blame and demand reparation but himself. What he earned was free from the ravages of inflation: "Productive private property represents a kind of sanctuary against robbery through adulteration, for the individual getting his substance from property which bears his imprint and assimilation has a more real measure of value."[28]

Weaver went on to explicate the lost nexus between property and a personal sense of honor. Laissez-faire capitalism had created corporations whose names mirrored their anonymity: "General," "Standard," "International." These were facades, he complained, that served to cover up mischief, for what *individual* can be held responsible for tainted or inferior products? The Spanish phrase for corporation, *sociedad anonima,* made the point very well. "Having a real name might require having a character, and character stands in the way of profit." Made-up names were abstractions that, like advertising slogans, were intrinsically dishonest. In sum, Weaver said, the right of private property ought to be particularly cherished and fostered by modern man because it opens the window for spiritual values. This was the only sanctuary, he was convinced, where pragmatism had not won the day.[29]

The close study he gave to the meaning of *corporation*, and what the word implied, underscores the point that the careful use of language bulked large in Weaver's thinking. Nominalism has stamped its imprint in this area as well, but perhaps less so, he believed. Since words have *intrinsic* meanings, he contended, they have been less yielding to the assaults of those who see communication as the mere arranging and rearranging of counters in order to get one's way. The recovery of right communication in some measure depended on the revival of the venerable notion that language was of divine origin. Vestiges of this idea survived in the case of oaths that bound individuals without regard to their feelings or the demands of a particular moment. That Adam named the animals underlined an important dimension of education, "learning to name rightly." Speech was a means of both understanding and "the *principle* of intelligibility." Along those lines, it is interesting to note that Calvin translated the first verse of John's Gospel as "In the beginning was [the] Speech."[30]

Weaver took the study of the "science" of semantics to be yet another noxious outgrowth of nominalism. Widespread interest in the subject derived in part, he contended, from the conviction that words by themselves carry a dynamic that cannot be denied. When Occam's view triumphed over that of Aquinas, ontology yielded to pragmatism. Philosophy reflected this shift from Occam to Bacon, Hobbes, and our own present day, when to some "ideas become psychological figments, and words become useful signs." Semanticists were almost universally devotees of the idea of change, which to them meant progress. They resisted the concept that language describes that which is; instead, they wanted words to "reflect . . . qualities of perceptions, so that man can, by the pragmatic theory of success, live more successfully." When asked to explain Coleridge's account of the two tourists at the waterfall, when the poet accepts one's description as "sublime" and rejects another's description as "pretty," those who see language as only a mirror of perception reason as follows: "When the man said 'That is sublime,' he appeared to be saying something about the waterfall. . . . Actually . . . he was not making a remark about the waterfall, but a remark about his own feelings. What he was saying was really 'I have feelings associated in my mind with the word *Sublime*,' or shortly, 'I have sublime feelings.' " Contrary to what many semanticists contended, Weaver fervently held that language was not a veil of obfuscation between human beings and reality, but an indispensable tool for definition.

> Definition then must depend on some kind of analogical relationship of a thing with other things, and this can mean only that definition is ultimately circular. That is to say, if one begins defining a word with synonyms, he will, if he continues, eventually complete a circuit and arrive at the very terms with which he started. . . . This concerns one of the most fundamental problems of philosophy; and I am ready to assert that we can never break out of the circle of language and seize the object barehanded, as it were, or without some ideational operation. It must surely be granted that whatever is unique defies definition.[31]

What this pointed to, Weaver concluded, was a truth uttered millennia ago by Plato, that all learning is based on defining a thing by what one already knows. Hence, language was not a barrier, but rather a foundation by which one can break the fetters of the present in order to find real meaning. "The community of language gives one access to significances at which he cannot otherwise arrive. To find a word is to find a meaning; to create a word is to find a single term for a meaning partially distributed in other words. Whoever may doubt that language has this power to evoke should try the experiment of thinking without words." What was essential to education in the truest sense, Weaver concluded, was education in languages (especially Latin and Greek), which demands rigor in the use of words, and in Socratic dialectic, which he saw as men's "means of coping with the datum of the world after they have established their primary feeling toward it." Dialectic is crucial because it required one to properly *name* things. "Dialectic comes to one's aid as a method by which, after our assumptions have been made, we can put our house in order."[32]

Weaver's final chapter was devoted to the idea that modern man was impious. Young Euthyphro in Plato, who wanted to prosecute his father for murder, has his twentieth-century counterparts who hate their past and revel in helping to destroy anything associated with it. One manifestation of this phenomenon is the desire to conquer nature, which is seen as a "thing" to be tampered with incessantly, a machine that needs not just repair but redesign. And when each "victory" creates additional problems that were not foreseen, those wedded to such a view do not pause for sober reflection about motive or method but press on to new projects of conquest.[33]

Moderns were also impious toward other people, Weaver contended. He saw the phrase "unconditional surrender" as a superb word picture of such an attitude. It was the arrogant posturing of men bent on usurping divine prerogative. In contrast to the ideal of chivalry, modern man assumed that his enemies do not even have the right to exist. Thus his talk about the brotherhood of man was nothing more than cant.[34]

The final way moderns manifested their impiety, Weaver contended, was by their contempt for the past. This was fraught with terrible consequences since reflection in any real sense is, perforce, about the past. "The present is a line, without width; the future only a screen in our minds on which we project combinations of memory."

Feminism, in Weaver's view, was one of the more perverse manifestations of the twentieth century's impiety, a reckless abandonment of one of the most basic givens of the human condition. He could not understand why so many women had so readily embraced it. "With her superior closeness to nature, her intuitive realism, her unfailing ability to detect the sophistry in mere intellectuality, how was she ever cozened into the mistake in going modern? Perhaps it was the decay of chivalry in men that proved too much. After the gentlemen went, the lady had to go too. No longer protected, the woman now has her career, in which she makes a drab pilgrimage from two-room apartment to job to divorce court."

Weaver called for a recovery of the idea of personality as a way of combating impiety toward others. Here again, he insisted, using the right word was crucial. Those who deplored the "loss of respect for individuality" were on to something but had opted for the wrong term. Individuality could become an excuse for "mere eccentricity or perverseness." *Personality* stressed selfhood *and* relationship with others. Individuals could all too easily become mere counters, he went on to argue, pointing out that bureaucrats and dictators were fond of stressing individual rights. And hatred of nonconformity was not confined just to totalitarian countries. The astute study he did of America a century and half ago convinced Tocqueville that Americans have a greater fondness for equality than liberty, and the majority, given the choice, would probably choose the former even if it were at the expense of the latter.[35]

In conclusion, Weaver admitted that he had tried to write his book in a secular style but insisted that religious belief was, finally, the pons asinorum that modern man must cross in order to avoid being overtaken and overwhelmed by the folly of modernity. He was convinced that a scrutiny of history, ancient and modern, left little doubt that loss of belief has yielded the bitter fruit of self-destruction:

Ancient cynicism, skepticism, and even stoicism, which were products of the decline of Greek religion, each concealed a bitterness. There is bitterness in the thought that there may be no hell; for—in the irrefutable syllogism of the theologians—if there is no hell, there is no justice. And bitterness is always an incentive to self-destruction. When it becomes evident that the world's rewards are not adequate to the world's pain, and when the possibility of other reward is denied, simple calculation demands the ending of it all.[36]

What, then, was to be done? Weaver made an urgent appeal for what he called "deep reformation." Using religious terminology, he said America desperately needed an "upward conversion." What worried him was the prospect that moderns had become so insensitive that to awaken them from their stupor was a task of Herculean proportions. *Ideas Have Consequences* resulted from his own deeply felt responsibility to sound the alarm. His final words reflect a sober but determined refusal to give in to despair: "It may be that we are awaiting a great change, that the sins of the fathers are going to be visited upon the generations until the reality of evil is again brought home and there comes some passionate reaction, like that which flowered in the chivalry and spirituality of the Middle Ages. If such is the most that we can hope for, something toward that revival may be prepared by acts of thought and volition in this waning day of the West."[37]

It seems clear that *Ideas Have Consequences* stood both as a cultural critique of American life and society as he had come to view it in the 1940s and 1950s and as a plan of action for reform. Weaver was not alone in sounding an alarm about where America seemed to be heading. George Nash has written that there were really three strands of protest at the time. Those who especially feared that an expanded state was a genuine threat to liberty can be referred to in general terms as classical liberals or libertarians. A second group was composed of many who had broken with communism and had then become its outspoken and passionate opponents, seeing an implacable threat to America in that movement; at stake as these men saw it was nothing less than the future of the world. Weaver belonged, Nash believed, to a third group who believed that the nation's only hope was a recovery of absolute values. The country's woes during the thirties and forties were the result of its having abandoned traditional beliefs and substituted any secular ideology that came along.[38] A close scrutiny of what Weaver wrote, however, makes it clear that while he was an ardent defender of tradition and spiritual values, his defense was neither reactionary nor conventional. He minced no words in pointing to the state as a threat to liberty and did not hold back in describing what he felt to be the dangers and horror of communism. That Weaver's works manifest characteristics of what Nash insists were three separate strands of an emerging conservatism in the 1940s and 1950s would seem to indicate that he was not a self-conscious member of that movement. A close study of *The Southern Tradition at Bay* and *Ideas Have Consequences* reveals the influence of the Agrarians and their holistic view of the world in every chapter of these two books by Weaver. It was natural that the emerging conservative movement and its self-appointed spokesmen, such as William F. Buckley Jr., would claim such an original thinker and articulate writer as Weaver as one of their own. But they sought him out and not the other way around. It is significant that the word *conservative* almost without exception is used by Weaver only when he is referring to the South's stubborn adherence to the four traditions earlier discussed and not to a particular political philosophy.[39] Weaver was a loner who had virtually no social life while he was at Louisiana State University and during all the years he was at the University of Chicago. His two most important works, *The Southern Tradition at Bay* and *Ideas Have Consequences,* were the expression of a highly original mind anxious and eager to communicate his conviction that cultural renewal in America and the West had to be based on a spiritual view of man that would enable the proper relationships once again to be established between the many and the one.

Even though there would seem to be little room for optimism in such a diagnosis as was presented in *Ideas Have Consequences,* Weaver had shown himself to be a fighter. As a prep student at Lincoln Memorial Academy, he first flexed his rhetorical muscles in practicing the art of persuasion. At the University of Kentucky, he was a fierce competitor on the track team and in the debate forum while maintaining an A average and taking an active part in the Liberal Club. The gloomy depression years saw him become a dedicated worker in the American Socialist Party doing his part to put Norman Thomas in the White House. At Vanderbilt he sampled the intellectual springs of Agrarianism, reluctantly giving up his socialism some three years later. His teaching years at Texas A & M disabused him of the notion of change as progress and of progress as only that which is quantifiable, making bigness something praiseworthy in and of itself. At Louisiana State University he focused on the lost cause of the American South without forgetting to contribute to what would turn out to be another lost cause— the Spanish civil war. The modern West's malaise was confirmed beyond all doubting to Weaver during World War II. Those years had shorn him of any lingering notions he may have had about the innate goodness of man and the inevitability of human progress. That disillusionment, along with his conviction that the southern experience could provide some important lessons to twentieth-century America and the world, found poignant expression in *Ideas Have Consequences*.

7 | Civil Disobedience against Language

LANGUAGE IS A COVENANT AMONG THOSE WHO USE IT. IT IS IN THE NATURE OF A COVENANT TO BE MORE THAN A MATTER OF SIMPLE CONVENIENCE, TO BE DEPARTED FROM FOR LIGHT AND TRANSIENT CAUSES. A COVENANT—AND I LIKE, IN THIS CONNECTION, THE RELIGIOUS OVERTONES OF THE WORD—BINDS US AT REALITY. WHEN WE COVENANT WITH ONE ANOTHER THAT A WORD SHALL STAND FOR A CERTAIN THING, WE SIGNIFY THAT IT IS THE BEST AVAILABLE WORD FOR THE THING IN THE PRESENT STATE OF GENERAL UNDERSTANDING. THE POSSIBILITIES OF REFINEMENT TOWARD A MORE ABSOLUTE CORRECTNESS OF MEANING LIE WITHIN AND BEHIND THAT CONVENTION. BUT AS LONG AS THE CONVENTION IS IN EFFECT, IT HAS TO BE RESPECTED LIKE ANY OTHER RULE, AND THIS REQUIRES THAT DEPARTURES FROM IT MUST JUSTIFY THEMSELVES.[1]

Having articulated in unmistakable terms his vision of what was wrong with the West in *Ideas Have Consequences,* Richard Weaver concluded with a clarion call for action. He had decided that what was needed was not one more jeremiad on decline but a blueprint for positive change. He would spend the next five years working out how he believed a basic reformation might be brought about through the recovery of what he termed *noble rhetoric.* While he made some preliminary observations on the topic in an article that first appeared in *College English* in 1948,[2] the full exposition and argument appeared in his book *The Ethics of Rhetoric,* which was published in 1953.

The word *rhetoric* in the eyes of many—journalists and politicians come readily to mind—has come to mean little more than balderdash or persiflage, or the cynical use of words to obscure real issues. An example of such confusion can be illustrated by what occurred during a committee meeting at the University of Chicago shortly before Weaver received an appointment to its English faculty.

In the atmosphere charged with the doomsday sense of urgency that followed the detonation of the first atom bomb in 1945, President Robert M. Hutchins of the University of Chicago appointed a committee to frame a world constitution. Two distinguished members of that group were poet and professor Giuseppe Antonio Borgese of the University of Chicago and the dean of Harvard's law school, James Landis—men who were a study in contrast. Mortimer Adler recalls that, at one meeting, Professor Borgese spoke with such intensity of feeling as to reduce his hearers to silence, except for Landis, who "Fixed Borgese with a cold stare and said in a low voice, 'That's just rhetoric!' Borgese, equally cold but with anger, and pointing a finger at Landis that might have been a pistol, replied: 'When you say that again, smile!'" Landis's remark and Borgese's retort well illustrate the ambivalence often felt toward the word *rhetoric*, as well as the two ways of understanding what it means.

The dean could not have meant that what Borgese said made no sense or ignored commonly accepted rules of expression. Borgese's mastery of the written and spoken word was well known by his colleagues, who admired his "flair for embellishing his remarks with imagery, with metaphor, with well-timed pauses and staccato outbursts that riveted attention on what he was saying and drove home the points he was trying to make." His words had a dynamic that Landis's utterances did not have, as polished and reasonable as the latter's remarks were. It may well have been that Landis's critique of Borgese was that he was not engaging in rhetoric, pure and simple, but that he "was *more* rhetorical than the occasion required." This exchange took place before a small group of colleagues who were in agreement on essentials; there was no need for Borgese to hold forth as though he were speaking to a large audience he was trying to move to certain beliefs and consequent actions. What

Landis wanted the committee to do was to stick "closely and coolly, to the pertinent matters, eschewing all irrelevant digressions that added more heat than light to the discussions. Hence his curt rebuff to Borgese that, in effect, said, 'Cut the unnecessary rhetoric out.'"

To agree with Landis that there was unnecessary rhetoric begs the question: When, if ever, would such rhetoric be needed? An answer in the negative would be to affirm that "speaking grammatically and logically always suffices for the purpose at hand. That it almost never does. One might just as well say that speaking to others never requires any consideration of how to get them to listen to what you have to say or how to make what you have to say affect their minds and hearts in ways that you wish to achieve."[3]

Defining rhetoric is no easy task. Peter Dixon at the beginning of his study of it notes its slipperiness and lack of precision: "It has been invoked in order to praise . . . and to condemn. So invertebrate is the word that we can apparently turn it inside out." Weaver recognized this difficulty without making heavy weather of it. "Rhetoric," he wrote, "is the most humanistic of all the disciplines." It "speaks to man in his whole being and out of his whole past and with reference to values which only a human being can intuit." He went on to say, "The most obvious truth about rhetoric is that its object is the whole man."[4] Thus, rhetoric dealt with something that was ever multifaceted and complex—human nature.

The Ethics of Rhetoric dealt at length with the topic and laid the foundation for all Weaver's subsequent treatment of it. One strand that runs unmistakably through the very different chapters of this book is that rhetoric was language designed to persuade. Plato's *Phaedrus* was Weaver's point of departure in this exploration of the nature of rhetoric. He held that whether Socrates really believed the Greek myths was irrelevant. This sort of higher critical approach missed the point. In the *Phaedrus,* "beneath the surface of repartee and mock seriousness," Plato "is asking whether we ought to prefer a neuter[ed] form of speech to the kind which is ever getting us aroused over things and provoking an expense of spirit."[5]

Language, Weaver wrote, can affect human beings in only three ways: "It can move us toward what is good; it can move us toward what is evil; or it can in a hypothetical third place, fail to move us at all." What could not be avoided in Plato's time and cannot be avoided now, Weaver averred, was the timeless truth that "any utterance is a major assumption of responsibility," and to tamper with language does nothing to mitigate that responsibility. The second of Plato's alternatives, what Weaver called "base rhetoric," was speech that pushed its audience in the direction of evil and deserved the qualifying adjective "because its end is . . . exploitation. . . . In the last analysis, it knows only its will." He had already explored this topic in some depth in *Ideas Have Consequences* in "The Great Stereopticon," where he scored journalism for its underlying sophistry. He believed it was generally true that journalists did not write so as to set forth clearly and in an unbiased fashion the alternatives. "By discussing only one side of an issue, by mentioning cause without consequence or consequences without cause, acts without agents or agents without agency . . . [they] often successfully block definitions and cause and effect reasoning."[6]

Weaver believed that rhetoric contained an element of "madness," as Plato understood it, simply because it is always more than a mere sequence of words that make logical sense. "There is always in its statement a kind of excess or deficiency which is immediately discernible when the test of simple realism is applied." What he called a "simple realism" insisted on an exact correspondence where "one thing must match another." This was why the true rhetorician was always first cousin to the poet. Each refused to submit to a reductionist view of language that attended only to denotation. Both appealed to the imagination. Note here that while Weaver is not making *poet* and *rhetor* interchangeable, he is saying that they perform the same tasks, using similar methods. "If the poet, as the chief transformer of our picture of the world, is the peculiar enemy of this mentality, the rhetorician is also hostile. . . . The 'passion' in his speech is revolutionary, and it has a practical end."[7]

One of rhetoric's intrinsic problems with which Plato grappled at some length in the *Phaedrus* is how to distinguish true rhetoric from sophistry. He did not quarrel with the sophists on the point that rhetoric's chief end is persuasion: It aimed to move hearers to belief or action. Where he parted company with them was on their point that one did not need to know whether what one was trying to convince others of was essentially true or not. The sophists believed that "all that is necessary is ability to make one's conclusions seem probable." Plato disagreed, insisting that a successful rhetorician must know both the truth and his hearers in order to know what will seem probable to *them*.[8] Weaver adopted this dictum and held that rhetoric is an indivisible alloy of truth and its right presentation.

Although dialectic is a vital component of rhetoric, the two may be artificially separated in order to study each in its turn. Weaver understood dialectic to be "a method of investigation whose object is the establishment of truth about doubtful propositions" and quoted Aristotle with approval: "A dialectical problem is a subject of inquiry that contributes either to choice or avoidance, or to truth and knowledge, and that either by itself, or as a help to the solution of some other problem. It must, moreover, be something on which either people hold no opinion either way, or the masses hold a contrary opinion to the philosophers, or the philosophers to the masses, or each of them among themselves."[9]

Weaver noted that Plato differentiated the "positive" terms *iron* and *silver* from such dialectical terms as *justice* and *goodness*. Socrates told Phaedrus that a good dialectician has the gift of properly grouping things "by classes, where the natural joints are" and will not "break any part, after the manner of a bad carver." The kind of dialectic to which rhetoric is frequently joined, Weaver said, is one that presses its hearers to make a decision. Such rhetoric deals with "questions of policy, and the dialectic which precedes it will determine not the applications of positive terms but that of terms which are subject to the contingency of evaluation. Here dialectical inquiry will concern itself not with what is 'iron' but with what is 'good.' It seeks to establish what belongs in the category of the 'just' rather than what belongs in the genus *Canis*." Persuasion, then, will begin with "a dialectic establishing terms which have to do with policy." Proper education is thus concerned not with bringing people to conform to their environment but with affecting their innermost being in the direction of the true and the good. If the soul's impulse is moving in the right direction, then, "its definitions will agree with the true nature of intelligible things."[10]

Once dialectic has performed its office by properly defining terms, it can go no further. But what can the rhetorician do if his or her logical arguments fail to persuade? At this point rhetoric properly shifts from logic to analogy.

> To look for a moment through a practical illustration, let us suppose that a speaker has convinced his listeners that his position is "true" as far as dialectical inquiry may be pushed. Now he sets about moving the listeners toward that position, but there is no way to move them except through the operation of analogy. The analogy proceeds by showing that the position being urged resembles or partakes of something greater and finer. It will be represented, in sum, as one of the steps leading toward ultimate good. Let us further suppose our speaker to be arguing for the payment of a just debt. The payment of the just debt is not itself justice, but the payment of this particular debt is one of the many things which would have to be done before this could be a completely just world. . . . It is by bringing out these resemblances that the good rhetorician leads those who listen in the direction of what is good. In effect, he performs a cure of souls by giving impulse, chiefly through figuration, toward an ideal good.[11]

Weaver summarized the point by saying, "The true rhetorician [is] a noble lover of the good, who works through dialectic and through poetic or analogical association." Much of the *Phaedrus* is taken up with a dispute about love; the commonplace that love was something to be praised is countered by the notion that love was blameworthy. Socrates concluded that love, properly defined, is a laudable thing. Weaver believed that it was at this juncture that Socrates exemplified a true rhetorician. He extolled the beauty of love by making it analogous to a fine charioteer. "In the narrower conception of this art, the allegory is the rhetoric, for it excites and fills us with desire for this kind of love. . . . But in the broader conception the art must include also the dialectic, which succeeded in placing love in the category of divine things before filling our imaginations with attributes of divinity." In other words, love, when properly defined by dialectic, naturally becomes an object of praise that the true rhetorician rightly extols. Here Weaver notes with approval that "it is so regularly the method of Plato to follow a subtle analysis with a striking myth that it is not unreasonable to call him the master rhetorician."[12]

Some would argue that rhetoric is not a useful tool that a lover of truth can use since it necessarily involves exaggeration. Weaver granted that there was a kind of exaggeration that was "mere wantonness" but that is not the currency of the true rhetorician, any more than caricature is the method of a true portrait painter.

While conceding that exaggeration was a component of proper rhetoric, Weaver insisted that it must properly be prophecy rather than caricature since true rhetoric necessarily considered potential as well as present reality. It was necessary, he believed, to see that which may or could be as already having a kind of existence. Here he pointed to prophecy as a venerable example of the point; it dealt with "the tendency of things." The noble rhetorician was always careful to focus on "real potentiality or possible actuality, whereas that of the mere exaggerator is about unreal potentiality." Weaver's basic presupposition is crucial to his argument; namely, that the noble rhetorician is possessed of discernment as well as a desire to set before his listeners a future that they perhaps would not otherwise consider. He illustrated by quoting from Winston Churchill's speech delivered during some of the darkest days of World War II when the British prime minister spoke of the "broad, sunny uplands" of postwar Europe. The exaggeration in this instance focused on what Germany's defeat would mean for the future of the continent. There was little reason for Churchill's bright vision if one looked only at the reality of the bombed-out city of London, Hitler's military triumphs in Europe, and America's reluctance to enter the war. "Yet the hope which transfigured this to 'broad sunlit uplands' was not irresponsible, and we conclude by saying that the rhetorician talks about both what exists simply and what exists by favor of human imagination and effort."

Elaborating further on the distinction between dialectic and rhetoric, Weaver noted that rhetoric, "With its forecast of the actual possibility . . . passes from mere scientific demonstration of an idea to its relation to prudential conduct." Rhetoric's "passion for the actual is more complete than mere dialectic with its dry understanding." It sees man not as a bloodless abstraction but as "a creature of passion who must live out that passion in the world. . . . Thus the complete man is the 'lover' added to the scientist; the rhetorician to the dialectician."[13]

The dialectician, pure and simple, is faced with another problem: motive. Weaver quoted with approval Kenneth Burke, who

heaped scorn on the notion that language ought to be purged from
any call to action since people naturally will be more inclined to take
the right course if left on their own initiative. He agreed with Burke
that such a "don't preach; just present the facts" approach ignored
the reality that language is sermonic by its very nature. "Insofar as
such a project succeeded," Burke wrote, "its terms would involve
a narrowing of circumference to a point where the principle of
personal action is eliminated from language, so that an act would
follow from it only as a non-sequitur, a kind of humanitarian after-
thought." The problem can be illustrated, Weaver said, by scruti-
nizing the work of government-appointed fact-finding committees.
The ideal language for such a group's report would be one in which
every word had only its denoted meaning and in which connotation
was utterly absent. But even if such a mode of expression was available, it would need an "attitude finding committee" to explain what
its findings really meant. Fact-finding committees knew they were,
in reality, attitude-finding committees. Their written reports belied
that they had been on a quest for mere facts by their statements
of purpose and conclusion and by how they *arranged* facts. "The
soul is impulse, not simply cognition," he concluded. Logic in and
of itself could only go so far in moving anyone to action.

> Rhetoric moves the soul with a movement which cannot finally be
> justified logically. It can only be valued analogically with reference
> to some supreme image. Therefore when the rhetorician encounters
> some soul 'sinking beneath the double load of forgetfulness and vice'
> he seeks to re-animate it by holding up to its sight the order of
> presumptive goods. This order is necessarily a hierarchy leading up
> to the ultimate good. All the terms in a rhetorical vocabulary are like
> links in a chain stretching up to some master link which transmits
> its influence down through the linkages. It is impossible to talk about
> rhetoric as effective expression without having a term giving intelligi-
> bility to the whole discourse, the Good. Of course, inferior concepts of
> the Good may be and often are placed in this ultimate position. . . . Yet
> the fact remains that in any piece of historical discourse, one rhetorical
> term overcomes another rhetorical term only by being nearer to the
> term which stands ultimate.[14]

Tragedy's endurance and appeal as a literary form illustrated his
point, Weaver insisted, with its stress on timeless truths about

human nature and behavior rather than mere history. Like rhetoric, it manifested an overriding concern with values.

He believed that while the intense struggle in every society over who shall control the flow of information may discourage some from learning the truth about anything and make them cynical about any "official" line, such a response was ill-informed. It simply is a given that people will try by means of language to influence each other. To assume otherwise is fallacious. It is at this point that true rhetoric provides its great service in clarifying; its "duty is to bring together *action* and *understanding* into *a whole that is greater than scientific perception"* [emphasis mine].[15]

Rhetoric rightly understood is, Weaver believed, "something very much like Spinoza's 'intellectual love of God.' This is its essence and the *fons et origo* of its power. It is 'intellectual' be- cause . . . there is no honest rhetoric without a preceding dialectic. The kind of rhetoric which is justly condemned is utterance in support of a position before that position has been adjudicated with reference to the whole universe of discourse." Love as Weaver used the word here means not only adhering to a theoretical truth intellectually but also longing to see its potential realized. He was particularly cautious in how he approached the phrase *of God,* realizing that in an increasingly secular age some would find it offensive, and satisfied himself with asserting that the real point was to "have in ultimate place the highest good man can intuit. . . . We shall be content with 'intellectual love of the Good.' It is still the intellectual love of the good which causes the noble lover to desire not to devour his beloved but to shape him according to the gods as far as mortal power allows." Concluding his lengthy look at the *Phaedrus,* Weaver wrote, "Rhetoric at its truest seeks to perfect men by showing them better versions of themselves, links in that chain extending up toward the ideal, which only the intellect can apprehend and only the soul have affection for. This is the justified affection of which no one can be ashamed, and he who feels no influence of it is truly outside the communion of minds. Rhetoric appears, finally, as a means by which the impulse of the soul to be ever moving is redeemed." It would not be difficult to conclude that in spite of his self-conscious distancing from religion, Weaver offered a view of human nature remarkably like that of Paul and

Augustine. It is fallen and restless. Or, as Augustine put it in one of his best-known statements in the *Confessions,* "You have made us for Yourself, and our hearts are restless until they rest in You."[16]

While conceding that he had drawn out of the *Phaedrus* more than Plato intended, Weaver nonetheless believed those with eyes to see would recognize that, though it appeared to begin as a straightforward discussion of love, this work ended up as an allegorical treatment of all human spoken communication.

Muddled thinking will always result, Weaver held, when dialectic and rhetoric are not properly understood and sharply distinguished. Many who carefully craft their arguments are surprised when they win no converts, just as some who deliver eloquent speeches may have their appeals dismissed out of hand. A superb illustration of this problem, Weaver held, was the Scopes trial held in Dayton, Tennessee, in 1925, when a high-school biology teacher was prosecuted by the state of Tennessee for teaching the theory of evolution in violation of state law. Taking a chapter in this book to explore the matter, he agreed that while the whole episode "had many aspects of the farcical . . . it was considered serious enough to draw the most celebrated trial lawyers in the country, as well as some of the most eminent scientists; moreover, after one has cut through the sensationalism with which journalism and a few of the principals clothed the encounter, one finds a unique alignment of dialectical and rhetorical positions."

The defense, led by Clarence Darrow and championing science, played the rhetorician; the prosecution for the state of Tennessee, led by William Jennings Bryan, consistently argued from a dialectical perspective. The former repeatedly insisted that evolution was true, while the latter simply stated that teaching it in any Tennessee public school had been forbidden by the state legislature. "These two arguments depend on rhetoric and dialectic respectively. Because of this circumstance, the famous trial turned into an argument about the order of knowledge, although this act was never clearly expressed, if it was ever discerned, by either side."[17]

Following Adler, Weaver noted that there were different orders of knowledge. The most basic was factual information—ordinary scientific data. The interpretations of those facts made up the next order as exemplified by scientific theories. Finally, there were explanations about the meaning of scientific propositions and theories. The Tennessee law that Scopes violated fell into this third category.[18] "It was neither a collection of scientific facts, nor a statement about those facts (i.e., a theory or a generalization); it was a statement about a statement . . . purporting to be based on those facts. It was, to use Adler's phrase, a philosophical opinion, though expressed in the language of law." The question became whether one could put together a case of facts and generalizations based on those facts "sufficient to overcome a dialectical position." Darrow and his team "throughout the trial . . . tended to take the view that science could carry the day just by being scientific. But in doing this, one assumes that there are no points outside the empirical realm from which one can form judgments about science. Science, by this conception, must contain not only its facts, but also the means of its own evaluation, so that the statements about the statements of science are science too."

> The eyes of the nation focused on this remarkable case as the two sides lined up as dialectical truth and empirical fact. The state legislature of Tennessee acting in its sovereign capacity, had passed a measure which made it unlawful to teach that man is connatural with the animals through asserting that he is descended from a "lower order" of them. (There was some sparring over the technical language of the act, but this was the general consensus.) The legal question was whether John T. Scopes had violated the measure. The philosophical question, which was the real focus of interest, was the right of a state to make this prescription.[19]

What was the nature of the state's case? Weaver averred that the truth or falsehood of the theory of evolution had no significant part in it so long as the prosecution adhered to its dialectical position. Both parties conceded the state's sovereignty over its public schools. Legislation had been passed that prohibited the teaching of the Bible in its public schools. It naturally followed that the same legislature could forbid its schools from teaching the theory of evolution.

Clarence Darrow, who gained additional notoriety for defending Scopes, had, as Weaver pointed out, previously used the same kind of argument that his protagonist Bryan took up at Dayton.

A year earlier, Darrow had taken on the famous Leopold and Loeb case in which two young college men who had committed murder were convinced that their intellectual prowess would prevent their perfect crime from being solved. Darrow had pointed the finger of blame at society rather than at the defendants. The central argument he made in their defense was that these two young men could not be held responsible for the murder they committed, because they had been forcibly exposed to ideas that negatively influenced their behavior. Since Nietzsche had been required reading in their college philosophy classes, Darrow insisted that Leopold and Loeb were not culpable; they had only turned the philosopher's ideas into actions. The guilty party was society for permitting such materials to be taught in its educational institutions.

Darrow had not asked the jury at Leopold and Loeb's trial, Weaver observed, to render a verdict on the validity of Nietzsche's philosophy.

> He was asking precisely what Bryan was asking of the jury at Dayton, namely that they take a strictly dialectical position outside it, viewing it as a partial universe of discourse with consequences which could be adjudged good or bad. The point to be especially noted is that Darrow did not raise the question of whether the philosophy of Nietzsche expresses necessary truth, or whether, let us say, it is essential to an understanding of the world. He was satisfied to point out that the state had not been a sufficiently vigilant guardian of the forces molding the character of its youth.

Darrow's position that reading Nietzsche had had a bad influence on these youths' impressionable minds may be compared with Bryan's holding that teaching the theory of evolution in the public schools of Tennessee would have an immoral influence on the students.

The defense at Dayton thus found itself, willy-nilly, having to resort to a rhetorical rather than a scientific argument, since "rhetoric deals with subjects at the point where they touch upon actuality or prudential conduct. Here the defense looks at the policy of teaching evolution and points to beneficial results. The argument then becomes: these important benefits imply an important beneficial cause."[20]

Summing up what had happened at Dayton, Weaver conceded that most people who took an interest in the Scopes trial probably concluded that the state of Tennessee had taken an

> absurd [position] because they are unable to see how a logical position can be taken without reference to empirical situations. . . . We see the nature of this distinction when we realize that there is never an argument, in the true sense of the term, about facts. When facts are disputed, the argument must be suspended until the facts are settled. Not until then may it be resumed, for all true argument is about the meaning of established or admitted facts. And since this meaning is always expressed in propositions, we can say further that all argument is about the systematic import of propositions.

Those who felt that science was somehow on trial in Dayton and that its cause was vindicated by the resulting publicity did not understand that science does not contain within itself the means by which it must ultimately be evaluated. They, no doubt, were encouraged by "the embarrassment to which Darrow brought Bryan in questioning him about the Bible and the theory of evolution (during which Darrow did lead Bryan into some dialectical traps). But in strict consideration all this was outside the bounds of the case because both the facts of evolution and the facts of the Bible were 'items not in discourse,' to borrow a phrase employed by Professor Adler."[21]

After developing a definition of noble rhetoric from Plato's *Phaedrus* in the initial chapter of *The Ethics of Rhetoric* and contrasting Darrow's argument for the defense with Bryan's for the prosecution in Dayton as archetypal examples of dialectical and rhetorical discourse, Weaver moved on to treat two types of argumentation: the argument from circumstance and the argument from definition. He illustrated the former from the writings and speeches of Edmund Burke and the latter from the works of Abraham Lincoln. Weaver believed that a proper understanding of any line of reasoning must begin with a scrutiny of its sources. Those setting forth systematic arguments will have almost certainly made use of more than one rationale, but a closer look often reveals that one will be favored over all the others. This source will tell us much, he held, about the author's essential presuppositions. At the time he was writing this book, the early 1950s, Weaver had been on the English faculty at the University of Chicago for some eight years and was well aware that Burke was being lauded as both a fountain of conservative wisdom and a founding father of their cause, while Lincoln was seen as having paved the way for excessively centralized government.[22]

Weaver began with a look at classical antecedents: *Genus, similitude,* and *circumstance* were the three sources of rhetorical argument that classical writers recognized. The first form of argument could be understood by alluding to the word *generic.* To begin with the nature of something and then make applications from it was to use this kind of rhetorical argument. In other words, one arguing from *genus* will base his or her argument on the *intrinsic* nature of the case. Lincoln's "refusal to hedge on the principle of slavery is referable to a fixed concept of the nature of man . . . [as] an argument from *genus.*"[23]

Those who argued from *similitude* were wont to use analogy and to look for correspondences. A belief in some sort of ultimate vision that gave coherence and meaning to everything is characteristic of those who use this style. Weaver chose poets and theologians such as Emerson and Bunyan as examples of those whose works betrayed a fondness for similitude.

The argument from *circumstance* differed from that of *genus* and *similitude* in several ways. It merely takes into account the immediate environment as pivotal in reaching conclusions and making decisions. The expedient course of action is always the one recommended; cause and effect are either ignored or subordinated to the pressures of the moment. This was the least reflective argument of all. Weaver wondered why Edmund Burke had become a kind of icon to political conservatives in America, since a close scrutiny of Burke's writings revealed his undeniable preference for the argument from circumstance. This favorite argument of the liberals, he noted, was critically at odds with conservatism. Even in Burke's railings against the French Revolution and his praise of tradition, he was, Weaver emphasized, anything but a conservative, since one's "method of argument is a truer index to his beliefs than his explicit profession of principles."

Given that persuasion was central to politics and that rhetoric perforce played a critical role, Weaver warned about the danger of the argument from circumstance, because its very potency was based on myopia. This sort of rhetoric casts its partisans into the role of those whose sole "policy [is one] of opposing an incumbent"—ultimately no policy at all. This led to an intellectually dishonest know-nothing conservatism.[24]

A much better rhetorical model for American conservatives, Weaver believed, was Abraham Lincoln. Lincoln's well-known biographer Albert Beveridge noted that the attorney Lincoln rarely argued from precedent in circuit court trials; he preferred to base his cases on "first principles." Two other biographers scrutinized speeches he made to republican gatherings in the year of that party's founding and concluded that while "these fragments of addresses give us only an imperfect reflection of the style of Mr. Lincoln's oratory during this period, they nevertheless show its essential characteristics, a pervading clearness of analysis, and that strong tendency toward axiomatic definition which gives so many of his sentences their convincing force and durable value." Speaking from personal knowledge as Lincoln's law partner, W. H. Herndon remembered: "Not only were nature, man, and principle suggestive to Mr. Lincoln; not only had he accurate and exact perceptions, but he was causative; his mind apparently with an automatic movement, ran back behind facts, principles, and all things to their origin and first cause—to the point where forces act at once as effect and cause. . . . All opponents [lawyers] dreaded his originality, his condensation, definition, and force of expression." Weaver believed that was why Lincoln towered above Washington, Jefferson, and Wilson. "Our feeling that he is a father of the nation even more convincingly than Washington, and that his words of wisdom when compared with those of the more intellectual Jefferson and the more academic Wilson strengthen the supposition that he argued from some very fundamental source."[25]

That "very fundamental source" of Lincoln's persuasive prowess was, Weaver believed, his adherence to a rhetoric based on the argument from definition. This presuppositional sort of thinking insisted "that there exist classes which are determined and therefore predictable. Whatever is a member of that class will accordingly have . . . [its] attributes." Fully cognizant of the hackles that statement would raise among those who do not hold to universal givens, Weaver simply observed that most people generally are divided into

"Those who seem to feel that genera are imprisoning bonds which serve only" to fetter the mind and others who see "such genera . . . [as] the very organon of truth. . . . It seems safe to assert that those who believe in the validity of the argument from genus are idealists, roughly, if not very philosophically defined." Lincoln fell into this camp as his writing and speeches spanning his entire career made clear. He believed that certain givens about man do not change, and, thus, human nature is to a considerable degree predictable.[26]

In the great debate over the national bank, for example, Lincoln opposed the idea of depositing national revenue in district subtreasuries until needed, because it would create a conflict of interest. "And who knows anything of human nature doubts that in many instances interest will prevail over duty, and that the subtreasurer will prefer opulent knavery in a foreign land to honest poverty at home." A national bank run by a board of directors would be able to use the monies until needed but would be required to pay interest on deposited funds at the prevailing rate, thus making responsibility and self-interest coincide. The hardships undergone by this president during the course of his child and adult years contributed much to his discernment, Weaver believed. "Lincoln's theory of human nature was completely unsentimental; it was the creation of one who had taken many buffetings and who, from early bitterness and later indifference, never affiliated with any religious denomination. But it furnished the means of wisdom and prophecy."[27]

Weaver believed this way of thinking fitted Lincoln peculiarly well for the challenge he would face on the slavery issue. Peel away the extraneous matters and one found, Weaver insisted, a fundamental inquiry about human nature. Douglas and Calhoun fixed their attention on law and politics as slavery touched on these matters. "Lincoln looked—as it was his habit already to do—to the center; that is, to the definition of man. Was the negro a man or was he not? It can be shown that his answer to this question never varied. . . . The answer was a clear 'yes,' and he used it on many occasions during the fifties to impale his opponents." Slaveholding states might tinker with their law codes and take pride in the legal protection afforded the bondsmen, but the slaves were *still property*—the Supreme Court had said so in the Dred Scott decision.

Lincoln cut through these legal niceties, dealing them damaging blows by pointing out that the black man "was very much a man when it came to such matters as understanding orders, performing work, and, as the presence of the mulatto testified, helping to procreate the human species. All of the arguments that the pro-slavery group was able to muster broke against the stubborn fact, which Lincoln persistently thrust in their way, that the negro was somehow and in some degree a man." Because Lincoln argued primarily from fixed principles, he displayed a quality of leadership that sets him apart, Weaver held, from *all other* American leaders.

> To define is to assume perspective; that is the method of definition. Since nothing can be defined until it is placed in a category and distinguished from its near relatives, it is obvious that definition involves the taking of a general view. Definition must see the thing in relation to other things, as that relation is expressible through substance, magnitude, kind, cause, effect, and other peculiarities. It is merely different expression to say that this is a view which transcends: perspective, detachment, and capacity to transcend are all requisites of him who would define, and we know that Lincoln evidenced these qualities quite early in life, and that he employed them with consummate success when the future of the nation depended on his judgment.[28]

The fact that claims to Lincoln have been staked from those all over the political spectrum, Weaver insisted, was the result of a one-dimensional or, at best, a partial approach to his rhetoric based solely on his stands on particular measures such as the tariff. "It seems right to assume that a much surer index to man's political philosophy is his characteristic way of thinking, inevitably expressed in the type of argument he prefers. In reality, the type of argument a man chooses gives us the profoundest look we get at his principle of integration." Here we get not only Weaver's view of "noble" rhetoric but his definition of conservatism as well. "Those who prefer the argument from definition, as Lincoln did, are conservatives in the legitimate sense of the word. . . . The true conservative is one who sees the universe as a paradigm of essences, of which the phenomenology of the world is a sort of continuing approximation. Or, to put this in another way, he sees it as a set of definitions which are struggling to get themselves defined in the real world." Lincoln's analysis of the Declaration of Independence was, among other things, a superb definition of conservatism as Weaver understood it.

> They [the writers of the Declaration] meant to set up a standard maxim for a free society, which should be familiar to all, and revered by all; constantly looked to, constantly labored for, and even though never perfectly attained, constantly approximated, and thereby constantly spreading and deepening its influence and augmenting the happiness and value of life to all people of all colors everywhere. The assertion that "all men are created equal" was of no practical use in effecting our separation from Great Britain; and it was placed in the Declaration, not for that, but for future use. Its authors meant it to be, thank God, it is now proving itself, a stumbling block to those who in after times might seek to turn a free people back into the hateful paths of despotism.[29]

The standard was set in Philadelphia in 1776. That the nation had often come up short when measured against this standard did not detract from its validity but served as a timeless spur to goad America on to greater efforts to realize the declaration's promises and meet its high standards.

Weaver was convinced that Lincoln's using the declaration as his point of departure guarded against either reckless action or apathy. This sort of conservative was often a reformer. But, like Lincoln, such reformers' tactics were guided by law—not future precedent or shifting societal norms, but law as the essence of unchanging justice. Weaver never wavered from this understanding of conservatism. In 1960 he noted that he had been labeled a conservative but made clear his hostility to that kind of conservatism that was nothing more than a knee-jerk preference for the status quo and that was loath to embrace change out of a nervous and fearful apprehension about what it might bring in its wake.

> It is my contention that a conservative is a realist, who believes that there is a structure of reality independent of his own will and desire. He believes that there is a creation which was here before him, which exists now not by just his sufferance, and which will be here after he's gone. This structure consists not merely of the great physical world but also of many laws, principles, and regulations which control human behavior. Though this reality is independent of the individual,

it is not hostile to him. It is in fact amenable by him in many ways, but it cannot be changed radically and arbitrarily. This is the cardinal point. The conservative holds that man in this world cannot make his will his law without any regard to limits and to the fixed nature of things. . . . The conservative I therefore see as standing on the *terra firma* of antecedent reality; having accepted some things as given, lasting, and good, he is in a position to use his effort where effort will produce solid results.[30]

Political parties understood and defined themselves to a great extent, Weaver wrote, in the public utterances of their leaders; that is why their appeal to principles may be costly in the short term but often yield success in time. Focusing only on pragmatic results made them, whether they wanted to or not, play a simple power game with their opponents. If they stressed only present circumstances, long-range perspective was lost. Thus, it was critically important that party leaders, like Lincoln, had the fortitude to define. Those who demonstrated that kind of courage were properly using noble rhetoric.

Moving from a scrutiny of Lincoln's argument from defini-tion, Weaver devoted a further chapter in *The Ethics of Rhetoric* to an analysis of the oratory and writings typical of the time during which the sixteenth president lived. Remarking that the nineteenth-century style created discomfort in the modern era, he wondered whether such unease perhaps may be attributed to that earlier generation's fondness for generalization. Admiring what he called the "spaciousness" of the older rhetoric, he observed, "Instead of the single note (prized for purposes of analysis), the[re] are widths of sound and meaning" that served two vital roles: They were dramatic pauses and connecting links "between what is said and the thing being signified." Weaver wondered how could the practitioners of such a rhetoric get by with it then and not now. Perhaps it was because they wrote and spoke from a more or less common set of assumptions or at least a great common ground shared with the audience. This spacious rhetoric of the nineteenth century was not designed to provoke new ways of thinking in most cases but served instead to articulate and reinforce already-held convictions.[31]

This spacious, older rhetoric rested on the importance of the *enthymeme,* an argument or syllogism in which one of its three propositions is not stated because the missing element is expected to be supplied by the audience. Put another way, it is a rhetorical argument that is compelling because it is based on values commonly shared between speaker and hearers. The latter *assume* the unstated premises and often supply the conclusion as well. Thus the hearers are in instinctive accord with the rhetor. The spaciousness of the older rhetoric rested, then, on the audience's holding certain fundamental assumptions shared with the speaker or writer. But it also had an important aesthetic dimension: that of maintaining a proper distance from the subject. The right perspective ruled out both excessive familiarity and too much distance. A rhetorically intense focus on the particular would be analogous to an artist's portrait of "the wart on Cromwell's face—because the *singular* is the *impertinent*" [emphasis mine]. Proper distance is necessary to proper perspective—for the artist and the rhetorician.[32]

Weaver's analysis of Lincoln anticipates similar points made by Garry Wills in his book *Inventing America.* Wills discusses at some length Lincoln's repeated insistence that the Declaration of Independence was America's true founding document. The enthymeme, or unstated proposition, of the Gettysburg Address's preamble was that the nation's true beginning occurred in 1776, not in 1789. The sixteenth president did not intend that his audience immediately validate his arithmetic; rather, he wanted his listeners to agree with "the recontracting of our society on the basis of the Declaration as our fundamental charter" instead of the Articles of Confederation or the Constitution since they were "messier enterprises, with the stamp of compromise upon them."[33] He was not being disingenuous or cynical but was appealing to the common Protestant assumptions of nineteenth-century Americans who had imbibed the King James Bible with their mother's milk.

Weaver's admiration of Lincoln was rooted, then, in the great emancipator's spacious rhetoric, which was typical of nineteenth-century oratory and in his consistent use of the argument from definition. There was probably another source as well: the Civil War president's religiousness, which was not creedal in any orthodox sense since he was not a practicing member of any particular church. Yet he could hardly be described as a secular man.[34] Such was exactly the case with Richard Weaver.

In a final observation on the older rhetoric's spaciousness, Weaver took note of another of its facets, a polite style that accorded with the rhetorician's assumption that his audience was made up of some who would readily understand his message and of others who decidedly would not. He found an apt analogy in nutrition.

> It is known that diet must contain a certain amount of roughage. This roughage is not food in the sense of nutriment; its function is to dilute or distend the real food in such a way that it can be most readily assimilated. A concentrate of food is, therefore, not enough, for there has to be a certain amount of inert manner to furnish bulk. Something of a very similar nature operates in discourse. When a piece of oratory intended for a public occasion impresses us as distended, which is to say, filled up with repetition, periphrasis, long grammatical forms, and other impediments to directness, we should recall that the diffuseness all this produces may have a purpose.[35]

Weaver took the rhetorical measure of the twentieth century in the final chapter of *The Ethics of Rhetoric,* which focused on what he called this age's *ultimate terms.* These were words or names with great inherent potency. Such linguistic devices, standing alone, invited their hearers to invest them with association and meaning.

In casting about for what he called the most important "god term" of the twentieth century, Weaver takes up the word *progress.* Whatever can be successfully labeled as progressive thereby becomes virtually unassailable. How did this come to be? He began his explanation by pointing out that mankind in all ages and places has insisted on having fixed reference points. Metaphysics, religion, and history each has served its turn. But since the sixteenth century there has developed the notion that man's increasing dominion over nature was an unmixed blessing. The Industrial Revolution accelerated the process and encouraged a mind-set that by the mid-twentieth century saw all development as inevitable and good in spite of the fact that doubts were expressed by a few. Still, it may well be that an appeal to progress was the one thing by which a majority of Westerners today could be convinced to make a personal sacrifice. "This capacity to demand sacrifice is probably the surest indicator of the 'god term,' for when a term is so sacrosanct that the material goods of this life must be mysteriously rendered up for it, then we feel justified in saying that it is in some sense ultimate."[36]

Fact had taken a place not far below *progress* as another god term of our day. To take note of the "facts of the case" in any speaking or writing was one of those declarative utterances designed to settle a matter once and for all. This attitude had its genesis, Weaver was convinced, during the Renaissance and was due to a shift in understanding how one arrives at the truth.

> Prior to that time, the type of conclusion that men felt obligated to accept came either through divine revelation, or through dialectic, which obeys logical law. But these were displaced by a system of verification through correspondence with physical reality. Since then things have been true only when *measurably true* [emphasis mine], or when susceptible to some kind of qualification. Quite simply, "fact" came to be the touchstone after the truth of speculative inquiry had been replaced by the truth of empirical investigation. Today when the average citizen says that he "knows the facts of the case," he means that he has the kind of knowledge to which all other knowledge must defer. Possibly it should be pointed out that his "facts" are frequently not facts at all in the etymological sense; often they will be deductions several steps removed from simply factual data. Yet the "facts" of his case carry with them this aura of scientific irrefragability, and he will likely regard any questioning of them as sophistry. In his vocabulary a fact is a fact, and all evidence so denominated has the prestige of science.[37]

Science also had its place in Weaver's lexicon of god terms, its rhetorical strength lying in its general acceptance as the means by which progress takes place. An associated problem with the widespread and popular use of this word was that it was frequently invoked without any referent. Examples were numerous: Any declaration that began with "science says" carried all the authority of pontifical pronouncements in the medieval church. Science, rightly understood, Weaver protested, was never a monolithic entity that spoke in unmistakable accents. The devotees of this god term would seem to envision "that scientists meet periodically in synod and there decide and publish what science believes." Weaver warned that railing against such credulity would be a mistake because it would overlook an important truth. All people have a "primal

need for a touchstone . . . [and] . . . a direction-finder." A very basic problem arose when one recognized that science was simply
another word for knowledge and that we are logically forced to say
"Knowledge knows." Here is "reflect[ed] the deeply human feeling
that somewhere somehow there must be people who know things
'as they are.' Once God or his ministry was the depository of such
knowledge, but now, with the general decay of religious faith, it is
the scientists who must speak *ex cathedra,* whether they wish to
or not."38

The mirror image of god terms, said Weaver, were *devil terms.*
Scanning American history, he pointed to the obvious: *Tory* was
the ultimate term of repulsion among the patriots during the
Revolutionary War. *Rebel* and *Yankee* served in their turn during
the Civil War. *Nazi* and *Fascist* replaced almost all others during the
Second World War. *Un-American* fit the bill during the late forties
and early fifties but was pushed aside by *Communist.* A particular
problem in trying to understand the dynamic of devil terms, Weaver
wrote, was that they were impervious to analysis. "One cannot
explain how they generate their peculiar force of repudiation. One
only recognizes them as publicly-agreed upon devil terms." *Nazi,
Fascist,* and *Communist* were, for many, terms of opprobrium that
needed no explanation. Devil terms perhaps could be understood,
Weaver thought, only as a subset of *charismatic terms,* to which he
turned next in his discussion.39

Unlike the god terms that had readily comprehensible referents,
the charismatic terms were free-floating. They had a powerful
dynamic that inhered in the words standing alone. Each one was a
potent noun in an adjectiveless void, or mirror image of C. S. Lewis's
"potent adjective in a nounless void." They appeared to draw their
strength from "a popular will that they shall mean something."
Weaver saw freedom and democracy as falling into this category
and feared that at some point enemies of both freedom and democracy would seek to appropriate both words by cleverly emptying
them of significance or redefining them in some Orwellian sense.40

The ethical use of rhetoric, Weaver said in his concluding chapter, rendered it imperative that these "ultimate terms" be used
in some logical fashion. And that meant that individuals who
used rhetoric must be self-disciplined. Without using theological

or philosophical terms, Weaver yet again made quite clear his belief that man was in some sense a fallen creature. "Every one of psychological sophistication knows that there is a pleasure in willed perversity and the setting up of perverse shibboleths is a fairly common source of that pleasure. War cries, school slogans, coterie passwords, and all similar expressions are examples of such creation." Aware that some would accuse him of special pleading, he conceded: "There may be areas of play in which these are nothing more than a diversion; but there are other areas in which such expressions lure us down the roads of hatred and tragedy . . . [by persuading us] . . . to do what the adversary of the human being wants us to do. It is worth considering whether the real civil disobedience must not begin with our language."

Weaver was no doubt being autobiographical when he pointed out that despair can readily result from recognizing that since all language is freighted with meaning, it will move people to action—good or bad. The twentieth century witnessed the control and management of information on a scale never before seen. Widespread propaganda efforts by all the conflicting parties during the two world wars and thereafter provided a vivid example. Government was but one instance. The private sector did the same thing through national and international networks of correspondents able to report to communication centers more or less instantaneously. That state of affairs, Weaver insisted, was all the more reason such a temptation to despair must be overcome. The practitioner of noble rhetoric had an obligation to resist modern sophists who treated words as mere counters, bowdlerizing language without a qualm. The original meaning of barbarian meant not a savage but someone far more dangerous—one who did not understand; thus, his task was all the more urgent.

What, exactly, could one person do? Or, what is more to the point, what *ought* he do? He could fight the good fight in one of the most unglamorous and demanding but critically important arenas—the freshman English composition class. Devoting himself to that task with a will, Weaver never seemed to mind that he was doing what most of the English faculty saw as time in purgatory where all newcomers were expected to serve until blessed seniority enabled them to leave the odious job and the memory of it behind them forever. Such skills courses periodically came under fire during his years at the University of Chicago by both administrators and faculty who wanted to combine the course in composition with some "content" class such as history or literature. Whenever that happened, Weaver responded with a "defense [that] was always vigorous and trenchant. To the charge that composition is merely a skills course and therefore deserves no independent status in the curriculum, he replied that the course has a content, that its content is rhetoric, and that rhetoric is the key to a liberal education."[41]

The Ethics of Rhetoric followed a natural progression in Weaver's intellectual development. It provided a definition of rhetoric, using historical antecedents to explain how one can distinguish noble rhetoric from mere sophistry. It also set forth his understanding of an authentic conservatism as one rooted in the eternal verities of Platonic idealism and Augustinian theology. Spinoza wrote about the intellectual love of God. Weaver insisted that the noble rhetor is dedicated to the intellectual love of the Good. The rest of his life and career is a study in a ceaseless battle to meet and hold up these very high standards in his speaking, writing, and teaching.

Richard M. Weaver passionately held to the belief that a society's health or declension was mirrored in how it used language. Language must be kept pure, he insisted. Communication was difficult enough to begin with. Words were the medium of exchange of human discourse, and if people lost faith in them as expressing commonly accepted ideas and feelings, conflict of some sort was inevitable. He feared the pernicious and pervasive notion that words were relative to time, place, and speaker and were devoid of inherent content. He believed the inevitable result would be that truth and meaning themselves would be drowned in a sea of relativism. The *Ethics of Rhetoric* was a Weaverian manifesto declaring that words had vital referents, and that meaning might be saved *only* if they were used properly.

8 | The Years in Exile
CHICAGO, 1944–1963

IT IS A FACT THAT THE AGRARIANS ISOLATED THEMSELVES BY BECOMING MORE INTELLECTUAL, MORE PERCEPTIVE MEN, BUT THEY LEFT A LEGACY OF THOUGHT. THEY LEFT A DOCTRINE WHICH IN SOME FORM WILL HAVE TO BE ASSIMILATED BEFORE WE STAND THE SLIGHTEST CHANCE OF SEEING THE REINTEGRATION OF MAN. BUT THERE WERE PERHAPS SPECIAL REASONS WHY THEY COULD NOT BE PROPHETS IN THEIR OWN COUNTRY. . . . THE PROPOSAL OF THE AGRARIANS NEVER TOOK INTO ACCOUNT A PROFOUND PSYCHOLOGICAL FACT [THAT] OF ALL THE LINGERING EVILS THE SOUTH SUFFERED AS A RESULT OF MILITARY DEFEAT, NONE WAS GRAVER THAN THE ALMOST TOTAL EXTINCTION OF INITIATIVE. . . . THE SOUTH SLIPPED INTO THE HABIT OF FOLLOWING THE NATIONAL TREND IN EVERYTHING BUT A FEW LOCAL CUSTOMS AND PREROGATIVES. . . . *THE TRUTH ABOUT THE AGRARIANS IS THAT THEY WERE BECOMING HOMELESS. THE SOUTH NO LONGER HAD A PLACE FOR THEM, AND FLIGHT TO THE NORTH BUT COMPLETED AN ALIENATION LONG IN PROGRESS.*[1] [EMPHASIS MINE]

That statement by Weaver, which appeared in his essay "Agrarianism in Exile" in 1950, was more than just an important insight into that movement; it also described his own odyssey. This becomes all the more clear in the light of his speech to his family's annual meeting the same year, held as always in Weaverville, North Carolina.

Having taught English at the University of Chicago for six years, he invited his kin to look with him at family, home, and community through the prism of Chicago. "That most brutal of cities," he lamented, was "a place where all the vices of urban and industrial society break forth in a kind of evil flower." Seeing himself exiled from what he held most dear, he spoke in unmistakable terms about his charge. "I sometimes think of the University to which I am attached as a missionary outpost in darkest Chicago. There we labor as we can to convert the heathen, without much reward of success. But of course we learn many things about what is happening in this country." Distance gives perspective and insight that propinquity often renders difficult, if not impossible. But his exile was more than just a withdrawal from the South: It was an hegira. "In the battle against anti-humanist forces," he wrote, "one does not desert by changing his locale for the plain reason that the battle is world wide. . . . Thus what has been represented as the flight of the Agrarians may appear on closer examination to be a strategic withdrawal to positions where the contest can be better carried on." Like most of the Agrarians, he had left his beloved and true home in order to better serve a cause. Weaver was, like them, part of a "community of enlightened but truculent alienation [that] constituted an independent polity of mind, a Republic of Letters."[2] If he could return to it someday, so much the better. But what really mattered was that was at his post doing his duty.

Weaver deplored the lack of community as he and his audience of kinfolk knew it. They grew up assuming that family and geography are indispensable components of self-identity. No doubt he had in mind the traditional way the rural South labeled farms: "the Boyd Place," "the Barlow Place," "the Prince Place." The use of the word *place* emphasized an inseparable link between family and geography. Flannery O'Connor, who has written perceptively about the South, once reacted to certain New York literary critics with the retort: "You know what's the matter with all that kind of folks? They ain't *frum* anywhere!" Weaver stressed to his hearers that *place* did not translate into *community* in the Midwest's famous capital. Chicago had "a politically defined area, . . . local laws and institutions, but that which makes true community, namely association on some non-material level and common attachment to some non-material ends, is lacking." It seemed particularly strange to him "that the more closely people are crowded together, the less they know about one another." He believed that many of the people he saw every day were bereft of any true sense of personal identity.[3] They lacked the security that comes from knowing their parents gave them a name as well as a particular legacy of strength and weakness that defines character. Mary Hood has written an amusing and apt illustration of the point.

> Suppose a man is walking across a field. To the question, "Who is that?" a Southerner would reply: "Wasn't his granddaddy the one whose dog and him got struck by lightning on that steel bridge? Mama's third cousin—dead before my time—found his railroad watch in that eight-pound catfish's stomach the next summer just above the dam. The way he married for that new Cadillac automobile, reckon how come he's walking like he has on Sunday shoes, if that's who it is, and for sure it is." To which a Northerner would reply to the same question, "That's Joe Smith." To which the Southerner might think (but be much too polite to say aloud), "They didn't ask his name—they asked who he is."[4]

To urban man, a name was all too often *merely* descriptive and not evocative:

> I am not here speaking of names that rest on empty genealogical pretense—the silliness of a coat of arms. Names can gather weight in even the humblest communities; they can become names for industry, for loyalty, for kinds of expertness, or for simple truthfulness. But in the overgrown and falsely glamorized city of which I speak, all the forces are against the establishment of names in this way. Instead, the very conditions of existence combine to make one anonymous. It has been said that the masses of a great city are people without faces. But they do have faces, and often you can see the marks of frustration on them. It would be more revealing to say that they are people without names. They come to be like mass-produced parts, polished, machined, and what is worst of all to say—interchangeable.[5]

Weaver conceded that there was a certain sort of natural defensiveness by some who insist that urban man does have a sense of pride, but he believed it was little more than a sort of knee-jerk assumption that their rural counterparts are provincial bumpkins. Country-boy and city-slicker jokes could better be understood as expressing an underlying tragedy. Convinced there is a crucial distinction between the parochial and the provincial, he thought it was too bad that they were often seen as synonyms. "What the big city fails to see, or wilfully ignores, is that provincialism is one of the chief supports of character. To be of a place, to reflect it in your speech and action and general bearing, to offer it as a kind of warranty that you will remain true to yourself—this is what it means to have character and personality. And without these things there is no individuality."[6]

Belonging to a particular family gave one a history that included burdens and responsibilities; the pleasing limbs of the family tree were there as well as the less attractive and asymmetrical ones whose very unsightliness served as a spur or reproach to succeeding generations. Weaver buttressed his point by noting that "all the great art of the world has been provincial." Talk of national art was problematic; to imagine such an entity as international art was virtually impossible. It was the very provincialism of art that gave it universal appeal and spoke to what is common to all humanity. Celebrating the sort of southern community that he knew at Weaverville, Weaver extolled the ties of neighborhood, village, and county—bonds that were most decidedly other than commercial. He encouraged his audience to ignore those who would point the finger of ridicule; they really did not know what they were talking about. Communities like Weaverville, characteristic of, but not confined to the South—he pointed to rural New England and the Ozarks as well—served as a sort of cultural gyroscope; they were "the great fly wheel of American society. If the machine speeds up too much, the fly wheel holds it back; if it slows down too much, the fly wheel speeds it up. The South, with its massive weight of tradition, with its pace regularized by a steady contact with nature, seems to perform that essential function. Our role has been, and I think will continue to be, that of the indispensable conservative counterpoise."[7] Such a part would sometimes irritate the whole or seem to sound a discordant note. Weaver probably had in mind Franklin D. Roosevelt's description of the South as the nation's economic problem child. But problem children often bring to the family's attention matters their parents ignore at their peril.

Appealing to his kin to avoid self-congratulation and laziness, Weaver challenged them to take up arms "against the dehumanization of life," even though that struggle had seemed to yield nothing but failure for four generations. Ending on a note of hope, he believed that at some point, "as society begins to look back, to ascertain the real sources of its strength, it is not presumptuous to say that we shall have to be recognized."[8]

Although Weaver without question came to see himself as taking up the same role as the other Agrarians in exile about whom he wrote, his sister remembered that he originally joined the University of Chicago faculty for a more prosaic reason: "It was a decent job—a paying job and he was just glad to have it." His dissertation adviser at Louisiana State University, Cleanth Brooks, coeditor of the *Southern Review*, had helped with a strong letter of recommendation. But it is equally true that the University of Chicago wanted him as part of their faculty. A representative of the college on a bus trip to recruit new faculty to teach in their "Great Books" program stopped in Asheville to interview Weaver and hired him on the spot.[9]

Henry Regnery has written about the irony that Weaver, a man suspicious of progress as it is popularly perceived and anxious not to bow down before the altar of science, should have spent his most productive years "at a university founded by John D. Rockefeller, where, not long before he arrived, the first chain reaction had taken place . . . and in the city where fifteen years before there had been a great exposition, 'A Century of Progress,' celebrating achievements of science and technology." Regnery observed, no doubt correctly, that while Weaver might have in some sense been out of place in Chicago, "the challenge and intellectual stimulation of the university . . . contributed to his creative achievement."[10]

Weaver joined the University of Chicago and taught there during the era when that institution was making its name. In looking back on the thirties, forties, and fifties, when he was on the faculty there, Edward Shills remembers how diverse a group his colleagues were.

[They differed] in temperament, in politics, religion, and ethnic origin. Some—very few—came from wealthy families, some—a larger number—came from families of very modest standing; most of them came from hard-working families in the learned professions and the mercantile lower middle class, some came from farmers' families. But whatever their origins, tempers, and affections, they all cared for their subjects. They were not above spending seven days a week on their work, week in week out, year in year out. They were not working for promotions, although they usually welcomed them when they came. Permanence of tenure was rarely a consideration for them. They did not fear that if they did not publish they would perish.

One important integrating principle for the carefully selected faculty and student body was the focus on intellectual rigor. The Red Scare following World War I, which flared up again in the early 1930s and in the McCarthyism of the 1950s, is characterized by Shills as "times when rude politicians, silly journalists, and demagogic priests were seeking to advance their respective interests at the cost of universities; businessmen sometimes joined them. The University of Chicago was as safe from [such] storms as a sheltered inland sea."[11]

Lest one should conclude that the campus was a rarefied ivory tower whose inhabitants took no note of politics, Shills adds that he and his colleagues "did have political views but their politics did not affect the honesty of their teaching or their research." And this at a time "when many universities were highly politicized." Such academic freedom has continued to characterize the University of Chicago, he holds, and is usually exercised not in the direction of politics, "but for the pursuit of knowledge with full fervor and with only the limitations of our own intellectual powers."[12]

During the tenure of President Robert M. Hutchins from 1929 to 1950, collegiality and strong sense of community provided a framework within which a spirited give-and-take "on educational and philosophic questions reached an extraordinary intensity" involving the trustees, the faculty, and the students as well. Perhaps there was a tinge of self-righteousness and provinciality in the attitudes of some that only on their campus were vital educational issues being squarely faced. Still, the case can be made "that Hutchins, and the professors and students who responded to him, were entirely right in trying so hard to make the goals of higher education explicit. Serious debates on such questions were weak and anemic elsewhere, whereas at Chicago almost the entire faculty and a substantial part of the student body—especially among undergraduates—took part."[13]

Hutchins's criticisms of the modern university in the 1930s generally received a warm reception from the academic community. His ideas for reform, however, were not so popular. Perhaps a majority of professors and large numbers of students were just as disillusioned as he about overspecialization, the hardening of departmental lines, and scientific research as a be-all and end-all. But many took alarm at his enthusiastic support of making classical liberal arts the center of a college education. "His prescriptions seemed more appropriate to Aristotle's Greece or to the scholastic universities of the Middle Ages than to the University of Chicago . . . in the twentieth century." Not a particularly original thinker among America's past university presidents, he still was a determined leader who built a strong faculty and inspired many "to develop their research and teaching in unique and significant ways." One man whom Hutchins hired early in his tenure was Mortimer Adler, who helped convince him that the study of philosophy was pivotal to what a university ought to be about. The social scientists in Adler's view "lacked methods of research and analyses of date sufficiently rigorous to support claims to truth." Lacking training in logic, physics, and mathematics, how could their work be called anything but a "mess"? Weaver quoted Adler's writing on rhetoric and dialectic with approval, although the two apparently never formally met even though they were on the same campus.[14]

Even though the University of Chicago played a critical role in the development of the atomic bomb and provided the setting for the famous experiment by Professor Enrico Fermi and his team on December 2, 1942, Hutchins determined that once fascism had been defeated, he would have his university lead the way in the peaceful development of atomic energy. The University of Chicago Research Institutes were established with the president announcing as their main purpose: "to advance knowledge and not primarily to develop the military or industrial applications of nuclear research," since "for the past six years the United States has abandoned both basic research and the training of a new generation of scientists. It is essential to our progress and our welfare that we overcome that deficiency."[15]

Richard Weaver was profoundly ambivalent about atomic research for peaceful uses or otherwise. He viewed South Carolina's allowance of a research center for the hydrogen bomb as a great betrayal. Earlier known for upholding the southern ideal of chivalry, the Palmetto State had capitulated to a project "which prepares for indiscriminate slaughter on a scale not hitherto contemplated." He was also appalled by a scene he saw every day that poignantly reminded him of what had been "a few years ago," where

> there stood on the edge of the campus of the University of Chicago a small café. It was a poor affair, without style or pretensions; but here in the afternoons members of the liberal arts faculties were wont to go for a cup of coffee, to get out of their professional grooves for an hour, to broach ideas and opinions, to be practicing humanists, you might say. Today a monstrous gray structure given over to atomic research covers the site: the little café is no more; and the amiable *Kaffeeklatsches* no longer take place.[16]

While that scene might dishearten him, Hutchins's stated belief that "the College curriculum should be prescribed, since if students were capable of selecting the subjects they were to study, they would already have had the general education we have prepared for them" no doubt was music to Weaver's ears. F. Champion Ward, who was dean of the college at the time, believed there was not widespread resentment of the prescribed curriculum for three primary reasons. The faculty were careful to explain to the students why everyone was required to follow the same path. Most of the students appeared to genuinely like their courses. But, perhaps most important of all, "there was the belief—delightful to the young—that faculty and students, by defying the prevailing 'cafeteria' model of undergraduate study, were engaged together in an important heretical movement."[17]

While his university colleagues were well aware of Weaver's political convictions and knew that he was occasionally in touch with such conservatives as William F. Buckley Jr., Russell Kirk, the publisher Henry Regnery, and others, he worked comfortably on campus in what James Sledd remembers as "a careful scheme of general education, or 'education for freedom' as president

R. M. Hutchins liked to put it." Weaver found this an amicable
workplace and discovered "a niche where he could do his own
respected work in his own responsible way." Sledd recently wrote
that "most academics do not enjoy the freedom that Weaver enjoyed and cannot educate for freedom when they are bidden to
educate for economic growth."[18] And one might add—to hew the
line of political correctness.

Those acquainted with the conviction and passion of Weaver's
writings might assume that he would have taken advantage of
the forum and captive audience offered by weekly staff meetings
at the university to proselytize for his views. Not so. Professor
Wilma R. Ebbitt recalled the "tremendous amounts of energy and
imagination we poured into our weekly debates about curriculum
and pedagogy." Weaver, "aside from his own impressively struc-
tured formal presentations, . . . spoke rarely—but then with im-
mense deliberation and to great effect. Tom Rogers, a newcomer
in 1955, recalls Dick as the austere elder statesman of the staff,
'either sitting in judgment on our discussions or waiting in the
wings to straighten things out if we needed help.' He adds, 'he
could be forcefully silent, pregnantly quiet.' True." Professor Ebbitt
remembers him in much the same way.

> Dick was a few years older than the rest of us and in some ways he
> seemed to be of another generation. I don't mean he was a father
> figure—far from it—but his presence at staff meetings was very
> important to us. We counted on him for a temperate approach to the
> issues we debated, sometimes in a very lively fashion. He held deep
> convictions, but he was never shrill in expressing them. He didn't
> have campus fame in any sense. He wasn't a big wig in the eyes of
> the faculty in other departments, but he was deeply respected by
> everybody who worked with him in English composition and the
> humanities.[19]

The two years he spent writing *Ideas Have Consequences* no
doubt clarified and focused Weaver's thought and lent a special
poignancy and conviction to the remarks he made before his family
reunion in 1950. Some of the depth of feeling that lay behind
the book was made plain in a letter Weaver wrote to his former
teacher, the Agrarian Donald Davidson. "I think it is going to put
the opposition in a spot where they will have to put up or shut up.

As we both know, they have not a great deal to put up." Surprised at the dispatch with which the University of Chicago Press accepted the manuscript for publication, he confessed to Davidson: "I wrote it with the feeling that the important thing was to hit and to hit hard—not of course at the expense of truth, but time did not permit an equal research into every area. I sensed that in some places I was over-generalizing. I have probably done so in my treatment of the arts as well as in my treatment of the American frontier. I shall . . . inform myself better there." Elaborating on his use of the term *bourgeois*, Weaver said that he was taking aim at "the American philistine, the sort of person who thinks that the greatest thing in life is to own and display a Buick automobile. It seems to me that it is this soulless, desiccated middle class which has done most to destroy the concept of non-material value. The levelling process results in everyone's being pushed into it. Its characteristic mentality is perfect ideological befuddlement." Relishing the controversy *Ideas Have Consequences* had stirred up, he went on,

> Whatever else may be said about the book, I am forced to conclude that it carries a whip lash. People seem to be for or against it violently. I was warned from the first that it would be attacked with fury, and the attack is materializing. The most ferocious assault I have yet seen appeared in *The Texas Spectator.* It was a two-page review (if such it may be called) by C. E. Ayers, bearing the caption "The Ideology of the Big Lie." Howard Mumford Jones was allowed to parade his asininity in the last issue of the *New York Times Book Review.* But people are rallying to the defense also.

Ending his letter on a note of defiant optimism, Weaver told Davidson that he had "felt from the beginning that there must be many persons in this country who are eager to hear the truth said about these matters, and to hear it said in words as hard as cannon balls. Anyhow, that is the way I tried to say it. . . . You can rely on us up here to fight the battle stubbornly."[20] This letter provides one more graphic example of Weaver's contempt for capitalism.

Ideas Have Consequences created quite a stir on campus when it was published in 1948; reaction was more negative than anything else, according to a fellow English teacher. "Some on the faculty who did not know Weaver personally found the book to be excessively dogmatic. But the campus was a different place then; it had not been politicized to the degree that one finds today."[21]

Cleanth Brooks, who had moved to Yale University, sent a congratulatory letter to his former student. Brooks was delighted with the adulatory comments penned by Paul Tillich and John Crowe Ransom that appeared on the book jacket. Effusively praising the work, Brooks warned Weaver that he should "expect to be flayed alive in the metropolitan liberal press. Maybe they will show more sense, but don't count on it." He promised to send a copy to his colleague Wilmoore Kendall, associate professor of government at Yale, who was "so placed as to help with the reviews, particularly those in political science circles." Almost four decades later, Brooks spoke of Weaver with much fondness and respect and observed that while he personally preferred "strategy and maneuver" to communicate his ideas, his former student had often taken the direct approach.[22]

In *Ideas Have Consequences,* Richard Weaver insisted that words have intrinsic meanings and stand for realities: "Language . . . appears as a great storehouse of universal memory, or it may be said to serve as a net, not imprisoning us but supporting us and aiding us to get at a meaning beyond present meaning through the very fact that it embodies others' experiences." He made no secret that this was an attack on the view set forth by S. I. Hayakawa in his *Language in Action,* understood by Weaver to insist that words merely reflect the perceptions of individuals living in a world characterized by change. Weaver concluded this chapter in *Ideas Have Consequences* with "a call for a fresh appreciation of language—perhaps, indeed, respect for words as things. Here is an opening for education to do something more than make its customary appeal for 'spiritual revival,' which is itself an encouragement to diffuseness and aimlessness."[23]

In an article he wrote for *College English* a year later, Weaver expanded on the idea. It had a revealing title—"To Write the Truth." That college composition courses were essential was a commonplace with which few, if any, teachers of English would take issue, he noted; but the ceaseless changes made in such courses revealed an underlying disquiet about the whole endeavor that he suspected covered up a fundamental problem. What, exactly, were composition teachers about? To make students more articulate? Perhaps. But that truism begs a further question. In a quick historical survey of the matter, Weaver noted that those who went back to Plato found that students were taught to speak and write the truth. No longer. "From speaking truthfully to speaking correctly to speaking usefully" traces, he believed, the sorry history of the endeavor. The proper role of an English teacher (practicing rhetorician) was for him to be a definer, one who teaches students to call things by their *proper names.* Well aware of the chorus of criticism such a view would provoke, Weaver anticipated some of the objections:

> It will be asked: By what act of arrogance do we imagine that we know what things really are? The answer to this is: By what act of arrogance do we set ourselves up as teachers? There are two postulates basic to our profession: the first is that one man can know more than another, and the second is that such knowledge can be imparted. Whoever cannot accept both should retire from the profession and renounce the intention of teaching anyone anything. Let those who consider such prerogative unreasonable consider what remains. If we cannot be sure that one person knows better than another the true nature of things, then we should follow the logic of our convictions and choose our teachers as the ancient Greek democracies chose their magistrates—by lot.[24]

Weaver confessed to Donald Davidson that he "had been a little brash. But there is no doubt in my mind about the essential rightness of the position," in spite of the controversy it aroused. The National Council of Teachers of English invited him to speak to them the next month to further explain his views. He looked forward to such a battle—but on his terms. "I have accepted on condition that I be given second place on the program instead of the first [as] originally assigned—I want to do some shooting myself. I should be very grateful for any more ammunition you can send me." Writing to Davidson, he said, "The big debate over whether the English teacher can be concerned with truth or substance was held yesterday before the National Council of Teachers of English. According to my friends and a good many strangers, victory fell on our side." The account of this fray as it appeared a month later in *College English* is bland, though the final sentence leaves little doubt that Weaver got his point across: "The opening session on concepts basic to courses had James M. McCrimmon, Galesburg Branch of the University of Illinois, and Richard M. Weaver, University of Chicago, as principal speakers. It made clear the dichotomy of professional opinion. Freshman composition should deal primarily with the medium of expression (semantics, for example) *versus* Freshman composition should go beyond correctness and accuracy to help the student to feel ethically responsible for his utterances." In a follow-up letter to Davidson, Weaver displayed his eagerness for another such clash and was optimistic about its outcome: "We shall get a hearing yet."[25]

The controversy stirred up by *Ideas Have Consequences* at the University of Chicago Press resulted in Weaver's seeking out a commercial publisher for his second work, *The Ethics of Rhetoric,* published in 1953 by Regnery of Chicago, some five years after his first book appeared. *Ideas Have Consequences,* however, did well for its publisher and has been in print for most of the over four decades since it first appeared. His new book, Weaver wrote to Davidson, was an effort to "work out some of the thoughts on language implicit in *Ideas Have Consequences.*" Warning his friend about the chapter on Lincoln, Weaver wrote, "Although I have said in it a few things critical of the South, my main intention was to show that Lincoln was a very different type of man from what the nation, under the influence of sentimental biography, popularly conceives. If it is successful, it will have the effect of making him *unavailable* to that crowd of anti-Southern rabble-rousers who have often used him in the past."[26] Noteworthy here are Weaver's fierce loyalty to the South and his deference to Davidson, whose good opinion he was eager to keep.

Davidson responded to *Ethics of Rhetoric* with effusive praise. From Nashville he wrote, "Your book is bound to be, for all who are even in a small measure alive to the present crisis, an intervention that will seem like God's special blessing. For the smaller company who have been following you closely all along, it will seem— with no less thanks to God for bringing the man and the moment together—that it is the book you have been all along destined to write. No book could be more important for these times or any

times. I can't find words to tell you how excited I feel about it."
For many years thereafter, Davidson used this book in his advanced
writing class.[27]

In his autobiographical essay, "Up from Liberalism," Weaver
recalled that it was during his graduate-school days at Vanderbilt
when he "began to perceive that many traditional positions in our
world had suffered not so much because of inherent defect as because of the stupidity, ineptness, and *intellectual sloth* of those who
for one reason or another were presumed to have their defense in
charge" [emphasis mine]. That sense of vocation as one duty-bound
to defend those traditional positions was reflected in his disciplined
and austere style of living at Chicago. Had he not set aside inviolate
periods of time to write, *Ideas Have Consequences* and *The Ethics of
Rhetoric* might never have appeared. Albert Duhamel, who shared
an office with Weaver for four years at the University of Chicago,
recalled his colleague was "as methodical in his daily regimen as he
was in his thinking, thereby affording another illustration of one
of his favorite principles—that style reflects substance."[28]

Professor Ebbitt remembers that the English department ac-
commodated Weaver's preference for two early morning classes so
that the rest of his day could be a virtually unvarying regimen. "At
precisely 11:30 he went to the Campus Commons for a solitary
lunch of soup and sandwich or soup and pie, walked a mile to
the house where he rented a room, wrote two pages, had a nap,
returned to campus to teach a 2:30 class, and then conferred with
students, attended a meeting, or assaulted the library stacks. At
5:30 he ate dinner at the Commons, again almost always alone. He
walked home, worked until 9:30, had a beer, and retired."

His weekends were no less organized and began with a half day
at his office on Saturday. After spending the afternoon browsing
through various Chicago used-book stores, he might end up at
Berghoff's, where he enjoyed German food and beer. He sometimes finished the day off with a conversation with his colleague
Duhamel. "In later years, he'd sit at the bar of Jimmie's until a
newsboy came through selling the early edition of the *Chicago Tribune*. Sundays he wrote." His zeal for order was also reflected in his
frequent and delighted reference to Konigsbergers' checking their
watches for accuracy when they saw Kant on his daily promenade.

Each spring brought a break and foretaste of another summer at home to which Weaver especially looked forward. Every March he fled to Weaverville for a prized ten-day southern parenthesis during Chicago's brutal winters. "Good to change the fantasies," he remarked to Professor Ebbitt, whom he chided for not taking advantage of the chance to leave town for the week-and-a-half respite. The pattern varied only twice: when he took a course in Greek at the University of Wisconsin in 1946 and on the occasion of his mother's visit several years later. Determined to make the most of the latter, Weaver bought a car with the thousand-dollar stipend that came with the Quantrell Award for Excellence in Teaching. Mrs. Ebbitt recalls that "Dick's friends would never forget his heroic but vain efforts to cope with Chicago traffic. He simply could not steel himself to make a left turn at a busy intersection. Driving Bob Streeter home one day—a distance of three blocks—he made four right turns to avoid the unnerving left one. At the end of the year he abandoned the car to a relative in Weaverville."

However happy he was to give up driving, Weaver never shrank from the opportunity to defend his political convictions. He scandalized some of his acquaintances at the university by stoutly defending the *Chicago Tribune*'s editorial policy: What Colonel McCormick had to say was logically and philosophically consistent. But his was not a know-nothing, anti-intellectual conservatism as evidenced by his lending his signature to a petition protesting the Mundt-Nixon Bill, which would have compelled the registration of communists.

Weaver's disciplined writing style was congruent with the way he spoke. He was deliberate and formal in speech and highly articulate, not just speaking in well-shaped sentences. "He often talked in substantial, coherent paragraphs; to a large degree, his talk resembled his writing." Eliseo Vivas of the University of Chicago's philosophy department similarly observes that "It was his habit to listen. When he spoke, it was deliberately, giving evidence that he had thought long about the matter to which he addressed himself. I often disagreed with him, but I do not remember ever catching him uttering opinions that came from the top of his head."[29] But the austere scholar could also relax on occasion. Professor Ebbitt's husband recalled how at small gatherings of friends, he would, after a few beers or the more traditionally southern bourbon and branch water, cheerfully lead group renditions of folk ballads such as "On Top of Old Smoky" and "Down in the Valley" in his off-key baritone. "He loved to tell yarns. He would laugh as he told them, laugh and slap his knee. He loved to quote his favorite authors. Nobody relished a felicitous phrase more than he; nobody was more given to aphorisms. He loved *friends,* and he was a good friend to people (like us) who disagreed totally with his politics."

While Weaver could and did enjoy such infrequent gatherings of small groups of people, there was a virtually impenetrable reserve to the man when it came to his dealing face-to-face with individuals, as Eliseo Vivas well remembers:

> One impression that grew stronger the longer I knew him was that I would never get to know him intimately. I knew him for nearly two decades and toward the end saw him frequently. I am certain that he liked me as I did him; but I do not feel that I even peered into the depths of his mind. He did not put you off, he did not hold you forcefully at arm's length, as some people do; but somehow you did not breach the reserve that kept his inwardness inviolate and inviolable. Only once, in a hotel, on the occasion of a symposium arranged by the Volker Fund, over some drinks in my room, did he speak to me about his life. What he said was vague and short, and the subject never came up again. I never found out whether the next morning he regretted or merely forgot his confidences. You sensed in him a man of great depths, of depths with which he seemed familiar, but into which you were not able to penetrate. Not that you wanted to. The reserve of the man carried with it its own authority and justification.[30]

Professor Ebbitt's response to a query about Weaver's religion is consistent with other accounts about this dimension of his life. Phrases such as "genuine though not orthodox in the conventional sense" recur. He was

> religious in his devotion to high principles and to spiritual values as opposed to materialism. He also had a philosophical cast of mind that led him to inquire about the basic assumptions underlying an argument, whether it was in religion, politics, or literary criticism.

When in public debate he challenged assumptions or had to defend his own, his expression was always temperate and his tone moderate. Though I know he was a man of firm convictions and deep feeling on many subjects, I don't think I ever saw him betray anger.[31]

Weaver was scrupulous in posting and keeping office hours. Students did not flock to him, though a steady stream did visit him for serious conferring but not for chats. Mrs. Ebbitt remembered that she often saw him "engaged in earnest conversation with students who came in to see him, and it struck me that he talked with them in much the way that he talked to colleagues. He never treated them as if they were kids but as if they were adults engaged in the pursuit of truth. He was somewhat formal with them even in that context of greater formality than at present. Students respected him as a learned, scholarly member of the faculty and as an extremely effective teacher of writing."[32]

Russell Kirk, whose *The Conservative Mind* has played a seminal role in the revitalization of conservatism since 1945, became a friend of Weaver's during the latter's tenure at Chicago and, on at least one occasion, had Weaver come to his home in Michigan as a guest. Conservatives have tried to lay claim to Kirk much as they have to Weaver, but as John B. Judis pointed out in his tribute to Kirk that appeared in the May 30, 1994, issue of the *New Republic,* less than a month after Kirk's death:

> Kirk hewed to his own path. In 1954 Buckley wanted him to be an editor of *National Review,* but he preferred to keep an arm's length from the publication. . . . He fretted about Buckley's affinity for Senator Joseph McCarthy. . . . Remarking on John Birch Society founder Robert Welch's charge that Dwight Eisenhower was a "Red," Kirk quipped, "Eisenhower's not a Communist, but a golfer." . . . He once told historian George Nash that he felt closer to socialist Norman Thomas than to anarcho-capitalist Murray Rothbard. He was especially critical of those "who abjure liberalism but seem incapable of conserving anything worth keeping."[33]

Kirk, who grew up in rural Michigan, wrote about southern conservatism's provincialism and described its way of life as "a set of assumptions and characteristics only dimly expressed but none the less real, which give the Southern conservative tradition its curious tenacity." There is "a preference for the slow processes of natural change, distinguished from the artificial innovation—the spirit of 'easy does it.' " He fretted that southern conservatism "cannot be said to obey consciously conservative ideas—only conservative instincts, exposed to all the corruption that instinct unlit by principle encounters in a literate age." Here Kirk recoiled from the perverse racism of Mississippi's Senator Bilbo, contrasting him to John Randolph of Roanoke, and wondered how it could have happened that the same region produced such contrasting men. There is, however, no more scornful and telling attack on Bilbo than that found in the work of a conservative Mississippi planter who himself was active in local and state politics, William Alexander Percy, uncle of the distinguished novelist Walker Percy. Kirk ought to have known "that southern conservatives despised Bilbo as a demagogue whose socioeconomic policies stamped him as a New Deal progressive—as a man whose only claim to being a conservative stemmed from a selected invocation of state rights to support personal ambition and a virulent racism."[34]

Weaver and Kirk were probably introduced by Canon Bernard Iddings Bell, a mutual friend and colleague of Kirk, who was the Episcopal chaplain at the University of Chicago. In his *The Crowd Culture* Bell excoriated the mindless, unreflective materialism of most Americans whose highest good was their own comfort. This, he wrote, was the inevitable condition of a society that worshiped democracy. His solution? What was needed was "skilled, critical leadership . . . a democratic elite" to lead the masses to "a more urbane and humane way of living." Bell wrote to Weaver in September 1948, apologizing for the fact that he would miss an upcoming presentation of Weaver to the Canterbury Club at the University of Chicago but promising that he would stop by Weaver's office upon his return from a speaking engagement at Marshall College in Huntington, West Virginia. In the same letter, Bell told Weaver that he had written an article for the *Christian Century* on religious instruction in secular universities and wanted his opinion on it. Weaver may well have discussed the article with Bell. At any rate, it was expanded to a book and appeared the next year under the title of *Crisis in Education*. In it, he emphasized the same themes that would appear in *Crowd Culture* but put the stress on diagnosing the ills of education and prescribing a cure. Bell's thinly disguised hostility to John Dewey came out in his insistence that education must be based on belief in God: "If there is no God," he wrote, "free love is entirely defensible and politics based on force is inevitable." He also aimed barbs at some intellectuals' uncritical adulation of science in the abstract as mankind's new savior.[35]

Russell Kirk's gregariousness and determination to get conservatives to cooperate and meet regularly impressed Weaver, who wrote to Donald Davidson that he hoped Kirk would "look you up before long. . . . In addition to being a fine personality, he is a great organizer and 'head-pusher,' so to speak. I think he is capable of doing a great deal for the nascent conservative movement in this country. Right now he is promoting the establishment of an organ, one function of which will be to combat the cultural and intellectual decadence of the East." In spite of the fact that that was a rather daunting challenge, Weaver felt that "Kirk is the kind of person who is not easily discouraged."[36] In such men as Bell and Kirk Weaver recognized allies with whom he shared many basic convictions.

Two years later, Kirk wrote Weaver that the new review would make its appearance in January 1957 with financial assistance from the publisher Henry Regnery's Foundation for Foreign Affairs. The fact that there was not yet enough money did not daunt Kirk in the least: He expected the support to come only when the fledgling journal and its supporters demonstrated their seriousness of purpose. Six years later, Weaver took pleasure in noting the success of the project: The journal *Modern Age* had progressed to the point of naming as its editor-in-chief Eugene Davidson, who had been with Yale University Press some twenty-eight years. He had been forced out of his former position, "after long tenure, by some machinations of the liberals."[37]

In 1955, just shy of his thirtieth birthday, William F. Buckley Jr. introduced *National Review,* a periodical that would become the standard publication of a renascent conservatism in America. "Its function," Buckley wrote to Weaver, "was not solely to renew the attack against the Left but to consolidate the Right." Buckley had begun corresponding with Weaver the previous year, and the magazine published occasional articles and book reviews by Weaver during the next decade.[38]

In 1957, Holt, Rinehart, and Winston published Weaver's text-book entitled *Composition: A Course in Writing and Rhetoric*. He con-fessed to Davidson that the demanding work of putting it together had almost gotten the best of him. "The labor was enormous, and several times I was on the point of throwing it up in despair. I believe that a college rhetoric must be harder to write than any other kind of textbook. . . . I am so glad to have the infinite details . . . behind me that I feel like a new man."[39]

That same year, Frank S. Meyer, one of several former commu-nists whose "god had failed" and who aligned themselves with the postwar conservative movement, wrote to Weaver to congratulate him on his essay "The Middle Way." Meyer admired the deftness with which Weaver "wove a beautiful web around the shifting posi-tions relativism assumes in the political sphere." He also expressed a desire to meet Weaver and, anticipating that the latter would not be making a trip east, said that he would "be in the Midwest some time this Spring and in Chicago for a few days, in which case, mahomet-like, I shall bring our meeting about." Such an attitude toward Weaver was not shared by his associates at the university, to whom "he was anything but a conservative icon." While "he was known for being thoroughly political in his thinking, he did not proclaim his views or seek converts. It would be more accurate to say that he was a conservative in a nest of liberals."[40]

That Weaver was not entirely comfortable with being pigeon-holed as simply and purely a conservative came out in his review of Frank S. Meyer's book *In Defense of Freedom: A Conservative Credo,* published by Regnery in 1962. Although this book was received with great enthusiasm by many conservatives at the time, Weaver expressed his reservations and qualifications in a lengthy and thoughtful review essay that appeared in the December 4, 1962, issue of *National Review.* He lauded the book as "brilliant with destructive analysis" and praised the author's criticisms of both "Liberal collectivism and . . . a dangerous strain he sees in some of the New Conservatives." Weaver agreed with Meyer that the state was a significant threat to true freedom and, in the only instance that I have seen in any of his other writings, used the adjective *brilliant* to describe Meyer's characterization of liberalism, which appeared as follows: *"Emotionally, it prefers psychoanalysis to*

the dark night of the soul, 'adjustment' to achievement, security to freedom.
It preaches 'the end of ideology,' admires experts and fears prophets,
fears above all commitment to value transcending the fact"[41] [Weaver's
emphasis]. Rousseau's idea of the "general will," mischievous in
its conception, had come to mean the will of a social and cultural
elite who would decide what was best for the masses of people and
then would use the power of the state to carry out their program.
The means might vary; a military coup would serve the purpose
in a country with an authoritarian government, while in a democracy the momentum created by landslide election results might be
used. Weaver agreed with Meyer's scolding of those he called the
new conservatives, such as Russell Kirk, Robert Nisbet, and John
Hallowell, for their extravagant admiration of the Greek polis as
a proper starting point for community. The logical conclusion at
the end of that path would be the exaltation of the state and the
consequent diminution of individual freedom.

At this point in his review of this book, Weaver distanced
himself from both Meyer and those he characterized as the new
conservatives. Conceding that the new conservatives exalted the
notion of community almost to the point of idolatry, Weaver
took aim at what he thought would be an equally spurious result
of carrying Meyer's concept of freedom too far. Pushed to its
logical conclusion, the outcome would be "Thoreau's anarchic
individualism." That the community was a threat to Thoreau
made no particular difference to him: His simple solution had
been to withdraw from it. All too simple, Weaver believed. One
could not really leave a community so easily; a community is
something that one was born into and that had provided nurture.
The liberals who defined community as nothing more than just a
group of people living in the same area, and Meyer, who saw it as
a "deadly environment of hereditarily or geographically imposed
association," were both wrong, Weaver averred.

The part of Meyer's work that disturbed him the most was the
author's insistence that the word *freedom* itself was a self-justifying
term that could stand alone. The question of what freedom was for,
which Meyer had dismissed out of hand, troubled Weaver a great
deal. Granted that freedom to do only good or only evil would
presuppose a determinism that would make of the whole idea a

mockery, Weaver insisted that freedom's worth was derived: It was a means that ought always to be subordinated to greater values and ends.[42]

What Weaver did in this review was to distance himself clearly from the type of conservatism Frank S. Meyer was exalting. While he was fulsome in his praise of Meyer's writing ability and felicitous style in this book, he clearly rejected *In Defense of Freedom: A Conservative Credo* as *his* creed and questioned whether a genuine conservatism could ever exalt freedom to such a high position that it became the be-all and end-all of political society. Weaver was an independent thinker whose conservatism, if it may be properly so called, was anything but a reflection, dim or otherwise, of that associated with William F. Buckley Jr. and the men who founded and ran *National Review*. But where would be a better place to make his reservations known? By the end of his essay-review, Weaver had defined and qualified conservatism in such a way that the thoughtful and honest reader would almost have to conclude that his brand was unique. Some might even say that what Weaver had set forth was not conservatism at all—or if it were, it was sui generis.

The point is further made by the fact that Buckley had decided not to publish Weaver's article "The Southern Tradition" in the *National Review*. Donald Davidson told Weaver he suspected "that Buckley didn't find in it just that nuance and twist—something like the Ivy College nuance with a little of the *New Yorker* twist—that *National Review* seems to be cultivating as a dominant style. . . . You mention irony as not being your *forté*. I don't think it's irony they want so much as a kind of comic innuendo. A rather la-de-da kind of innuendo." Davidson lavishly praised the essay and especially liked Weaver's metaphor about the South being a kind of flywheel that brought stability to America. He went on to suggest that Weaver ought to pursue "the flywheel figure, which is a new idea that you leave undeveloped, but that you could develop with telling results. In fact I'd guess that Buckley *et al* might prefer to see some expansion of your characteristic thought and are in that direction *because* they feel and also *need* the push of that flywheel."[43]

Randall Stewart, chairman of the Vanderbilt English department, was another occasional correspondent of Weaver's who began writing to him in the 1950s. Remarking to Stewart on "Middle

Western deference toward the East," Weaver remained puzzled by the phenomenon:

> I have been aware of this ever since I became a resident of this section eleven years ago. And it struck me as strange when I first encountered it because I knew that in the South we never had this attitude toward the East. It now seems to me that the Middle West simply does not know how to fight the East (of course I am using "fight" in the general sense of "compete with"). And this leaves me vexed because I like most Middle Westerners. They are solid, decent, well-meaning people, though they are naive enough about a lot of things. But at the thought of taking on the East, they run up the white flag before the first shot has been fired. Goodness knows, we in the South have taken a good many beatings from the East, but I think we have administered a few ourselves, and we don't run from the fight. I keep thinking how the Middle Westerners need somebody to show them how to fight. They could do so much better than they have done with a different attitude and a somewhat better technique. I think a prime example of this self depreciation (along with a kind of lingering defiance) is F. Scott Fitzgerald. And the idea of an East-West polarity is of course one of the implicit themes of *The Great Gatsby*.[44]

The generous use of military terminology—"fight," "run up the white flag," "the first shot has been fired," "don't run from the fight," "show them how to fight"—again revealed in unmistakable terms the passion of a man determined to do battle against what he perceived to be cultural philistinism by teaching and using noble rhetoric, but who had no illusions about gaining easy victories.

Weaver went to New York City in March 1962 for a Madison Square Garden meeting of Young Americans for Freedom, organized in William F. Buckley Jr.'s Connecticut home two years earlier. It was one of the few times that he would travel so far away from his post in Chicago. The master of ceremonies at the organization's annual awards rally thanked Weaver for his "arguing for and extolling the virtues of classical learning and the values of individualism. In an age of sputniks, . . . his has been a very lonely, though eloquent voice reminding us of the necessity of returning to first principles and of recapturing the *areté* of the Greeks and the *virtus* of the Romans. It is with pride and pleasure," the presenter concluded, "that I present an award to a Platonist, a humanist, and a conservative—Professor Richard Weaver of the University of Chicago."[45]

Shortly after his return to Chicago from this New York trip, Randall Stewart spoke to him about possibly coming to Vanderbilt. Weaver could hardly contain his enthusiasm. It was, he admitted, the only place in the country he would be willing to leave Chicago for. Yet there was a great deal of hardheaded realism on his part. He wondered whether Vanderbilt would really want a fifty-three-year-old man who had published only three books. "Since coming to Chicago eighteen years ago I have given so much of my effort (virtually all of it, in fact) to our courses in general education that I am hardly a specialist in anything any more, unless it is the theory of rhetoric," he wrote. "I have kept up fairly well with American literature, especially the Southern sector. Still, I think I could teach the courses you mention, and others we might devise." Warming to the idea, Weaver concluded by suggesting to Stewart that a one-year appointment would be ideal; at the end of that time, Vanderbilt and he could decide whether their mutual interests would be best served by his being given a permanent teaching position there. He could take a leave of absence from Chicago for the 1963–1964 school year to do the trial year in Nashville. By February 1963, things had progressed to the point where he and Stewart were discussing the specifics of his teaching responsibilities—to include a class on the theory of rhetoric "and Don's course in Advanced Writing if this is agreeable to everyone, but I certainly would feel like a pygmy stepping into his shoes."[46]

Writing to his mother on January 9, 1963, Weaver confided that Harold Luhnow, president of the Francis Volker Fund, had asked him whether he would be willing to take a position with the fund at his current salary. He responded that he would have to honor his one-year commitment to Vanderbilt, but after that he might be receptive to such an offer and believed that he would hear from the fund again at the end of the year. In a letter to her on his birthday two months later, he complained that he was tired. "I sort of wish to myself that I could stop now and rest up for six months before going to Vanderbilt. But two or three things make this impossible.

First of all, I need the money that working brings. And second, it is important that I keep my academic title here for some while longer. I want that to appear on the revised textbook."[47]

His move to Vanderbilt was not to be; it was cut short by his untimely death on April 1, 1963. He had just celebrated his fifty-third birthday. His sister believed he died due to a cerebral hemorrhage brought on by overwork. A similar problem had claimed his father at forty-five. When Weaver had complained about chest pains while at home in North Carolina the year before, his brother-in-law Kendall Beaton suggested that they were probably symptoms of stress. Wilma Ebbitt remembers that the sense of loss felt by Weaver's colleagues at his decision to leave the University of Chicago had been tempered by their sharing his joy over the prospect of going to Vanderbilt. They were heartbroken by news of his death. On a 1962 Christmas card to Ralph T. Eubanks, Weaver had written "There is much to be done."[48] His fighting spirit remained unabated to the end.

9 | Epilogue

WE HAVE TO INFORM THE MULTITUDE THAT RESTORATION COMES AT A PRICE. SUPPOSE WE GIVE THEM AN INTIMATION OF THE COST THROUGH A SERIES OF QUESTIONS. ARE YOU READY, WE MUST ASK THEM, TO GRANT THAT THE LAW OF REWARD IS INFLEXIBLE AND THAT ONE CANNOT, BY CUNNING OR THROUGH COMPLAINTS, OBTAIN MORE THAN HE PUTS IN? ARE YOU PREPARED TO SEE THAT COMFORT MAY BE A SEDUCTION AND THAT THE FETISH OF MATERIAL PROSPERITY WILL HAVE TO BE PUSHED ASIDE IN FAVOR OF SOME STERNER IDEAL? DO YOU SEE THE NECESSITY OF ACCEPTING DUTIES BEFORE YOU BEGIN TO TALK OF FREEDOMS? THESE THINGS WILL BE VERY HARD; THEY WILL CALL FOR DEEP REFORMATION. . . . YET IT IS THE DUTY OF THOSE WHO CAN FORESEE . . . TO MAKE THEIR COUNSEL KNOWN. NOTHING IS MORE CERTAIN THAN THAT WE ARE ALL IN THIS TOGETHER. . . . IF THE THINKERS OF OUR TIME CANNOT CATCH THE IMAGINATION OF THE WORLD TO THE POINT OF EFFECTING SOME PROFOUND TRANSFORMATION, THEY MUST SUCCUMB WITH IT. THERE WILL BE LITTLE JOY IN THE HOUR WHEN THEY CAN SAY, "I TOLD YOU SO."[1]

Richard M. Weaver saw his vocation as teaching right rhetoric to all who would hear, especially to the young. In this he was self-consciously emulating the Agrarians who had played a pivotal role in his conversion to the "ethical and poetic view of life." Modern man, Weaver held, is locked in the prison of the present—and, even worse, in the cell of himself. He thinks he can survive on his own. Weaver would hardly have been surprised that "I survived" has become a fashionable and flippant popular retort used today to describe any difficulty that many such sufferers would label as a "negative experience"—from the sublime to the ridiculous.

Of Weaver it can be truly said, as E. B. White declared of himself in a letter to the *New York Herald Tribune* protesting the blacklisting of alleged communists in 1947, that he was "a member of a party of one."[2] This was not because Weaver was a loner, but because he was a seminal thinker. His works are original in a manner that evokes from readers not startled amazement at a completely new idea, but rather a thought-provoking way of seeing the familiar and commonplace in a new light. He began with man as a fallen creature who nonetheless was more than just "mind." That man is a rational creature is beyond dispute; that he is *merely* rational Weaver spent a lifetime disputing. Tradition and sentiment, soul and spirit, he believed, were intrinsic to humanness.

Weaver learned much from the Agrarians. Although he was a generation younger than they and different from them in many respects, he admired their willingness to exile themselves in order to do battle against cultural philistinism. Although their numbers were never large, they comprised a Gideon's band, doing the work of the doctors of culture and holding the fort against cultural decline. To be sure they (and he) were sons of the traditional South, but their education and experience gave them that perspective essential to prescribing the proper palliatives to a sick culture. Their time in Europe during the Great War and its aftermath was critical to the Agrarians' development of a sense of distance. The sojourn stripped them of a bare provincialism, while it reinforced their conviction that true identity was inextricably intertwined with and bound to a place. Richard Weaver's analogous experiences were his undergraduate days at the University of Kentucky and his teaching tenure at Texas A & M University. Torn away from the security of family and home, he was forced to face not another continent separated from his by an ocean, but rather the contrasting culture of modernity. It was alien to him because it understood progress in terms of economic growth and technological advancement measured and certified by numbers and graphs and charts.

Weaver became disdainful of the Whig interpretation of history, which tended to dismiss lost causes as deserving their fate. To him, the mere fact that this or that particular cause had failed was not "the lesson itself, but simply the text of the lesson."[3] A mere reading of history might yield the conclusion that things turned out the way they did because of the inevitable march of both progress and freedom. Reflection, however, yielded probing questions about why the great issues had been joined and what motivated the combatants. By the time he had finished his doctoral dissertation at Louisiana State University, Weaver was convinced that an uncritical adulation of modernity was at best an idolatrous kowtowing to a false deity and was at worst a cultural betrayal, especially if the worshipers happened to be southerners. They ought to know better.

The immediate cause of Weaver's joining the College of Arts and Sciences at the University of Chicago as an English teacher was prosaic and simple. He needed work, and the university offered him a position. But it proved to be more than just a job. After he had been at Chicago for only two years, he wrote "Agrarianism in Exile," an essay in which he sought to explain why many of the Agrarians had left their native South for northern universities. In so doing, they gained the separation essential to right perspective. Distance framed the culture and brought into focus its unique beauty and virtue as well as its flaws and weaknesses. It is almost certain that this essay is autobiographical. Even though a draft was submitted to Donald Davidson at Vanderbilt for comments, he did not substantially change it. Suggesting only minor emendations, Davidson fulsomely praised Weaver's analysis. Like the Agrarians, Weaver came to denounce both socialism and capitalism as systems. In their stead he extolled a conservative social order that respected tradition without indulging in a mindless worship of the past. This, he believed, avoided both socialism's inevitable need to coerce and capitalism's compulsive embrace of technology.

The publication of *Ideas Have Consequences* in 1948 caught the attention of Russell Kirk, William F. Buckley Jr., Wilmoore Kendall, and others who would play a pivotal role in the budding post–World War II conservative intellectual movement in America. It was to be expected that they saw in Weaver an ally. But, while he did not

shy away from these men and their movement, he wore the label
conservative only after carefully qualifying it.

Weaver's correspondence and friendship with Donald Davidson no doubt clarified and reinforced his understanding of himself
while at the University of Chicago. In the setting of a family reunion at Weaverville, he let his guard down and stoutly declared to
them that he served at a "missionary outpost in darkest Chicago."[4]
As a practicing rhetorician he no doubt chose the words not only for
their particular connotations, but also for how they would resonate
with his audience. The phrase itself is a study in the economical use
of language. A missionary is one sent out on a redemptive task—a
life-and-death matter for the hearers of the message. The religious
meaning here can hardly be ignored. He was not making a living
by taking the same *job* year after year: His was a vocation in the
etymological sense of the term. "Outpost" is a military word that
brings to mind a beleaguered band or perhaps a solitary soldier
on guard far from the security and comfort of headquarters—near
enemy territory, vulnerable to attack at any moment. Speaking to
his relatives in Weaverville, he confided that the braggart capital of
the Midwest was really a benighted asphalt jungle.

What was the task, then, to which Weaver set himself for the
rest of his life at his duty station in Chicago? He understood it to
be the teaching and spirited advocacy of right rhetoric. This was no
retreat to a merely academic cloister. Throughout his career he consciously saw himself as being eminently practical and maintained
that the world of ideas was ultimately the source of all human
actions. One can see this illustrated in the titles of his best-known
books: *Ideas Have Consequences, The Ethics of Rhetoric,* and *Visions
of Order.* In each instance the connecting of the theoretical (ideas,
rhetoric, and vision) with the practical (consequences, ethics, and
order) is obvious.

Weaver was well within the platonic tradition when he insisted that tampering with language—whether in writing or in
speaking—is not only irresponsible but also an impious blow at
truth itself. He scorned efforts by some semantic theorists to reduce
words to a mere geometric congruence or pragmatic denotation as
a misguided effort to attain scientific precision. Such an approach
blithely ignored the special way in which poetry communicates

to man at his deepest level and, at any rate, set an unattainable goal. The gift of language is what sets humankind apart from the animals; hence, what Weaver called the "power of the word" is critical to humanity in all its dimensions. The "Word of God," according to the Gospel of John, best describes God incarnate. Since language is such a dynamic and powerful gift, it must be carefully safeguarded from sophistic perversion and, above all, taught properly to the young. He wrote at length about the importance of the rehabilitation of the word, rescuing language from those who saw it as nothing more than a tool to be used for one's selfish purposes or as a means to smuggle a hidden agenda.

In sum, rhetoric rightly defined, Weaver insisted, was Spinoza's "intellectual love of God." While he makes a concession to twentieth-century secularism by modifying the definition to "intellectual love of the Good," the essential meaning, for Weaver, does not change.

Circular argument is essential in the sense that all communication begins with certain presuppositions or "first principles." They are premises and cannot be reached as conclusions. Any analytic discussion of these underpinnings of all writing and speaking is futile. Efforts to dissect and explicate are truly useless, because such an approach is itself based on definite presuppositions. To see *through* something, one writer has observed, is the same as not seeing it at all.[5] Weaver strongly believed that words have a real existence and are not bound to the temporal; rather, they are rooted in that which is immutable and lasting.

The religious base of Weaver's thought is never far away from the surface in his writing and is often explicit. While this does not necessarily translate into orthodox, creedal Christianity, he frequently uses language associated with that traditional formulation. It is noteworthy that "The Older Religiousness of the South" was his first published essay. In it he openly admired a faith that could be simply stated as a professed belief in biblical Christianity, admission to the brotherhood of faith, and a recognition of sacred Scripture as divine revelation. His dissertation advisor and English professor at LSU, Cleanth Brooks, has scored those who practice a religion of what might be called dogmatic agnosticism: " 'The Search for God' is all very well for a party of religious explorers; it hardly does for a religion which maintains that it has found Him. . . . If the religious values are *true,* if they are worth adhering to, shall they determine the civilization; or shall the economic order into which we drift determine our values by allowing to us whatever values an economic order will permit?"[6]

At any rate, Weaver's writings are liberally laced with terminology unmistakably religious in meaning: "apostasy," "sanctified," "damnation," "reformation," "spiritual progress," "pious," "impious," "providential," "orthodoxy." The use of such terms was integral to his idea of true rhetoric, which, he held, always seeks to move hearers to the noble and good. Rhetoric at its finest ennobles men by appealing to both the mind and the soul. It necessarily touches the intellect and feelings simultaneously. Noble rhetoric appeals to the intellect not through a bare reason and heartfelt sentiment. "As a man thinketh in his heart, so is he," wrote the psalmist. Weaver held, furthermore, that true rhetoric provided guidance for rudderless and restless souls by teaching them to love what is good and turn away from evil.

In his *Confessions,* Augustine looked back with distaste on what he called his "Chair of Lies" as professor of rhetoric at the University of Milan, where he had been a mere vendor of words. All his skills had been focused on the pragmatic use of language for self-serving purposes. Words were nothing more than counters to further his own career. He said as much in remembering a speech containing a great many lies that he had written fulsomely praising the emperor.[7] Following his conversion, his great skill for expression was devoted to the service of what he was convinced was Truth. Weaver's odyssey to his conversion to the ethical and poetic vision of life had been his Milan; like Augustine after his conversion, Richard Weaver devoted himself utterly to the task of teaching and promulgating right rhetoric for the rest of his life.

Both the Left and the Right in America speak of a culture war. Throughout his career Weaver believed that such a conflict had been going on for some time. His last work bore the subtitle "The Cultural Crisis of Our Time." Thirty-odd years after this book was published, Francis Fukuyama observed, "It should not be surprising that the strength of community life has declined in America. This decline has occurred not *despite* liberal principles, but because of them. This suggests that no fundamental strengthening of community life will be possible unless individuals give back certain of their rights to communities." Weaver anticipated Fukuyama's conclusion that exalting an atomistic individualism at the expense of community exacts a terrible price. Weaver's spirited defense of the reconsideration of the central role played by true community, the givenness of human nature and the world in which we find ourselves contained some of the bluntest words he ever wrote. The alternative he foresaw was a brutishness that saw humankind as nothing more than an "eating, defecating, mating animal."[8] Richard Malcolm Weaver gave passionately of himself during his all too brief life in the classroom, lecture hall, and printed page to forestall just such an outcome.

Notes

Introduction

1. David Middleton, "The Patriarch," in *The Burning Fields.*
2. Catherine Dunne, conversation with author, Lexington, Ky., July 22, 1985. Miss Dunne is a retired teacher, an acquaintance of the Weaver family, and a life-long resident of Lexington, Ky.
3. Russell Kirk, letter to author, December 8, 1993; George Core, telephone conversation with author, November 17, 1993.
4. E. B. White, "Salt Water Farm," 34.
5. Thomas Molnar, *The Counter Revolution,* 147; W. H. Auden and Louis Kronenberger, eds., *The Viking Book of Aphorisms,* 236.

1. A Social Bond Individualist

1. Mark Van Doren, introduction to *Two Years before the Mast,* x.
2. Richard M. Weaver, *The Southern Tradition at Bay,* 390–91, 396.
3. Eugene D. Genovese, *The Southern Tradition: The Achievements and Limitations of an American Conservatism,* 39.
4. Richard M. Weaver, "Conservatism and Libertarianism: The Common Ground," in *Life without Prejudice and Other Essays,* 159.
5. Richard M. Weaver, "Two Types of American Individualism" (1963), in *The Southern Essays of Richard M. Weaver,* 77–103.
6. Bruce Clayton, *W. J. Cash: A Life,* 153–91.

2. The Early Years

1. Richard M. Weaver, "Address to Family Meeting," August 10, 1950, in Pearl M. Weaver, *The Tribe of Jacob: The Descendants of the Reverend Jacob Weaver of Reems Creek, North Carolina, 1786–1868 and Elizabeth Siler Weaver,* 114.
2. Ibid., vii; Richard M. Weaver, *Visions of Order: The Cultural Crisis of Our Time,* 23.
3. Polly Weaver Beaton, interview by author, tape recording, Brevard, N.C., October 19, 1985; Richard M. Weaver, *Ideas Have Consequences,* 113–28; Henry Regnery, *Memoirs of a Dissident Publisher,* 191; Henry Regnery, "A Southern Agrarian at the University of Chicago"; Richard M. Weaver, "Up from Liberalism," in *Life without Prejudice and Other Essays,* 143–44.
4. Weaver, *Tribe of Jacob,* 112.
5. Beaton, interview; Weaver, *Tribe of Jacob,* 113.
6. Beaton, interview.

7. Weaver, *Ideas Have Consequences,* 113–28; Charles Kellogg Follette, "A Weaverian Interpretation of Richard Weaver," 55–56.

8. Richard M. Weaver, "Agrarianism in Exile" (1950), in *The Southern Essays of Richard M. Weaver,* 34.

9. Kendall Beaton, "Richard M. Weaver: A Clear Voice in an Addled World," 1–2.

10. Robert Hamlin, "Weaver's *Tribal Pietas:* The Beginnings and Early Years, 1910–1933," 6; Beaton, "Clear Voice," 2; Follette, "Weaverian Interpretation," 60.

11. Lester G. McAllister and William E. Tucker, *Journey in Faith: A History of the Christian Church (Disciples of Christ),* 279.

12. Richard M. Weaver, student notebook, quoted by permission of Mrs. Polly Weaver Beaton, literary executor of Richard M. Weaver; Fowler, trans., "Euthydemus," in *Plato in Twelve Volumes,* vol. 2: 443.

13. Weaver, student notebook; Richard M. Weaver, *The Ethics of Rhetoric,* 28.

14. Weaver, student notebook. "Our Holy and Gracious Father who art in Heaven; we ask that thy blessings descend upon that good man in whose recognition we have gathered here this night. We ask that he be comforted in his old age that he may have no cause to regret the great sacrifices which he has made in the interest of Christianity, that he receive the reward that is Virtue's, the peace that comes to righteousness and the recompense which is due honest effort. May his success be an example to those who are ambitious and may the influence of this great leader never be abated among his followers, but his reward be equal to his deserts. We ask this in behalf of one to whom we are indebted. Amen." and "Our Holy and Gracious Father who art in Heaven. We render up our thanks to Thee for the restful Sabbath thru [*sic*] which we have just passed. May thy Holy Spirit descend upon this congregation tonight and give each one who is to take part in these services the ability to expound thy word and doctrines as thou woudst have them expounded. We pray that all of our eyes may be opened to that great treasure of the Gospel and that we be not led astray by the sychisms [*sic*] and delusions of unfaithfulness. We pray that each may learn something here tonight which may instruct him the further how to keep the day consecrated to thy name. Give us strength to contend against the many temptations which now beset us on this day. We ask this in the name of Christ. Amen."

15. Ibid; Clifford Amyx, interview by author, tape recording, Lexington, Ky., July 23, 1985; Follette, "Weaverian Interpretation," 62.

16. Richard M. Weaver, "The Older Religiousness of the South" (1943), in *The Southern Essays of Richard M. Weaver,* 135.

17. Beaton, interview.

18. Weaver, student notebook; Weaver, *Ideas Have Consequences,* 170–71.

19. Weaver, student notebook.

20. Jesse Stuart to Richard M. Weaver, January 3, 1955, Weaver Family Papers. Quoted by permission of Mrs. Polly Weaver Beaton, literary executor of Richard M. Weaver.

21. Amyx, interview.

22. Ibid; Clifford Amyx, "Weaver the Liberal: A Memoir," 101–6.

23. Amyx, interview.

24. Ibid; Amyx, "Weaver the Liberal," 4.

25. Richard M. Weaver, "A Panorama of Peace in the Colleges," 72.

26. Amyx, interview.

27. Ibid.

28. Weaver, *Ideas Have Consequences,* 92–112; Amyx, interview; Amyx, "Weaver the Liberal," 6.

29. Amyx, interview.

30. Frederick Lewis Allen, *Only Yesterday: An Informal History of the 1920s,* 355–56.

31. Amyx, interview.

32. Ibid.

33. Clifford Amyx and Richard M. Weaver, "Looking over the Magazines," *Kentucky Kernel,* August 7, 1931, 4.

34. Richard M. Weaver, "The Revolt against Humanism."

35. Amyx and Weaver, "Looking over the Magazines," *Kentucky Kernel,* August 7, 1931, 3.

36. Ibid., *Kentucky Kernel,* August 14, 1931, 3.

37. Ibid; Julian S. Huxley, *What Dare I Think?,* 56, 277.

38. Weaver, "Up from Liberalism," in *Life without Prejudice,* 131; Weaver, transcript from University of Kentucky. Richard M. Weaver Papers, Special Collections, The Jean and Alexander Heard Library, Vanderbilt University, Nashville, Tennessee; Beaton, interview.

39. Weaver, "Up from Liberalism," in *Life without Prejudice,* 130–31.

40. Ibid., 131; Amyx, interview.

41. Weaver, "Up from Liberalism," in *Life without Prejudice,* 131; Weaver, *Visions of Order,* 5.

42. Weaver, "Up from Liberalism," in *Life without Prejudice,* 132–33; Amyx, interview.

3. Vanderbilt and the Agrarians

1. Richard M. Weaver, "The Tennessee Agrarians" (1952), in *The Southern Essays of Richard M. Weaver,* 11.

2. Weaver, "Older Religiousness," in *Southern Essays,* 134–36; Amyx and Weaver, "Looking over the Magazines," *Kentucky Kernel,* August 14, 1931, 3.

3. Lothar Hönnighausen, "Aspects of Rewriting the South," in *Rewriting the South: History and Fiction,* xi.

4. Paul K. Conkin, *The Southern Agrarians,* 1.

5. Weaver, "Agrarianism in Exile," in *Southern Essays,* 30; Conkin, *Southern Agrarians,* 1–2.

6. Weaver, "Agrarianism in Exile," in *Southern Essays,* 32–33.

7. Donald Davidson, *Southern Writers in the Modern World,* 2.

8. Conkin, *Southern Agrarians,* 3.

9. Ibid., 4–6.

10. John L. Stewart, *The Burden of Time: The Fugitives and Agrarians,* 15; Conkin, *Southern Agrarians,* 6.

11. Conkin, *Southern Agrarians,* 6–7.

12. Stewart, *Burden of Time,* 4; Conkin, *Southern Agrarians,* 7.

13. Davidson, *Southern Writers,* 12; Conkin, *Southern Agrarians,* 7.

14. Conkin, *Southern Agrarians,* 10.

15. T. D. Young, *Gentleman in a Dustcoat: A Biography of John Crowe Ransom,* 94; Conkin, *Southern Agrarians,* 17–18; Louise Cowan, *The Fugitive Group: A Literary History,* 24–25.

16. Cowan, *Fugitive Group,* 28–29; Conkin, *Southern Agrarians,* 12.

17. Conkin, *Southern Agrarians,* 14, 16.

18. Ibid., 17–18; *Fugitive* 1 (April 1922), 2.

19. Stewart, *Burden of Time,* 77–79; Conkin, *Southern Agrarians,* 20.

20. Conkin, *Southern Agrarians,* 23–25, 32.

21. Stewart, *Burden of Time,* 114–15; Donald Davidson to Richard M. Weaver, March 25, 1949, Weaver Papers; Genovese, *Southern Tradition,* 85; Conkin, *Southern Agrarians,* 32.

22. Conkin, *Southern Agrarians,* 33.

23. Davidson to Weaver, March 25, 1949, Weaver Papers.

24. John Crowe Ransom, "Reconstructed but Unregenerate," in *I'll Take My Stand,* by Donald Davidson and others, 1–27.

25. Ibid., 13, 14, 15–22.

26. Amyx and Weaver, "Looking over the Magazines," *Kentucky Kernel,* August 7, 1931, 3; Richard M. Weaver, "The Southern Phoenix" (1963), in *The Southern Essays of Richard M. Weaver,* 14.

27. Weaver, "Southern Phoenix," in *Southern Essays,* 17.

28. Mark G. Malvasi, "Risen from the Bloody Sod: Recovering the Southern Tradition," 7–8; Weaver, "Southern Phoenix," in *Southern Essays,* 18.

29. Donald Davidson, "A Mirror for Artists," in *I'll Take My Stand,* 60.

30. Frank Lawrence Owsley, "The Irrepressible Conflict," in *I'll Take My Stand,* by Donald Davidson and others, 61–91; Weaver, "Southern Phoenix," in *Southern Essays,* 20.

31. Allen Tate to Lincoln Kirstein (Malvasi, "Risen from the Bloody Sod," 112); Genovese, *Southern Tradition,* 88.

32. Weaver, "Southern Phoenix," in *Southern Essays,* 23, 27–28.

33. Ibid., 35–36.

34. John Crowe Ransom, *God without Thunder: An Unorthodox Defence of Orthodoxy,* 5.

35. Stephen Neill, *The Interpretation of the New Testament, 1861–1961,* 133–36, 191, 201, 212, 214.

36. John D. Godsey, "Neorthodoxy."

37. Ransom, *God without Thunder,* 16, 17, 19, 20–21.

38. Ibid., 22–24.

39. Ibid., 41, 49.

40. The son of a Methodist minister, Ransom resigned from teaching a Sunday school class in the mid-1930s in the Methodist church of which he was then a member since he said he could no longer subscribe to the Apostles' Creed (George Core, conversation with author, Sewanee, Tenn., April 23, 1990); Ransom, *God without Thunder,* 56–57, 67, 70.

41. Weaver, "Agrarianism in Exile," in *Southern Essays,* 36.

42. Ibid., 37.

43. Daniel Joseph Singal, *The War Within: From Victorian to Modernist Thought in the South, 1919–1945,* 73; Weaver, *Southern Tradition at Bay,* 224; Samuel Francis, *Beautiful Losers: Essays on the Failure of American Conservatism,* 131.

44. Follette, "Weaverian Interpretatation," 103; Ransom, *God without Thunder,* xii and *passim.*

45. Weaver, "Up from Liberalism," in *Life without Prejudice,* 133–34. On the subject of Ransom's influence in the Fugitive/Agrarian circle and on his students, see *The Vanderbilt Tradition: Essays in Honor of Thomas Daniel Young,* ed. Mark Royden Winchell. For example, on page 24: "The style and subtlety of Ransom's example naturally appealed to the others interested in poetry and criticism. Anyone can see that influence in the letters and memoirs of the other leading Fugitives and Agrarians. . . . The real leader, as Tate, Davidson, and others have said, was one who never directly asserted his leadership—John Crowe Ransom."

46. Weaver, "Up from Liberalism," in *Life without Prejudice,* 134.

47. Ibid; Weaver, "Tennessee Agrarians," in *Southern Essays,* 11.

48. In a recent work, John Shelton Reed marks the affinity of the 1960s New Left critique of capitalism to that of the earlier Agrarians (John Shelton Reed, "For Dixieland: The Sectionalism of *I'll Take My Stand,*" in *A Band of Prophets: The Vanderbilt Agrarians after Fifty Years,* ed. William C. Havard and Walter Sullivan, 41–64); Weaver, "Up from Liberalism," in *Life without Prejudice,* 134–35.

49. Philip Wheelwright, "Neo-Humanism," 565.

50. J. David Hoeveler Jr., *The New Humanism: A Critique of Modern America, 1900–1940,* vi–vii.

51. Weaver, "Revolt against Humanism," 66.

52. Henry Hazlitt, "The Pretensions of Humanism"; Allen Tate, "The Fallacy of Humanism," in *The Critique of Humanism,* by C. Hartley Grattan, 161; Weaver, "Revolt against Humanism," 69.

53. Weaver, "Revolt against Humanism," 74.

54. Ibid., 77; Follette, "Weaverian Interpretation," 76.

55. John Crowe Ransom, *The World's Body,* x–xi; Weaver, "Tennessee Agrarians," in *Southern Essays,* 7, 8.

56. Amyx, "Weaver the Liberal," 11; Amyx, interview.

57. Weaver, "Tennessee Agrarians," in *Southern Essays,* 8.

4. The Poetical and Ethical Vision of Life

1. Weaver, "Agrarianism in Exile," in *Southern Essays,* 48.

2. Weaver, "Up from Liberalism," in *Life without Prejudice,* 135.

3. Frank W. Powell to Richard M. Weaver, March 23, 1948, Weaver Papers.

4. Amyx, interview; Beaton, interview; Powell to Weaver, March 23, 1948.

5. "Diplome de Syndicat des Cordonniers, Piquers et Employés du Couse-Main," certificate in the Richard M. Weaver Papers in Weaverville, N.C.

6. Harvey Klehr, *The Heyday of American Communism: The Depression Decade,* 202–3; Malcolm Cowley, "Hemingway's Nevertheless," 361–62.

7. Jeffrey Hart, "The Spanish Civil War"; George H. Nash, *The Conservative Intellectual Movement in America since 1945,* 84; Allan Guttmann, *The Wound in the Heart: America and the Spanish Civil War,* 204.

8. George Orwell, *Homage to Catalonia.*

9. A. Walton Litz, ed., *American Writers: A Collection of Literary Biographies,* 139. Cowley began working for *New Republic* in 1929 and did not cut his ties with them until 1948. He was actively involved in the coal mining strikes in Pineville

and Harlan, Ky., in 1932 which were brutally put down. It would be interesting to know whether Cowley and Weaver met since this year was the high-water mark of Weaver's life as a Socialist. Cowley went on in the summer of 1932 to actively campaign for a communist candidate. " 'For the only time in my life I took part in a political campaign,' he has ruefully said. . . ." By 1980 he could not even bring himself to listen to the broadcast of a national convention. Like Weaver, he became virtually apolitical; William L. O'Neill, *The Great Schism: Stalinism and the American Intellectuals,* 18, 20, 34, 45, 97, 103, 179, 300, 344, 346, 364; Lewis P. Simpson, "Malcolm Cowley and *Exile's Return."*

10. Malcolm Cowley, "Hemingway's Wound—And Its Consequences," 428.

11. Weaver, "Up from Liberalism," in *Life without Prejudice,* 136–37.

12. Ibid., 135–36.

13. Ibid., 136–37.

14. William James, *The Varieties of Religious Experience,* 186; Richard M. Weaver, "Lee the Philosopher" (1948), in *The Southern Essays of Richard M. Weaver,* 174.

15. Thomas S. Kuhn, *The Structure of Scientific Revolutions,* 139; Owen Barfield, *Saving the Appearances: A Study in Idolatry,* 142–47.

16. Winchell, *A Blossoming Labor,* 427; Cleanth Brooks, letter to author, July 14, 1985; Weaver, *Southern Tradition at Bay,* 9, 16.

17. Robert B. Heilman, letter to author, November 15, 1987.

18. Robert B. Heilman, "Baton Rouge and LSU Forty Years After," 126.

19. Ibid., 126–27.

20. Ransom himself was already moving sharply away from Agrarianism to become a New Deal Democrat. T. D. Young, *Gentleman in a Dustcoat,* 365–78 *passim;* John Crowe Ransom, "Art and the Human Economy"; J. T. Fain and T. D. Young, eds., *The Literary Correspondence of Donald Davidson and Allen Tate,* 344–45.

21. Weaver, "Revolt against Humanism," 83–84.

22. Weaver, "Up from Liberalism," in *Life without Prejudice,* 131.

23. Ibid.

24. Amyx, interview; Weaver, "Up from Liberalism," in *Life without Prejudice,* 132.

25. Weaver, *Visions of Order,* 22–39; Amyx, interview.

26. Kuhn, *Scientific Revolutions,* 139.

27. Weaver, "Up from Liberalism," in *Life without Prejudice,* 132–33.

28. James, *Varieties of Religious Experience,* 186.

29. Weaver, "Up from Liberalism," in *Life without Prejudice,* 133.

30. Kuhn, *Scientific Revolutions,* 146.

31. Weaver, "Up from Liberalism," in *Life without Prejudice,* 133.

32. Ibid., 134; Andrew Nelson Lytle, "The Hind Tit," in *I'll Take My Stand,* by Donald Davidson and others, 205.

33. Kuhn, *Scientific Revolutions,* 171, 225, 260.

34. Weaver, "Up from Liberalism," in *Life without Prejudice,* 135; Kuhn, *Scientific Revolutions,* 139.

35. Kuhn, *Scientific Revolutions,* 139, 146, 184, 185, 266.

36. Perry Miller, *Errand into the Wilderness,* vii–viii; Weaver, "Up from Liberalism," in *Life without Prejudice,* 135–36.

37. Miller, *Errand into the Wilderness,* vi–viii; Weaver, "Address to Family Meeting," in Weaver, *Tribe of Jacob,* 114.

38. Weaver, "Up from Liberalism," in *Life without Prejudice,* 135; Weaver, "Agrarianism in Exile," in *Southern Essays,* 47.

39. Genovese, *Southern Tradition,* 2.

5. The Southern Tradition in Weaverian Perspective

1. Weaver, *Southern Tradition at Bay,* 391, 396.

2. Richard M. Weaver, "The Southern Tradition" (1964), in *The Southern Essays of Richard M. Weaver,* 209–29.

3. Ibid., 47–48.

4. Daniel J. Boorstin, *The Americans: The Colonial Experience,* 97–98; Genovese, *Southern Tradition,* 4, and Elizabeth Fox-Genovese and Eugene D. Genovese, "The Religious Ideals of Southern Slave Society"; Richard M. Weaver, "American Individualism," and "Two Orators" (1963), in *The Southern Essays of Richard M. Weaver,* 77–103, and 104–33; M. E. Bradford, *A Better Guide than Reason: Studies in the American Revolution,* 7.

5. Weaver, *Southern Tradition at Bay,* 48, n. 1, 49–50; Jackson Turner Main, *The Social Structure of Revolutionary America,* 67.

6. Weaver, *Southern Tradition at Bay,* 53.

7. Ibid., 35, 89; George Fitzhugh, *Sociology for the South,* 92.

8. Klehr, *Heyday of American Communism;* Weaver, *Ideas Have Consequences,* 132–33; Weaver, "American Individualism," in *Southern Essays,* 77–103.

9. Weaver, *Southern Tradition at Bay,* 54.

10. Ibid.

11. Thomas Jefferson, "Notes on the State of Virginia," 288.

12. Weaver, *Southern Tradition at Bay,* 57, 59.

13. Ibid., 59–69. Weaver developed the notion of chivalry as a check against the unrestrained warfare which was characteristic of World Wars I and II in an article entitled "Southern Chivalry and Total War" (1945) In ibid., 30 n. 1, Weaver makes an excellent statement on the nature of generalization: "It is useless to argue against generalization; a world without generalization would be a world without knowledge. The chaotic and fragmentary thinking of the modern age is due largely to an apprehensiveness, inspired by empirical methods, over images, wholes, general truths, so that we are intimidated from reaching the conclusions we must live by. The exception neither proves nor disproves the rule; in the original sense of the maxim it tests the rule: *exceptio probat regulam."*

14. Weaver, *Southern Tradition at Bay,* 71 n. 52, 77, 78, 79–80.

15. Ibid., 69–83; "In political theory, modern southern conservatives have built their work on their antebellum forbears, most notably John Randolph of Roanoke and John C. Calhoun" (Genovese, *Southern Tradition,* 23).

16. Weaver, *Southern Tradition at Bay,* 86.

17. Ibid., 87.

18. Ibid., 88.

19. Weaver, "Older Religiousness," in *Southern Essays,* 134–46; Weaver, *Southern Tradition at Bay,* 99.

20. Genovese, *Southern Tradition,* 25; Louis Filler, *The Crusade against Slavery: Friends, Foes, and Reforms, 1820–1860,* 183–85.

21. Weaver, *Southern Tradition at Bay,* 100.

22. Ibid., 101–2. For an excellent treatment on how the churches of the North and South diverged after about 1750, see Genovese, *Southern Tradition,* 25–26.

23. Weaver, *Southern Tradition at Bay,* 105.

24. Robert L. Dabney, *A Defence of Virginia and through Her of the South in Recent and Pending Contests against the Sectional Party,* 131–32.

25. Weaver, *Southern Tradition at Bay,* 107–9; William W. Bennett, *The Great Revival in the Southern Armies;* J. William Jones, *Christ in the Camp or Religion in the Confederate Army,* 242–389.

26. Weaver, *Southern Tradition at Bay,* 223, 224.

27. Ibid., 138.

28. Ibid., 138–39.

29. Ibid., 146; Dabney, *A Defence of Virginia.*

30. Dabney, *A Defence of Virginia,* 250; John Winthrop, "Liberty and Authority," in *Puritanism and the American Experience,* ed. Michael McGiffert, 39.

31. Weaver, *Southern Tradition at Bay,* 144, 148, 152–53.

32. Ibid., 167–68.

33. Ibid., 173–74.

34. Ibid., 176–79, 196–98, 206.

35. Weaver, "Lee the Philosopher," in *Southern Essays,* 171–80; Weaver, *Southern Tradition at Bay,* 209.

36. Weaver, "Lee the Philosopher," in *Southern Essays,* 180.

37. E. Porter Alexander, *The Military Memoirs of a Confederate,* 219; Weaver, *Southern Tradition at Bay,* 221–22.

38. Richard Taylor, *Destruction and Reconstruction,* 256–57.

39. Weaver, *Southern Tradition at Bay,* 230.

40. Ibid., 234; Beaton, interview.

41. Weaver, *Southern Tradition at Bay,* 241, 249–50, 340–42, 390.

42. Heilman, letter to author.

43. W. J. Cash, *The Mind of the South.*

44. Clement Eaton, review of *The Mind of the South,* 374–75; C. Vann Woodward, review of *The Mind of the South,* 400–401.

45. Michael O'Brien, *Rethinking the South: Essays in Intellectual History,* 112–76, 179–80, 234, 235, 240–53, 259–69, 276–342, 343–87.

46. Margaret Bourke-White, *You Have Seen Their Faces;* James C. Cobb, " 'Mind' in the Mainstream: *The Mind of the South* and the Mind of the Nation, 1941–1991," in *Rewriting the South: History and Fiction,* ed. Lothar Hönnighausen and Valeria Gennaro Lerda, 253; Richard H. King, *A Southern Renaissance: The Cultural Awakening of the American South, 1930–1955,* 147.

47. O'Brien, *Rethinking the South,* 179–80.

48. Richard M. Weaver, "Southern Chivalry and Total War" (1945), in *The Southern Essays of Richard M. Weaver,* 159–70; Cash, *The Mind of the South,* ix.

49. Donald Davidson, *Still Rebels; Still Yankees,* 191–200; Weaver, *Southern Tradition at Bay,* 395; Richard M. Weaver, "The South and the Revolution of Nihilism" (1944), in *The Southern Essays of Richard M. Weaver,* 186–88.

50. Weaver, "Southern Tradition," in *Southern Essays,* 229; Fred Hobson, *Tell about the South: The Southern Rage to Explain,* 328. Hobson notes that Weaver anticipated C. Vann Woodward's point in "The Irony of Southern History" that the South, in experiencing military defeat and poverty, had been taught hard lessons she could share with the rest of America.

51. George Brown Tindall, *The Persistent Tradition in New South Politics;* Weaver, "Southern Tradition," in *Southern Essays,* 217.

52. Weaver, *Southern Tradition at Bay,* 391; Daniel J. Boorstin, *The Americans:*

The Democratic Experience, 579–98; Robert Nisbet, *The Twilight of Authority,* 75–145, 230–37. William Barrett notes that "Technical requirements have led us to quantify and calculate a great many more parts of life; but preoccupied as we may be with objects and data, the human subject is still there, restless and unappeased, haunting the edges of the technical world. . . . Modern civilization has raised the material level of millions of people beyond the expectations of the past. . . . [T]echnological advance in itself is not sufficient to secure the happiness of mankind. The sources of that happiness seem to lie elsewhere" (William Barrett, *The Illusion of Technique,* 344–45). See also Boorstin, "Darwinian Expectations," in *Cleopatra's Nose: Essays on the Unexpected,* 136–40.

53. Weaver, *Southern Tradition at Bay,* 390–96.

54. Genovese, *Southern Tradition,* 1; Weaver, "Up from Liberalism," in *Life without Prejudice,* 144.

6. The Potency of Belief

1. Weaver, "Up from Liberalism," in *Life without Prejudice,* 148–49.

2. Jeffrey M. Gayner, "The Critique of Modernity in the Work of Richard M. Weaver," 97.

3. Weaver, *Ideas Have Consequences,* 1–2; Genovese, *Southern Tradition,* 12, 81.

4. Gerhard L. Weinberg, *A World at Arms: A Global History of World War II,* 462–63, 659–60, 702–4, 902; Fred Singleton, *A Short History of Finland,* 127–50; W. R. Mead, *Finland,* 169–88; Weaver, "Up from Liberalism," in *Life without Prejudice,* 148.

5. Weaver, "Up from Liberalism," in *Life without Prejudice,* 146–49.

6. Weaver, "Southern Chivalry," in *Southern Essays,* 159–70.

7. James J. Kirschke, "The Ethical Approach: The Literary Philosophy of Richard M. Weaver," 87; Weaver, *Ideas Have Consequences,* v; Weaver to Donald Davidson, February 28, 1948.

8. Ernst Troeltsch, *The Social Teachings of the Christian Churches,* vol. 2: 2, 464; William S. Sahakian, *The History of Philosophy,* 115–17.

9. Herbert Marshall McLuhan, "The Southern Quality," 107.

10. Weaver, *Ideas Have Consequences,* 3–5; C. S. Lewis, *The Abolition of Man,* 87; Weaver, *Ideas Have Consequences,* 4–5.

11. Weaver, *Ideas Have Consequences,* 5–6; Genovese, *Southern Tradition,* 24.

12. Weaver, *Ideas Have Consequences,* 6–7.

13. Weaver, *Ethics of Rhetoric,* 214–15; 214 n. 1, "It is surely worth observing that nowhere in the King James Bible does the word 'fact' occur"; Weaver, *Ideas Have Consequences,* 7–8.

14. Weaver, *Ideas Have Consequences,* 8.

15. Ibid., 11, 12–13.

16. Ibid., 18, 21–23.

17. Ibid., 24, 26–28, 29, 33.

18. Ibid., 41–42; Beaton, interview.

19. Weaver, *Ideas Have Consequences,* 41–42, 44, 51.

20. Ibid., 52–53.

21. Weaver, *Ethics of Rhetoric,* 214–15; Weaver, *Ideas Have Consequences,* 57–59; Weaver, *Southern Tradition at Bay,* 30; C. S. Lewis, *Letters to Malcolm: Chiefly on Prayer,* 55.

22. Weaver, *Ideas Have Consequences,* 75; Robert Goldwater and Marco Treves, eds., *Artists on Art, From the Fourteenth to the Twentieth Century,* 419.

23. Weaver, *Ideas Have Consequences,* 82, 85, 89.

24. Ibid., 91; John Fiske, *Civil Government in the United States Considered with some Reference to Its Origins,* 305–6.

25. Weaver, *Ideas Have Consequences,* 93.

26. Ibid., 94, 96; Dick Francis, *Enquiry,* 155; Malcolm Muggeridge, *Chronicles of Wasted Time, Chronicle I: The Green Stick,* 711.

27. Weaver, *Ideas Have Consequences,* 97, 100, 101, 102, 104, 109, 111.

28. Ibid., 113, 115–16, 126–27, 130–31, 132–35, 140.

29. Ibid., 141, 147; Genovese, *Southern Tradition,* 12.

30. Weaver, *Ideas Have Consequences,* 148–49; John Calvin, *Commentary on the Gospel according to John,* 25–29. Calvin takes four pages to explain why he chose this as the most appropriate term.

31. Lewis, *Abolition of Man,* 24; Weaver, *Ideas Have Consequences,* 150–51, 155–56, 158.

32. Weaver, *Ideas Have Consequences,* 159, 167, 168.

33. Ibid., 170–71.

34. Weaver, "Southern Chivalry," in *Southern Essays,* 159–70; Weaver, *Ideas Have Consequences,* 175.

35. Weaver, *Ideas Have Consequences,* 176, 179, 181; Alexis de Tocqueville, *Democracy in America,* 473–76.

36. Weaver, *Ideas Have Consequences,* 185.

37. Weaver, *Southern Tradition at Bay,* 394; Weaver, *Ideas Have Consequences,* 186.

38. Nash, *Conservative Intellectual Movement,* xiii.

39. Weaver, *Southern Essays,* 17–18, 21, 31, 58, 81, 94–99, 212–13, 223–24, 227–28, 232–39, 237, 252.

7. Civil Disobedience against Language

1. Richard M. Weaver, "Relativism and the Use of Language" (1961), in *Language Is Sermonic: Richard M. Weaver on the Nature of Rhetoric,* 136.

2. Weaver, "To Write the Truth" (1948), in *Language Is Sermonic,* 210–25.

3. Mortimer J. Adler, *How to Speak; How to Listen,* 21, 22–23.

4. Peter Dixon, *Rhetoric,* 1; T. S. Eliot, *Selected Essays,* 25–30; Weaver, *Visions of Order,* 71; Weaver, "Language Is Sermonic," in *Language Is Sermonic,* 205.

5. Weaver, *Ethics of Rhetoric,* 4, *passim.*

6. Weaver, *Ideas Have Consequences,* 92–112; Weaver, *Ethics of Rhetoric,* 6, 11–12.

7. Weaver, *Ethics of Rhetoric,* 14–15.

8. Fowler, trans., *Plato in Twelve Volumes,* vol. 1: 407.

9. Weaver, *Ethics of Rhetoric,* 15.

10. Fowler, trans., *Plato in Twelve Volumes,* vol. 1: 265E, 535; Weaver, *Ethics of Rhetoric,* 15–17.

11. Weaver, *Ethics of Rhetoric,* 17, 18, 20.

12. Ibid., 18–19.

13. Ibid., 19, 20, 21.

14. Weaver, *Language Is Sermonic,* 16; Kenneth Burke, *A Grammar of Motives,* 90; Weaver, *Ethics of Rhetoric,* 22–23.

15. Weaver, *Ethics of Rhetoric,* 24.

16. Ibid., 25; R. S. Pine-Coffin, trans., *St. Augustine's Confessions,* vol. 1: 1, 21.

17. Weaver, *Ethics of Rhetoric,* 26, 28–29, 30.

18. Mortimer J. Adler, *Dialectic,* 223–24. "Actuality is a class of entities, which are not statements, that is, which do not express propositions, or refer to entities in discourse. Let this class of entities be designated the first order of facts. The second order of facts is the class of entities which are statements about the first order of facts. The propositions which these statements express form a partial universe of discourse. This universe of discourse contains the body of propositions comprising the sciences. The third order of facts is the class of entities which are statements about the second order of facts, that is, statements about statements. The propositions which these statements express form a partial universe of discourse which is the body of philosophical opinion. A scientific proposition is expressed in a statement about facts of the first order, which are usually designated existences or existential relations, entities in the field of actuality. A philosophical proposition is expressed in a statement about facts of the second order, that is, about the statements expressing propositions in some partial universe of discourse."

19. Weaver, *Ethics of Rhetoric,* 30–31, 44.

20. Ibid., 45–46, 51.

21. Ibid., 52–53.

22. Ibid., 55; Nash, *Conservative Intellectual Movement,* 162–66, *passim.*

23. Weaver, *Ethics of Rhetoric,* 56.

24. Ibid., 57–58, 83.

25. Albert J. Beveridge, *Abraham Lincoln, 1809–1758,* vol. 2: 549; John C. Nicolay and John Hay, *Abraham Lincoln: A History,* vol. 2: 46; J. G. Holland, *The Life of Abraham Lincoln,* 72–86; W. H. Herndon, *Herndon's Lincoln,* vol. 3: 594; Weaver, *Ethics of Rhetoric,* 86.

26. Weaver, *Ethics of Rhetoric,* 86.

27. Ibid., 88, 89–90.

28. Ibid., 90–91, 108.

29. Ibid., 112–13; Don E. Fehrenbacher, ed., *Abraham Lincoln: Speeches and Writings, 1832–1858,* 398–99.

30. Weaver, "Conservatism and Libertarianism," in *Life without Prejudice,* 158–59.

31. Weaver, *Ethics of Rhetoric,* 114, 119, 169, 172–73.

32. Karlyn Kohrs Campbell, *The Rhetorical Act,* 203–4; Weaver, *Ethics of Rhetoric,* 184.

33. Garry Wills, *Inventing America: Jefferson's Declaration of Independence,* xiii–xviii.

34. Fehrenbacher, *Lincoln: Speeches and Writings,* 19, 107, 139–41, 256, 805, 809.

35. Weaver, *Ethics of Rhetoric,* 184.

36. Ibid., 211–14.

37. Ibid., 214–15.

38. Ibid., 216.

39. Ibid., 222–23.

40. C. S. Lewis, *That Hideous Strength,* 306; Weaver, *Ethics of Rhetoric,* 230–31.

41. Wilma R. Ebbitt, interview by author, tape recording, Newport, R.I., April 13, 1992.

8. The Years in Exile: Chicago, 1944–1963

1. Weaver, "Agrarianism in Exile," in *Southern Essays,* 41–44.

2. Weaver, *Tribe of Jacob,* 114; Weaver, *Southern Essays,* 41–42, 44; Malvasi, "Risen from the Bloody Sod," 393–94; John Crowe Ransom, "The Communities of Letters."

3. Weaver, *Tribe of Jacob,* 114; Robert Drake, *Flannery O'Connor: A Critical Essay,* 11; Weaver, *Tribe of Jacob,* 114. Flannery O'Connor thought highly of Weaver's *Ethics of Rhetoric* as a guide to proper speaking and writing. In a letter to Janet McKane, O'Connor wrote: "If I were you, I'd throw away *The Art of Plain Talk* and keep at your Milton & Shakespeare. Sometime at your library you might see if you could find *The Ethics of Rhetoric* by R. M. Weaver. I once had a copy but I gave it to somebody for a graduation present and now I'm sorry I did" (*The Habit of Being,* 595).

4. Mary Hood, "A Stubborn Sense of Place."

5. Weaver, *Tribe of Jacob,* 114.

6. Ibid., 114–15.

7. Ibid., 115, 116.

8. Ibid.

9. Beaton, interview; George Core, telephone conversation with author, March 15, 1994.

10. Henry Regnery, "Southern Agrarian."

11. Edward Shills, ed., *Remembering the University of Chicago,* xii, xv.

12. Ibid., xvi–xvii.

13. William H. NcNeill, *Hutchins' University: A Memoir of the University of Chicago, 1929–1950,* viii.

14. Mary Ann Dzuback, *Robert M. Hutchins: Portrait of an Educator,* ix, 88, 89, 92, 95; Weaver, *Ethics of Rhetoric,* 27, 30–31.

15. Mark Reutter, *One in Spirit: A Retrospective View of the University of Chicago on the Occasion of Its Centennial,* 104–5.

16. Weaver, "Southern Phoenix," in *Southern Essays,* 23; Weaver, "Up from Liberalism," in *Life without Prejudice,* 153.

17. F. Champion Ward, "Requiem for the Hutchins College," 82, 83.

18. Wilma R. Ebbitt, "Richard M. Weaver, Friend and Colleague." Talk delivered to the Conference on College Composition and Communication, St. Louis, Missouri, on March 19, 1988; James Sledd, "A Comment on 'Social Construction, Language, and the Authority of Knowledge,'" 587, 588.

19. Ebbitt, "Weaver, Friend and Colleague," 4; Ebbitt, interview.

20. Weaver to Donald Davidson, February 28, 1948.

21. Ebbitt, interview.

22. Brooks to Weaver, January 31, 1948; Cleanth Brooks, telephone conversation with author, January 23, 1985.

23. C. S. Lewis makes the same essential points in *Studies in Words,* 1–25; Hayakawa, *Language in Thought and Action,* 19–86; Weaver, *Ideas Have Consequences,* 151, 155, 169.

24. Weaver, *Language Is Sermonic,* 194–95.

25. Weaver to Davidson, March 8, 1949, and April 2, 1949; "NCTE News," 483; Weaver to Davidson, May 16, 1950.

26. Weaver to Davidson, October 5, 1953.

27. Davidson to Weaver, November 21, 1955; Core, interview, March 15, 1994.

28. Weaver, "Up from Liberalism," in *Life without Prejudice,* 135; Ebbitt, interview.

29. Ebbitt, "Weaver, Friend and Colleague," 1; Eliseo Vivas, introduction to *Life without Prejudice and Other Essays,* by Richard M. Weaver, ix.

30. Vivas, introduction to *Life without Prejudice,* by Richard M. Weaver, viii–ix.

31. Ebbitt, interview.

32. Ibid.

33. John B. Judis, "Three Wise Men," 20–21.

34. Russell Kirk, *The Conservative Mind in America: From Burke to Eliot,* 20; William Alexander Percy, *Lanterns on the Levee: Recollections of a Planter's Son,* 147–54; Genovese, *Southern Tradition,* 20.

35. Nash, *Conservative Intellectual Movement,* 46; Bernard Iddings Bell, *Crowd Culture,* 91; Bernard Iddings Bell to Richard M. Weaver, September 22, 1948; Bernard Iddings Bell, *Crisis in Education,* 124, 145.

36. Weaver to Davidson, January 27, 1954.

37. Russell Kirk to Weaver, October 5, 1956; Weaver to Davidson, October 5, 1961; Weaver to Davidson, September 7, 1960. Weaver named Henry Regnery as his source.

38. William F. Buckley to Weaver, June 10, 1954; Buckley to Weaver, June 10, 1954, January 3, 1957, and March 29, 1957.

39. Weaver to Davidson, April 23, 1957.

40. Richard H. S. Crossman, ed., *The God That Failed: Why I Left Communism,* 1–11, *passim;* Nash, *Conservative Intellectual Movement,* 97–98; Frank S. Meyer to Weaver, January 19, 1957; Ebbitt, interview.

41. Nash, *Conservative Intellectual Movement,* 175; Richard M. Weaver, "Anatomy of Freedom."

42. Weaver, "Anatomy of Freedom," 444.

43. Davidson to Weaver, October 17, 1956.

44. George Core, ed., *Regionalism and Beyond: Essays of Randall Stewart,* v; Weaver to Randall Stewart, May 4, 1955.

45. *Young Americas for Freedom,* copy of citation for award, Weaver Papers.

46. Weaver to Stewart, May 19, 1962.

47. Weaver to Stewart, February 3, 1963; Weaver to Mrs. C. E. Weaver, January 9, 1963, and March 3, 1963.

48. Beaton, interview; Ebbitt, interview; Weaver to Ralph T. Eubanks, December 15, 1962.

9. Epilogue

1. Weaver, *Ideas Have Consequences,* 186–87.

2. Dorothy Lobrano Guth, ed., *The Letters of E. B. White,* 285.

3. Weaver, *Southern Tradition at Bay,* 388.

4. Weaver, "Address to Family Meeting," in Weaver, *Tribe of Jacob,* 114.

5. Lewis, *Abolition of Man,* 91.

6. Weaver, "Older Religiousness," in *Southern Essays,* 134–46; Cleanth Brooks, "A Plea to the Protestant Churches," in *Who Owns America? A New Declaration of Independence,* ed. Herbert Agar and Allen Tate, 327–30.

7. R. S. Pine-Coffin, trans., *The Confessions of St. Augustine,* Book 6: 6, p. 118; Book 9: 2, p. 182.

8. Francis Fukuyama, *The End of History and the Last Man,* 328; Weaver, *Visions of Order,* 152.

Bibliography

Works by Richard M. Weaver

"Anatomy of Freedom." *National Review* 13 (December 4, 1962): 443–44.

The Ethics of Rhetoric. Chicago: Henry Regnery Company, 1948.

Ideas Have Consequences. Chicago: University of Chicago Press, Phoenix Books, 1953.

Language Is Sermonic: Richard M. Weaver on the Nature of Rhetoric. Ed. Richard Johannesen, Rennard Strickland, and Ralph T. Eubanks. Baton Rouge: Louisiana State University Press, 1970.

Life without Prejudice and Other Essays. Chicago: Henry Regnery Company, 1965.

"A Panorama of Peace in the Colleges." *The Intercollegian* 47 (December 1929): 69–72.

"The Revolt against Humanism." M.A. thesis, Vanderbilt University, 1934.

The Southern Essays of Richard M. Weaver. Ed. George M. Curtis III and James J. Thompson Jr. Indianapolis: Liberty Press, 1987.

The Southern Tradition at Bay Ed. George Core and M. E. Bradford. New York: Arlington House, 1968.

Student Notebook kept by Richard M. Weaver at Lincoln Memorial Academy in Harrogate, Tennessee. Mrs. Polly Weaver Beaton, Weaverville, North Carolina.

Visions of Order: The Cultural Crisis of Our Time. Baton Rouge: Louisiana State University Press, 1964.

With Clifford Amyx. "Looking over the Magazines." *Kentucky Kernel.* August 7, 1931, and August 14, 1931.

Other Works Cited

Adler, Mortimer J. *Dialectic.* New York: Harcourt Brace, 1927.
———. *How to Speak; How to Listen.* New York: Macmillan, 1983.

Agar, Herbert, and Allen Tate, eds. *Who Owns America? A New Declaration of Independence.* Boston: Houghton Mifflin, 1936.

Alexander, E. Porter. *The Military Memoirs of a Confederate.* New York: Charles Scribner's Sons, 1907.

Allen, Frederick Lewis. *Only Yesterday: An Informal History of the 1920s.* New York and Evanston: Harper and Row, 1957.

Amyx, Clifford. "Weaver the Liberal: A Memoir." *Modern Age* 31 (spring 1987): 101–6.

———. and Richard Weaver. "Looking over the Magazines." *Kentucky Kernel.* August 7, 1931, and August 14, 1931.

Arendt, Hannah. *Totalitarianism.* 1951. New York: Harcourt Brace Jovanovich, 1968.

Auden, W. H., and Louis Kronenberger, eds. *The Viking Book of Aphorisms.* New York: Viking Press, 1962.

Barfield, Owen. *Saving the Appearances: A Study in Idolatry.* New York: Harcourt, Brace and World, Inc., n.d.

Barrett, William. *The Illusion of Technique.* Garden City, N.Y.: Anchor Press/Doubleday, 1978.

Beaton, Kendall. "Richard M. Weaver: A Clear Voice in an Addled World." Speech presented to the annual Weaver family meeting, Weaverville, North Carolina, August 5, 1963.

Bell, Bernard Iddings. *Crisis in Education.* New York: McGraw Hill, 1949.

———. *Crowd Culture.* New York: Harper and Brothers, 1952.

Bennett, William W. *The Great Revival in the Southern Armies.* 1876. Harrisonburg, Va.: Sprinkle Publications, 1976.

Beveridge, Albert J. *Abraham Lincoln.* 2 vols. Boston and New York: J B Lippincott, 1928.

Boorstin, Daniel J. *The Americans: The Colonial Experience.* New York: Random House, 1973.

———. *The Americans: The Democratic Experience.* New York: Random House, 1958.

———. *Cleopatra's Nose: Essays on the Unexpected.* New York: Random House, 1994.

Bourke-White, Margaret. *You Have Seen Their Faces.* New York: Modern Age, 1937.

Bradford, M. E. "The Agrarianism of Richard Weaver: Beginnings and Completions." *Modern Age* 14 (summer–fall 1970): 249–56.

———. *A Better Guide than Reason: Studies in the American Revolution.* LaSalle, Ill.: Sherwood Sugden, 1979.

Burke, Kenneth. *A Grammar of Motives.* 1945. Berkeley and Los Angeles: University of California Press, 1969.

Calvin, John. *Commentary on the Gospel according to John.* Trans. Rev. William Pringle. 1848. Grand Rapids, Mich.: Baker Book House, 1981.

Campbell, Karlyn Kohrs. *The Rhetorical Act.* Belmont, Calif.: Wadsworth, 1982.

Cash, W. J. *The Mind of the South.* New York: Alfred A. Knopf, 1941.

Clayton, Bruce. *W. J. Cash: A Life.* Baton Rouge: Louisiana State University Press, 1991.

Conkin, Paul K. *The Southern Agrarians.* Knoxville: University of Tennessee Press, 1988.

Core, George, ed. *Regionalism and Beyond: Essays of Randall Stewart.* Nashville: Vanderbilt University Press, 1968.

Cowan, Louise. *The Fugitive Group: A Literary History.* 1959. Baton Rouge: Louisiana State University Press, 1968.

Cowley, Malcolm. "Hemingway's Nevertheless." In *Think Back on Us: A Contemporary Chronicle of the 1930s,* ed. Henry Dan Piper, 361–64. Carbondale and Edwardsville: Southern Illinois University Press, 1967.

———. "Hemingway's Wound—And Its Consequences." In *The Portable Malcom Cowley,* ed. Donald W. Faulkner, 417–35. New York: Viking-Penguin, 1990.

Crossman, Richard H. S., ed. *The God That Failed: Why I Left Communism.* New York: Harper and Row, 1950.

Dabney, Robert L. *A Defence of Virginia and through Her of the South in Recent and Pending Contests against the Sectional Party.* 1867. Harrisonburg, Va.: Sprinkle Publications, 1977.

Davidson, Donald. *Southern Writers in the Modern World.* Athens: University of Georgia Press, 1958.

———. *Still Rebels; Still Yankees and Other Essays.* Baton Rouge: Louisiana State University Press, 1957.

———. and others. *I'll Take My Stand.* 1930. New York: Harper and Row, 1962.

de Grazia, Alfred. *The Student at Chicago in Hutchins' Hey-day.* Princeton, N.J.: Quiddity Press, 1991.

Dixon, Peter. *Rhetoric.* London and New York: Methuen, 1971.

Douglas, George H. *H. L. Mencken: Critic of American Life.* Hamden, Conn.: Archon Books, 1978.

Drake, Robert. *Flannery O'Connor: A Critical Essay.* Grand Rapids, Mich.: William B. Eerdmans, 1966.

Dzuback, Mary Ann. *Robert M. Hutchins: Portrait of an Educator.* Chicago: University of Chicago Press, 1991.

Eaton, Clement. Review of *The Mind of the South,* by W. J. Cash. *American Historical Review* 47 (January 1942): 374–75.

Ebbitt, Wilma R. "Richard M. Weaver, Friend and Colleague." Paper presented at the Conference on College Composition and Communication, St. Louis, Mo., March 19, 1988.

Eliot, T. S. *Selected Essays.* New York: Harcourt Brace Jovanovich, 1950.

Fain, John Tyree, and Thomas Daniel Young, eds. *The Literary Correspondence of Donald Davidson and Allen Tate.* Athens: University of Georgia Press, 1974.

Fehrenbacher, Don E., ed. *Abraham Lincoln: Speeches and Writings, 1832–1858.* New York: Literary Classics of the United States, 1989.

Filler, Louis. *The Crusade against Slavery: Friends, Foes, and Reforms, 1820–1860.* Algonac, Mich.: Reference Publications, 1986.

Fiske, John. *Civil Government in the United States Considered with some Reference to Its Origins.* New York: Houghton Mifflin, 1890.

Fitzhugh, George. *A Sociology for the South.* Richmond, Va.: A. Morris, 1854.

Follette, Charles Kellogg. "A Weaverian Interpretation of Richard Weaver." Ph.D. diss., University of Illinois at Urbana-Champaign, 1981.

Fox-Genovese, Elizabeth, and Eugene D. Genovese. "The Religious Ideals of Southern Slave Society." In *The Evolution of Southern Culture,* ed. Numan V. Bartley, 14–27. Athens: University of Georgia Press, 1988.

Francis, Dick. *Enquiry.* New York: Harper and Row, 1969.

Francis, Samuel. *Beautiful Losers: Essays on the Failure of American Conservatism.* Columbia: University of Missouri Press, 1993.

The Fugitive 1 (April 1922).

Fukuyama, Francis. *The End of History and the Last Man.* New York: Free Press, 1992.

Gayner, Jeffrey M. "The Critique of Modernity in the Work of Richard M. Weaver." *The Intercollegiate Review* 14 (spring 1979): 97–104.

Genovese, Eugene D. *The Southern Tradition: The Achievements and Limitations of an American Conservatism.* Cambridge: Harvard University Press, 1994.

Godsey, John D. "Neorthodoxy." Vol. 10, *The Encyclopedia of Religion,* ed. Mircea Eliade, 360–62. New York: Macmillan, 1987.

Goldwater, Robert, and Marco Treves, eds. *Artists on Art, from the Fourteenth to the Twentieth Century.* 1945. New York: Random House, Pantheon Books, 1972.

Grattan, C. Hartley. *The Critique of Humanism.* New York: Brewer and Warren, 1930.

Guth, Dorothy Lobrano. *The Letters of E. B. White.* New York: Harper and Row, 1976.

Guttmann, Allan. *The Wound in the Heart: America and the Spanish Civil War.* New York: Free Press of Glencoe, 1962.

Hamlin, Robert. "Weaver's *Tribal Pietas:* The Beginnings and Early Years, 1910–1933." Paper presented at the Southern Speech Communication Association Convention, Biloxi, Miss., April 1979.

Hart, Jeffrey. "The Spanish Civil War." *National Review* 18 (January 11, 1966): 31.

Havard, William C., and Walter Sullivan, eds. *A Band of Prophets: The Vanderbilt Agrarians after Fifty Years.* Baton Rouge: Louisiana State University Press, 1982.

Hayakawa, S. I. *Language in Thought and Action.* New York: Harcourt Brace, 1939.

Hazlitt, Henry. "The Pretensions of Humanism." *The Nation* 130 (March 1933): 272–73.

Heilman, Robert B. "Baton Rouge and LSU Forty Years After." *The Sewanee Review* 88 (winter 1980): 126–43.

Herndon, W. H. *Herndon's Lincoln.* 3 vols. Springfield, Ill.: Herndon's Lincoln, 1921.

Hobson, Fred. *Tell about the South: The Southern Rage to Explain.* Baton Rouge: Louisiana State University Press, 1983.

Hoeveler, J. David, Jr. *The New Humanism: A Critique of Modern America, 1900–1940*. Charlottesville: University Press of Virginia, 1977.

Holland, J. G. *The Life of Abraham Lincoln*. Springfield, Mass.: Gurdon Bill, 1866.

Hönninghausen, Lothar, and Valeria Gennaro Lerda, eds. *Rewriting the South: History and Fiction*. Tübingen, Germany: A. Francke Verlag, 1993.

Hood, Mary. "A Stubborn Sense of Place." *Harper's* 273 (August 1986): 36.

Huxley, Julian S. *What Dare I Think?* New York: Harper and Brothers, 1931.

James, William. *The Varieties of Religious Experience*. 1902. New York: Modern Library, 1929.

Jefferson, Thomas. "Notes on the State of Virginia." In *Writings*, 123–325. New York: Literary Classics of the U.S., 1984.

Jones, J. William. *Christ in the Camp or Religion in the Confederate Army*. 1887. Harrisonburg, Va.: Sprinkle Publications, 1986.

Judis, John B. "Three Wise Men." *The New Republic* 210 (May 30, 1994): 20–24.

King, Richard H. *A Southern Renaissance: The Cultural Awakening of the American South, 1930–1955*. New York: Oxford University Press, 1980.

Kirk, Russell. *The Conservative Mind in America: From Burke to Eliot*. Chicago: Regnery-Gateway, 1986.

Kirschke, James J. "The Ethical Approach: The Literary Philosophy of Richard M. Weaver." *The Intercollegiate Review* 14 (spring 1979): 87–94.

Klehr, Harvey. *The Heyday of American Communism: The Depression Decade*. New York: Basic Books, 1984.

Krutch, Joseph Wood. *The Measure of Man: On Freedom, Human Values, Survival, and the Modern Temper*. Indianapolis and New York: Bobbs-Merrill, 1929.

Kuhn, Thomas S. *The Structure of Scientific Revolutions*. 2d ed. Vol. 2, *Foundations of the Unity of Science*, ed. Otto Neurath, Rudolf Carnap, and Charles Morris, 54–272. Chicago: University of Chicago Press, 1970.

Lamb, W. R. M., trans. *Plato in Twelve Volumes.* Vol. 2. 1924. Cambridge: Harvard University Press, 1977.

Lewis, C. S. *The Abolition of Man.* 1947. New York: Macmillan, 1972.

———. *Letters to Malcolm: Chiefly on Prayer.* New York: Macmillan, 1963.

———. *Studies in Words.* Cambridge, England: Cambridge University Press, 1960.

———. *That Hideous Strength.* 1946. New York: Macmillan, 1965.

Litz, A. Walton, ed. *American Writers: A Collection of Literary Biographies.* Supplement 2, Part 1. New York: Charles Scribner's Sons, 1981.

Main, Jackson Turner. *The Social Structure of Revolutionary America.* Princeton: Princeton University Press, 1965.

Malvasi, Mark G. "Risen from the Bloody Sod: Recovering the Southern Tradition." Ph.D. diss., University of Rochester, 1991.

McAllister, Lester G., and William E. Tucker. *Journey in Faith: A History of the Christian Church (Disciples of Christ).* St. Louis: Bethany Press, 1975.

McGiffert, Michael, ed. *Puritanism and the American Experience.* Reading, Mass.: Addison-Wesley, 1969.

McLuhan, Herbert Marshall. "The Southern Quality." In *A Southern Vanguard,* ed. Allen Tate, 100–121. 1947. Freeport, N.Y.: Books for Libraries Press, 1970.

McNeill, William H. *Hutchins' University: A Memoir of the University of Chicago, 1929–1950.* Chicago: University of Chicago Press, 1991.

Mead, W. R. *Finland.* New York: Frederick A. Praeger, 1968.

Middleton, David. "The Patriarch." In *The Burning Fields,* 5–7. Baton Rouge: Louisiana State University Press, 1991.

Miller, Perry. *Errand into the Wilderness.* Cambridge: Harvard University Press, 1956.

Molnar, Thomas. *The Counter Revolution.* New York: Funk and Wagnalls, 1967.

Muggeridge, Malcolm. *Chronicles of Wasted Time, Chronicle I: The Green Stick.* New York: William Morrow, 1973.

———. *A Twentieth Century Testimony.* New York: Thomas Nelson, 1978.

Nash, George H. *The Conservative Intellectual Movement in America since 1945.* New York: Basic Books, 1976.

"NCTE News." *College English* 10 (May 1949): 482–83.

Neill, Stephen. *The Interpretation of the New Testament, 1861–1961.* New York and London: Oxford University Press, 1966.

Nicolay, John C., and John Hay. *Abraham Lincoln: A History.* 10 vols. New York: Century, 1904.

Nisbet, Robert. *The Twilight of Authority.* New York: Oxford University Press, 1975.

O'Brien, Michael. *Rethinking the South: Essays in Intellectual History.* Baltimore: Johns Hopkins University Press, 1988.

O'Connor, Flannery. *The Habit of Being: Letters of Flannery O'Connor,* ed. Sally Fitzgerald. New York: Farrar, Straus and Giroux, 1979.

O'Neill, William L. *The Great Schism: Stalinism and the American Intellectuals.* New York: Simon and Schuster, 1982.

Orwell, George. *Homage to Catalonia.* 1938. New York: Harcourt Brace Jovanovich, 1980.

Percy, William Alexander. *Lanterns on the Levee: Recollections of a Planter's Son.* Baton Rouge: Louisiana State University Press, 1973.

Perry, Lewis. *Intellectual Life in America: A History.* New York: Franklin Watts, 1984.

Pine-Coffin, R. S., trans. *The Confessions of St. Augustine.* New York: Dorset Press, 1986.

Ransom, John Crowe. "Art and the Human Economy." *Kenyon Review* 7 (fall 1945): 683–88.

———. "The Communities of Letters." In *Poems and Essays,* 109–17. New York: Vintage Books, 1955.

———. *God without Thunder: An Unorthodox Defence of Orthodoxy.* London: Gerald House, 1931.

———. *The World's Body.* New York: Charles Scribner's Sons, 1938.

Regnery, Henry. *Memoirs of a Dissident Publisher.* New York: Harcourt Brace Jovanovich, 1979.

———. "A Southern Agrarian at the University of Chicago." *Modern Age* 32 (spring 1988): 99–110.

Reutter, Mark. *One in Spirit: A Retrospective View of the University of Chicago on the Occasion of Its Centennial.* Chicago: University of Chicago Press, 1991.

Sahakian, William S. *The History of Philosophy*. New York: Barnes and Noble, 1968.

Shills, Edward, ed. *Remembering the University of Chicago*. Chicago: University of Chicago Press, 1991.

Simpson, Lewis P. "Malcolm Cowley and *Exile's Return*." In *The Critics Who Made Us*, ed. George Core, 115–38. Columbia: University of Missouri Press, 1993.

Singal, Daniel Joseph. *The War Within: From Victorian to Modernist Thought in the South, 1919–1945*. Chapel Hill: University of North Carolina Press, 1982.

Singleton, Fred. *A Short History of Finland*. New York: Cambridge University Press, 1989.

Sledd, James. "A Comment on 'Social Construction, Language, and the Authority of Knowledge,'" *College English* 49 (1987): 585–88.

Stewart, John L. *The Burden of Time: The Fugitives and Agrarians*. Princeton: Princeton University Press, 1965.

Taylor, Richard. *Destruction and Reconstruction*. New York: D. Appleton, 1879.

Tindall, George Brown. *The Persistent Tradition in New South Politics*. Baton Rouge: Louisiana State University Press, 1975.

Tocqueville, Alexis de. *Democracy in America*. Trans. Henry Reeve. Ed. J. P. Mayer and Max Lerner. New York: Harper and Row, 1966.

Troeltsch, Ernst. *The Social Teachings of the Christian Churches*. Trans. Olive Wyon. 2 vols. London: Allen and Unwin, 1950.

University of Kentucky. Official Records: Student transcript of Richard M. Weaver.

Van Doren, Mark. Introduction to *Two Years before the Mast*, by Richard Henry Dana. New York: Bantam Books, 1959.

Ward, F. Champion, "Requiem for the Hutchins College." In *General Education in the Social Sciences: Centennial Reflections on the College of the University of Chicago*, ed. John J. MacAloon, 77–102. Chicago: University of Chicago Press, 1992.

Weaver, Pearl M. *The Tribe of Jacob: The Descendants of the Reverend Jacob Weaver of Reems Creek, North Carolina, 1786–1868 and Elizabeth Siler Weaver*. Weaverville, N.C.: The Weaver Family Historical Committee, 1962.

Weinberg, Gerhard L. *A World at Arms: A Global History of World War II.* New York: Cambridge University Press, 1994.

Wheelwright, Philip. "Neo-Humanism." In *Princeton Encyclopedia of Poetry and Poetics,* ed. Alex Preminger, 565–67. 1965. Princeton: Princeton University Press, 1974.

White, E. B. "Salt Water Farm." In *One Man's Meat,* 30–35. New York: Harper and Row, 1982.

Wills, Garry. *Inventing America: Jefferson's Declaration of Independence.* Garden City, N.Y.: Doubleday, 1978.

Winchell, Mark Royden. *A Blossoming Labor: The Life and Times of Cleanth Brooks.* Forthcoming.

———. ed. *The Vanderbilt Tradition: Essays in Honor of Thomas Daniel Young.* Baton Rouge: Louisiana State University Press, 1991.

Woodward, C. Vann. "The Irony of Southern History." In *The Burden of Southern History,* 167–91. Baton Rouge: Louisiana State University Press, 1960.

———. Review of *The Mind of the South,* by W. J. Cash. *Journal of Southern History* 7 (August 1941): 400–401.

Young, T. D. *Gentleman in a Dustcoat: A Biography of John Crowe Ransom.* Baton Rouge: Louisiana State University Press, 1976.

Manuscript Collections

Davidson, Donald. Papers. Special Collections. The Jean and Alexander Heard Library. Vanderbilt University. Nashville, Tenn.

Weaver, Richard M. Papers. Special Collections. The Jean and Alexander Heard Library. Vanderbilt University. Nashville, Tenn.

———. Weaver Family Papers. Mrs. Polly Weaver Beaton, Weaverville, N.C.

Index

Credits